BBC RADIO 6 MUSIC'S ALTERNATIVE JUKEBOX

500 EXTRAORDINARY TRACKS THAT TELL
THE STORY OF ALTERNATIVE MUSIC

First published in Great Britain in 2014 by Cassell,
an imprint of Octopus Publishing Group Limited,
Endeavour House, 189 Shaftesbury Avenue, London WC2H 8JY

www.octopusbooks.co.uk | www.octopusbooksusa.com

An Hachette UK Company | www.hachette.co.uk

Distributed in the US by Hachette Book Group,
1290 Avenue of the Americas, 4th and 5th Floors, New York, NY 10020

Distributed in Canada by Canadian Manda Group,
664 Annette St, Toronto, Ontario, Canada M6S 2C8

By arrangement with the BBC.

The BBC logo is a trademark of the British Broadcasting
Corporation and is used under licence.

BBC logo © BBC 1996

UK ISBN: 978-1-84403-784-1 / US ISBN: 978-1-84403-789-6

Printed and bound in China.

             loyd Bradley
        litor: Hannah Knowles
      r: Leanne Bryan
      r: Justin Lewis
     er: Eoghan O'Brien
    : Clare Barber
   ager: Giulia Hetherington
     Evans at Telegramme
    er: Sorrel Wood
     Vanessa Bird
   roller: Sarah Connelly

CONTENTS

INTRODUCTION

The word 'alternative' can mean so many things when applied to music. For us here at BBC Radio 6 Music, and for the purposes of this book and the 500 tracks selected for inclusion, it refers to an alternative spirit: music that is informed by the desire to experiment with ideas and sounds already in existence. It is about music that is not just a product of popular culture, but that also actively informs or responds to it.

Some of the artists we have chosen might now be deemed commercial figures, but they started off as part of underground scenes, which were only latterly embraced by the mainstream once they had transformed popular tastes. Other tracks have been selected for their experimental qualities, and how they influenced what was to come musically – whether or not the rest of the artist's output matched that particular track's ground-breaking impact.

The book starts with roots-based tracks, which set the tone and the standard for the alternative music movement. Where mainstream pop tends to produce artificial copies of its influences, at the heart of alternative music is both an understanding of – and a great respect for – the past. As the 1960s kicked in, the seeds planted by those early artists began

to germinate as they were mixed in with other cultures and scenes, eventually spawning all variety of genres, from hip-hop to electronica.

Some of our finest 6 Music presenters have chosen songs for the book and their song choices have the presenters' names alongside them throughout. Several of them have gone into more depth about the reasons behind their choices (see pages 12, 45, 53, 61, 75, 80, 116, 129, 133, 141, 234 and 247) as have we (see pages 88 and 217).

At BBC Radio 6 Music, we aim to connect the dots between what is happening now and where it all came from. In the vast ocean of music that is available to listeners today, a little navigation comes in handy, and we hope that this book will act as a map to help you chart a course around the very best of alternative music.

JEFF SMITH (HEAD OF MUSIC, BBC RADIO 6 MUSIC)
JAMES STIRLING (EDITOR, BBC RADIO 6 MUSIC)

THE FIRE STARTERS

Before we take a journey through
the decades, here are some of the
groundbreaking tracks that established a
standard for the alternative music scene to
follow. Carefully crafted, impassioned and
with a free spirit, from Robert Johnson to
Odetta to Aretha Franklin, these voices
were the spark that lit the flame.

Cross Road Blues
Robert Johnson
1937 • Sony Jazz

CRAIG CHARLES' CHOICE >> As a template for what would influence alternative music and its musicians, so much can be traced back to Johnson the Delta blues master (shown here on the left). He loved life on the road and all that went with it, to such a degree that he was said to have met his end in 1938, imbibing poisoned whiskey courtesy of the husband of the woman he was flirting with. He died aged 27, as would Janis Joplin, Jimi Hendrix, Brian Jones, Jim Morrison, Kurt Cobain and Amy Winehouse. Johnson was rumoured to have sold his soul to the devil at a road junction in Clarksdale, Mississippi in return for his phenomenal playing ability. Even leaving all this aside, Johnson established two important traditions that shifted blues forwards. One was that he wrote conventionally structured lyrics and music, rather than simply jamming and ad-libbing, although he was more than capable of that, too. The other was that he limited his compositions to around three minutes in length, specifically for the purposes of recording. But all this is window-dressing; what continues to inspire generations of would-be rock musicians is a dark, beautifully interpretive way with the guitar, and a singing voice so subtly expressive it could shift from pain to humour to roadhouse raucousness within the same line. 'Cross Road Blues' demonstrates all this perfectly.

Cold, Cold Heart
Hank Williams
1951 • MGM

MARK RADCLIFFE'S CHOICE << Originally the B-side of a lesser Williams hit, 'Dear John', radio DJs picked up on 'Cold, Cold Heart' to provide him with what became his most enduring song, covered by artists from Louis Armstrong to Norah Jones. Essentially a simple honky-tonk-ish country blues arrangement – he never learned to read or write music – the lyrics are Williams at his storytelling best, relating an unusual tale of a woman unable to return his love due to a traumatic incident in her past. 'Cold, Cold Heart' showed country music to be far more cerebral than the clichés afforded, and on its release in 1951, it effectively introduced the rest of the world both to Williams as a songwriter, and to the genre itself when Tony Bennett had a huge US pop hit with it that same year.

I Got a Woman
Ray Charles
1954 • Atlantic

 CRAIG CHARLES' CHOICE Some half a decade before Ray Charles' 'What'd I Say' became soul music's recognized starting pistol, there came 'I Got a Woman'. Although it was more rudimentary than what would follow from the singer and bandleader, all the elements can be seen to be already falling into place. It's a song constructed on a southern gospel platform with all that intense pace and those vocal mannerisms, but while Charles is making like a preacher of the secular sermon, behind him there's a summit meeting of rhythm and blues and big band jazz. At this point it's still more swing than soul, but there's a liveliness and infectiousness about this track that made a huge mark on the then nascent rock 'n' roll. The illustrious list of those who later covered it includes Elvis, Bill Haley, Roy Orbison, the Beatles, Adam Faith, Johnny Hallyday and Bobby Darin.

Aló! Quién Ñama?
Mon Rivera featuring Moncho Leña y los Ases del Ritmo
1956 • Ansonia

 CERYS MATTHEWS' CHOICE Remarkable as it may sound, this sparkling, salsa-ish Puerto Rican orchestral pop tune started life as a serious protest song. In its original form it was a *plena*, Puerto Rico's equivalent of the Trinidadian calypso, in which songs were spontaneously written to discuss political situations or comment on everyday life. 'Aló!, Quién Ñama?' originated as a song about a seamstresses' strike at a local factory. It's about the bringing in of scab labour, and the title (which translates as 'Hello! Who's calling?') refers to the strikers phoning each other to pass on news and information. 'Aló! Quién Ñama?' was first performed and recorded by Mon Rivera's dad, confusingly also known by the same name. Rivera the younger (born Efrain Rivera Castillo) wrote orchestral arrangements of many of his father's plenas in a big band style. This allowed a new generation to dance their way to solidarity with the workers.

That Old Black Magic
Louis Prima and Keely Smith
1958 • Capitol

HUEY MORGAN'S CHOICE ≫ For proof that a good song can be interpreted by any number of people in any number of styles and still remain a good song, look no further than this version of Arlen and Mercer's 'That Old Black Magic'. Originally written in 1942, and covered countless times, it was usually smooth or sultry or both – as performed by Jerry Lewis as Buddy Love in *The Nutty Professor* – but husband-and-wife team Louis Prima and Keely Smith took it somewhere else entirely. Upping the tempo to a kind of cabaret-like jump jive, Prima's gusto and infectiously enthusiastic gruff *Eye*-talian tones swapped lines with Smith's silky tunefulness, to give the song a massive injection of life. And as hugely and funkily entertaining as it was, it never crossed the line into parody.

Water Boy
Odetta
1959 • Vanguard

≫ In Martin Scorsese's documentary on Bob Dylan, *No Direction Home*, there's a clip of Odetta singing 'Water Boy' on US television in 1959, accompanying herself on acoustic guitar. At the end of each line she strums sharply across the strings and, quite literally, barks. Given this is pre-civil rights and pre-desegregation in many US states, such a display must have been truly terrifying to a large amount of its viewing public. But that was the passion and beauty of the singer, and this song is a heart-wrenching spiritual tune that is bluesier than the blues and more soulful than soul. Odetta was the foremost exponent of African-American folk music and in her singing you can hear the blues, jazz and church traditions that contributed to it. As the most powerful black female voice at the start of the civil rights movement, she has been hailed as an influence by such luminaries as Bob Dylan, Harry Belafonte, Joan Baez and Maya Angelou.

Black Snake
John Lee Hooker
1959 • Riverside

« If John Lee Hooker is the embodiment of blues, then 'Black Snake' is quintessential John Lee Hooker. With just an acoustic guitar and his vocals, the arrangement couldn't be sparser – rural blues using the simplest of repetitive, almost clanky chord progressions. The real beauty and aching qualities of the song – the blues, if you will – is in Hooker's weather-beaten careworn voice, creating its own meandering, bendy melody that hovers just above the backing. The 'Black Snake' of the title is a sneakin', low-down, backdoor man. The singer is going to kill him when he catches up with him – and Hooker sounds so utterly wronged you would happily load the gun for him.

Soulful Dress
Sugar Pie DeSanto
1964 • Chess Records

» An often overlooked inhabitant of the junction between rhythm and blues and rock 'n' roll is Sugar Pie DeSanto. With songs like 'Soulful Dress', she epitomized Chicago's Chess Records sound, which was infused with as much urban blues as country soul. This is a smart, hard-rocking guitar-led sound, which was just right for the storming, soulful singer with a stage presence to match her voice – you can see this in online clips of 'Rock Me Baby' – and the result is something the women's movement would be proud of, even in this pre-enlightenment era. 'Soulful Dress' concerns itself with the style of her evening attire: 'I'm gonna put on my dress/ That hits me way above the knees/With that V-cut back/ It has straps instead of sleeves'. But it's delivered with so much gusto that DeSanto unashamedly turns her wardrobe into a weapon.

CERYS MATTHEWS' SELECTION

(See Cerys' song choices on pages 9, 11, 40, 119, 261 and 293.)

When I choose tracks – for my 6 Music show, or for this book – it's important for me to pick out songs that are infectious; music that will put a smile on people's faces.

My first DJ set was at the World Music Awards with Gilles Peterson. I played 'Aló! Quién Ñama' by Mon Rivera there – it starts with a man answering the phone with the song's title ('Hello! Who's Calling?') before a brass section cuts in. It's a protest song, but it's hugely contagious.

Recorded in the days before overprocessing, John Lee Hooker's 'Black Snake' is just one man's voice and his guitar; yet it sounds like an orchestra, it's that big. He's a legend. You have to get behind the scratches on the records and poor recordings of his early tracks, but it's worth it. It's hard to know what he's talking about on 'Black Snake': 'He's a mean black snake / been sucking my rider's tongue' – Hooker leaves it open and that makes it all the more powerful to me.

Another pioneer that I've chosen here is Sugar Pie DeSanto – she's known as 'The Lady James Brown' – and she should be as famous as him. She went on tour with the James Brown Revue tour for two years, and claimed he got rid of her because she tired him out: she still does the splits as a live performer today, in her late seventies!

King Floyd's 'Groove Me' is a track I chose because as soon as you hear the opening section it's groove-tastic. He's a New Orleans legend and if this is playing, calling you, you need go nowhere else.

The Clash's 'I Fought the Law' is my favourite Clash song, although they didn't write it. What I love about them is that they had completely open ears: they were listening to music from all over the world, all different styles. They were sponges, taking it all in and throwing it back out of the Clash artistic machine. One of my favourite moments was interviewing them and discovering the noise at the end of the song is a urinal flushing.

'Mig, Mig' by Fanfare Ciocărlia featuring Jony Iliev is outrageously good. Like most standards, this track has centuries-old history. Fanfare Ciocărlia is a Roma band that plays music passed down from father to son. Historians believe Romanies originated from Rajasthan, brought as slaves from North India to Europe. With them they brought a tonal scale that was new to Europe. Fanfare Ciocărlia's 12-piece brass orchestra keeps that history and the spirit of Roma music alive.

With politics and religion affecting the musicians' lives and ability to play, it's incredible that 'Soubour' by Songhoy Blues remains the freshest-sounding music. In 2006 Damon Albarn founded Africa Express, a series of collaborations between western and Malian artists. They recorded several sessions, and this is the standout track for me. Right now, the most exciting, innovative sounds are non-Anglo-American.

> 'WHEN I CHOOSE TRACKS... IT'S IMPORTANT FOR ME TO PICK OUT SONGS THAT ARE INFECTIOUS; MUSIC THAT WILL PUT A SMILE ON PEOPLE'S FACES.'

Witch Hunt
Wayne Shorter
1965 • Blue Note

«

In 1964, the year before 'Witch Hunt' came out, saxophonist Wayne Shorter became one-fifth of what many people believe to be the greatest ever jazz group, or even one of the greatest musical ensembles of any kind – the Second Great Miles Davis Quintet. From his own *Hear No Evil* album, Shorter still seems to have his head in that group, which isn't at all a bad place to be. Recruiting pianist Herbie Hancock and double-bassist Ron Carter from Davis' Quintet and adding trumpeter Freddie Hubbard and drummer Elvin Jones, *Hear No Evil*'s six songs are textural, three-dimensional pieces moving the saxophonist closer to bebop once more. Composed by Shorter to evoke 'misty landscapes with wild flowers and strange, dimly seen shapes', 'Witch Hunt' marks the dark, brooding edge of that particular theme.

Respect
Aretha Franklin
1967 • Atlantic

> Otis Redding wrote this song in 1965, and recorded it almost as a plea for a bit of respect from the lady he's devoting his life to. When Aretha Franklin got hold of the same song two years later, there was a slight change in lyrics, but a seismic shift in attitude. Not that there was anything wrong with Otis' version, but Aretha hurled herself at it, demanding respect on the grounds that she's the best thing that's ever likely to happen to this slacker boyfriend. Even the music on Franklin's interpretation has a bit more sass about it and the backing singers seem to function like her gang – you can almost feel them neck-popping and finger-wagging. Unsurprisingly, this version of the song quickly became a civil rights rallying cry, then went on to assume the mantle of a feminist anthem.

THE 1960s

With such rich, provocative roots, it's no surprise
that the alternative music scene had hit its stride
by the 1960s. Here we take a small step back to
1964 to kick off the main show with the Kinks, whose
progressive, raw-edged sound moved away from the
easy-listening music that was dominating the charts at
the time. As the decade progressed there was an explosion
of experimentation: from psychedelia and punk to ska
and reggae, people's ears were being opened
to new and exciting sounds.

You Really Got Me
The Kinks
1964 • Pye

>> A huge step forwards from the easy-listening likes of Jim Reeves or The Bachelors, who were dominating record sales in 1964, which wasn't really that difficult, 'You Really Got Me' was sufficiently different from so much British Young Persons' music – mostly theatre variety-show-type pop groups and American impressionists – to move that on too.

Indeed, 'You Really Got Me' was a brief intuitive burst of gut-level musical emotion, with a chord progression that seems to fit snugly on top of the Kingsmen's 'Louie Louie'. A simple riff, simple lyric, raw power and nothing too much to think about – you either got on board or got out of the station.

The track was an instant and massive success, but one that very nearly never happened at all. After two badly performing singles, the North London band were on notice from their record label to come up with a hit. After recording a tepid version of the song, Ray Davies badgered the label to let them try again. Under pressure to come up with something special, his lead guitarist and brother Dave used a razor blade to slit the speaker on his amp and stuck drawing pins into this modified cone; and it was straight from this rattling, buzzy, fuzzy piece of kit that the riffs were recorded. It was a template, in attitude, for the next wave of rock bands to make the blues their own rather than simply copy it, and a blueprint, in technique, for the Kinks for the rest of their life.

Tainted Love
Gloria Jones
1964 • Champion

>> A record guaranteed to spark a lively originals versus covers debate, made all the more energetic by how Jones' original became so overshadowed by its cover versions. Check the videos online for a string of genuinely bewildered 'Is this a cover of Soft Cell/Marilyn Manson?'-type comments. The simple truth is, it's not better or worse than the covers, it's just *different*. It's neither the banging synth-pop nor the disco *moderne* of later readings, and while it doesn't neglect the big beat it's got the softer edges of cleverly rounded pop-soul. The lush orchestration allows a greater sense of drama, too, as Jones' powerful voice rides the arrangement to a series of peaks and troughs, building up to a sense of outrage that rises above them all.

Al Capone
Prince Buster
1965 • Blue Beat

« The gunfire, the car crash and the shouted 'Al Capone's guns don't argue' introduced so many youngsters to ska. True, 'My Boy Lollipop' had already been a hit in 1964, but that had always tried so hard to be a pop song it was generally taken as such. 'Al Capone' was always much skarier, simply because it was an instrumental and so made an instant impact and was unlike anything around at the time. The intensity of the beat, the playing and the passion in the horns – both in the choruses and solos – spurred on by the insane 'chk-a chk-a' vocal, opened so many doors for Jamaican music in general in the UK.

Subterranean Homesick Blues
Bob Dylan
1965 • Columbia

» Although Bob Dylan's first forays into that new-fangled electrification caused so much weeping and a-wailing, without it we wouldn't have 'Subterranean Homesick Blues'. It's a song both completely bonkers and utterly era-defining that would never have had the necessary drive without the gift of amplification. Dylan was an adolescent rock 'n' roll fan, and by the time he cut this record with a full band he was secure enough to let the chopped up rockabilly-ish riffs jangle out behind him, making the song so winningly jaunty that it would take a soul of stone not to engage with it. On top of this are apparently ad-libbed rhymes that took in pretty much everything relevant to young America, even offering up a few dire warnings. Dry as that might sound, it's hung together so inventively and with such lyrical dexterity it's difficult to imagine Dylan getting through a take with a straight face. 'Johnny's in the basement mixing up the medicine/I'm on the pavement thinking 'bout the government…Watch the plain clothes/You don't need a weatherman/To know which way the wind blows.' A counterculture primer, it was Bob Dylan's first top-40 hit in the US.

Do I Love You (Indeed I Do)
Frank Wilson
1965 • Soul

CRAIG CHARLES' CHOICE ⏬ A bouncy, run-of-the-mill early Motown tune, at one point during the 1970s it became Northern Soul's great white whale – the company opted not to release it and subsequently destroyed all but a handful of the few hundred original, unreleased pressings. A decade later it became a record so rare that if a DJ actually owned a copy that had survived Berry Gordy's crusher, that in itself was cause for celebration and dancefloor delirium. In 2009 one of these discs sold at auction in the UK for over £25,000, but such a price tag means that the song can never be judged purely on its merits. While there's nothing at all wrong with the music – a jangly, foot-stomping generic early-1960s Motown sound – technically there are better Northern Soul records. However, its dramatic dumping all those years ago secured it a treasured place in music history.

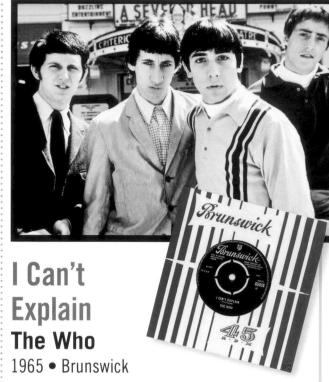

I Can't Explain
The Who
1965 • Brunswick

⏫ Their first single release under the name 'The Who', 'I Can't Explain' had just about everything it needed to appeal to the first generation of entirely post-World-War-II youth, experiencing the conflicting influences of rock 'n' roll and National Service. Masquerading as a love song, it has much wider implications and is so eloquently inarticulate at making its points it becomes a perfect manifestation of directionless teenage frustration – indeed, Pete Townshend was just 18 when he wrote it. Over the years, much has been made of what it borrowed from the Kinks, and while 'I Can't Explain' obviously draws on the Kinks' rhythms and constructions, it's far less instinctive-sounding. Instead it brings a sophistication to the proceedings – especially in the vocals – that added another endearing dimension, and would remain relevant to generations to come.

Dirty Water
The Standells
1966 • Capitol

>> By an unremarkable Californian garage rock band, which never had another hit, 'Dirty Water' has been cited as a punk influence a couple of generations removed. Written and produced by Ed Cobb who had previously written Gloria Jones' song 'Tainted Love' (see page 16) – you can hear the connection – at the same time there's a host of Stone-isms and splashes of psychedelia riding on a hacked-out beat. Somewhat paradoxically for such an archetypal West Coast band, it's a warts-and-all hymn to the city of Boston – the dirty water of the title is Boston's legendarily polluted harbour – and the song has been taken up by crowds at local sporting events.

Caroline, No
The Beach Boys
1966 • Capitol

<< The Beach Boys' seemingly-interminable summer of sun, surf and convertibles had to run out of road at some point, and if the doleful 'Caroline, No' pulls it up a bit sharpish, that's because it melodiously marks Brian Wilson's first solo track, rather than being a group effort. While it was released as Wilson's debut single, it cropped up on the group's *Pet Sounds* just six weeks later. Wilson is the only group member involved, his vocals being multi-tracked for the harmonies. A tale of both love lost and love unrequited, with a wistful, jazz-inflected backing, it's the product of both Wilson's and lyricist Tony Asher's collective disappointment. Wilson had a serious high-school crush on a girl named Carol, while Asher reportedly had a girlfriend who cut her hair (a main theme here) after dumping him. Presumably for somebody a bit more cheerful.

Eight Miles High
The Byrds
1966 • CBS

 A hugely influential example of psychedelic rock, and quite rightly so, as it doesn't get much better than this: comfortably woozy, it's intriguingly layered, featuring overlapping, cascading harmonies. The lyrics are entertainingly nuts and it's got a strong Indian influence, while nodding to the more inventive end of contemporary jazz. Mostly, though, it's got such an English feel to it, and is far closer to the Beatles or even the Yardbirds than anything particularly American. As the last Byrds single released with their original songwriter Gene Clark, 'Eight Miles High' represents the peak of how the band moved folk into the rock world while maintaining an easy-going identity. It was banned from American radio upon release for being about drug use, although the band protested that it was actually about flying to London for the first time. Unsurprisingly, nobody took them too seriously.

Hold On, I'm Comin'
Sam & Dave
1966 • Atlantic

As soul music developed out of what had been rhythm and blues, it was important it maintained the full breadth of musical and cultural traditions. This meant that the lusher, more string-heavy goings-on in Detroit had to be balanced out by something less evolved but equally high-profile. The Stax set-up, in Memphis, represented a gutsier counterpart to Motown, keeping things simple by augmenting a bass-heavy, driving rhythm section with fat, powerful horns, to throw down backing that was not for the nervous. As singers, Sam & Dave epitomized what was going on down in Memphis: visceral, instinctive and displaying blues and gospel traditions that thrived on emotion. 'Hold On' is them at their storming, raw-throated, unpolished and barely-produced best.

(I'm Not Your) Steppin' Stone
The Monkees
1966 • Colgems/RCA

Relative to the number of records they sold, there probably hasn't been a band that exerted less influence on what was going on around them than the Monkees. However, their contribution to 1960s pop was so comprehensively enjoyable nobody really cared whether they played their instruments. On this track, Micky Dolenz was the only actual Monkee in the recording studio and, as on much of their output, he was singing lead rather playing drums. 'Steppin' Stone' is what Brand Monkees did best: it jangles with contemporary, grown-up sounds and harmonies, but is also translating wider pop culture – psychedelia, mostly – into a form palatable for little kids while still keeping things faintly edgy. They took this approach this on their TV series too, which is why their psychedelic movie *Head* shouldn't have come as such a shock.

7 and 7 Is
Love
1966 • Elektra

Because this is a bit fast and very shouty, it's theoretically yet another candidate for the first punk single ever. But like so many of its rivals, it's not really – it was too well behaved, obviously intricately constructed and Arthur Lee's vocals are far too restrained. Instead, it was a very good and cleverly arranged, up-tempo rock 'n' roll song, closer to the Doors than anything overly garagey. There is a depth to the production that allows the layers to sit comfortably with no jarring or chafing against each other.

Tomorrow Never Knows
The Beatles
1966 • Parlophone

More than just the best song from the best Beatles album, here was a tune that moved rock music so far into psychedelia, in both thought and deed, that there could be no turning back: the recording of the song in April 1966 preceded Floyd's *Piper at the Gates of Dawn*, Hendrix's 'Purple Haze' and the Beach Boys' *Pet Sounds*. In fact, even to call 'Tomorrow Never Knows' a 'tune' is to do it a disservice. As the first number recorded for the *Revolver* album, it's a seismic leap forwards from *Rubber Soul*, and given the technology of the day, brought new levels of creativity from producer George Martin and his engineers. Tape loops, double tracking, reversed guitars, tape saturation, varied stereo panning…all were innovations at the time and in many cases equipment had to be modified on the spot to create the desired effect: of transcendental meditation on vinyl. Many liken it to a musical acid trip, but 'Tomorrow Never Knows' is a serious contender for the most inventive piece of music of the modern age. In barely three minutes, it demonstrates why the Beatles set a benchmark for just about everybody since.

Knock on Wood
Eddie Floyd
1966 • Stax

« Never quite as vocally unreserved as Sam & Dave (see page 20), Eddie Floyd was nonetheless a true Stax singer in that he could comfortably hold his own against a backing comprising Booker T's MGs and the Memphis Horns. 'Knock on Wood' isn't as straight-off-the-blocks explosive as other Stax offerings, but its chugging beat contains enough crescendos to pack quite a punch. Cowritten by Floyd, who penned many a Stax hit, it was originally written for (and would be covered by) Otis Redding, but Floyd's raw and more staccato style gives far more opportunity for the horns and the guitars to show off the crisp, locked-down playing that made that label so special.

Try a Little Tenderness
Otis Redding
1966 • Stax

CRAIG CHARLES' CHOICE » For a record label with a well-deserved reputation for footstompin', hollerin' soul music, Stax had a remarkably deft touch with the quieter stuff. Most of this came from an intrinsic gospel/country/soul-based understanding that throttling back on the histrionics could create a swelling, quiet storm of emotion. Otis Redding was the in-house king of this; when he held his voice back to tick-over level, as he does here, the obviously restrained power leaves you perched on the edge of your seat. What turns this tune into an absolute soul music killer is Isaac Hayes' arrangement of Booker T and the MGs' backing. Hayes would later stretch Bacharach and David songs into 20-minute epics by holding back until the very end. On 'Try a Little Tenderness', Hayes brings in instruments almost individually, pushing them forwards in turn, and creating a *background* more than a *backing*, offering splashes of colour during Redding's pauses. With considerable musical bravery, this works like an introduction that fills around two-thirds of the song, allowing the vocals to stand out so vividly they carry the whole melody. When all the elements unite, the tune clicks into place, pushing Redding into a glorious summit of emotion: an astonishing piece of work.

These Days
Nico
1967 • Verve

>> An interesting paradox is at work here: who knows best, the singer or the producer? In this case it was undoubtedly producer Tom Wilson. Originally this glum Jackson Browne-penned hymn to regret, yearning and loss was carried along by the writer's own nimble-fingered guitar picking and not much else. This was, apparently, how Andy Warhol (Nico was his muse) saw the song and he insisted on adding only an electric guitar to subtly modernize proceedings. After the recording was complete, it was Wilson who added mournful sweeping strings, a move that properly lifts the number out of the Greenwich Village coffee-house mire and creates something both arresting and memorable. Nico, of course, detested what had been done to it.

Tin Soldier
Small Faces
1967 • Immediate

<< While the Small Faces' excursions into psychedelic pop were always entertaining, it never seemed as if that particular route would lead anywhere. It was wig-out-by-numbers and their crisply turned-out mod hearts weren't really in it. So when they reverted to the R&B they did best, albeit retaining a few recently acquired, freaked-out flourishes, the reaction was a huge sigh of relief. Probably from the band as well, as this crisp soul stomper was originally written by members Steve Marriott and Ronnie Lane for soul diva and record label mate PP Arnold, but upon finishing it decided it was just too damn funky for them to give away.

You Don't Love Me
Dawn Penn
1967 • Studio One

DON LETTS' CHOICE A single song that demonstrates one of Jamaican music's central beliefs – if something's worth doing at all it's worth doing again. It's a gorgeous, oozing rock-steady tune, cut at Studio One and with all of influential producer Coxsone Dodd's hallmarks: great separation between the tracks; just enough echo; vocals riding on top; metronomic discipline from the players; and a grumbling and almost subconscious bass-line. Yet 'You Don't Love Me' wasn't entirely original – it's based on a country song from 1960, which was itself based on a Bo Diddley tune from five years earlier. Penn returned to the song again in 1994, under the title 'No, No, No', to even greater chart success.

See Emily Play
Pink Floyd
1967 • Columbia

>> 'See Emily Play' came from *Piper at the Gates of Dawn*, less an album and more a psychedelic masterclass. Bits of it are as odd as can be, others are pure whimsy, much of it has dark shadows cast across it, and some of its musical ideas exist right on the edge of what might have been possible. This was while Syd Barrett was still in the band, with both him and his superhuman acid intake driving Floyd in that particular direction. No matter how much LSD is dripping out of the grooves, though, it never forgets it's making pop music, and the musicians involved are good enough to do this instinctively. 'See Emily Play' is a vivid example – cascading, apparently random music that comes together with spectacularly cohesive and multi-textured results, coupled with lyrics that at first seem purely playful, but ultimately convey more sinister messages. It's never less than totally alluring – music through the looking glass – and is light years removed from the Sydless, joyless corporate rockers the band would become.

For What It's Worth
Buffalo Springfield
1967 • Atco

One of the psychedelic movement's earliest protest songs – from the more contemporary end of rock, as opposed to established folk singers – 'For What It's Worth' was not, as many believed, railing against the Vietnam war or the Kent State University shootings (which in any case happened later, in 1970), but was far more geographically and culturally parochial. Buffalo Springfield's quiet ire concerned a 10pm curfew enforcement at LA's Whiskey a Go-Go club, where they were the house band, and the police's efforts to discourage kids from loitering outside afterwards. The song is a mild-mannered gripe, and cleverly makes the point that while it seems a trivial matter, it's the thin end of an establishment wedge. It's also the group's best-known number, and because the title doesn't appear in the lyrics, it's often known by the line, 'Stop, children, what's that sound?'

Back in the USSR
The Beatles
1968 • Apple

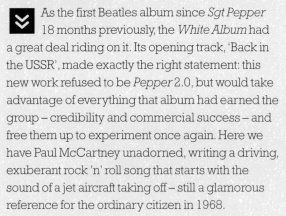

As the first Beatles album since *Sgt Pepper* 18 months previously, the *White Album* had a great deal riding on it. Its opening track, 'Back in the USSR', made exactly the right statement: this new work refused to be *Pepper* 2.0, but would take advantage of everything that album had earned the group – credibility and commercial success – and free them up to experiment once again. Here we have Paul McCartney unadorned, writing a driving, exuberant rock 'n' roll song that starts with the sound of a jet aircraft taking off – still a glamorous reference for the ordinary citizen in 1968.

On the face of it, the track is no groundbreaker: the title borrows from Chuck Berry ('Back in the USA'); Paul takes advice from Beach Boy Mike Love who urged him to pastiche his group's inimitable vocal style; and throws in a cheerful nod to Hoagy Carmichael's 'Georgia on My Mind'. Despite the group famously being at each other's throats during the recording – Ringo isn't on this track as he'd just 'quit' the band, for nearly two weeks – the result harks back to the group's early days fooling about in a Hamburg soundcheck. It was the sort of apparent spontaneity and straightforwardness that many wanted from the lovable moptops.

Of course not everybody liked it, and just as many didn't get the idea that Paul might also have had a sharp wit, a wicked sense of irony, a love of satire and no fear of social commentary. In the UK, each end of the political spectrum took this as evidence the Beatles were communists, in the US they were labelled 'commies', which was probably worse, and in the USSR itself, it didn't really matter because the group's recordings had long since been officially banned along with Levi's and Coca-Cola.

All Along the Watchtower
The Jimi Hendrix Experience
1968 • Reprise

MARY ANNE HOBBS' CHOICE « The opening chord sequence and the lead line that follows with the lyric, 'There must be some kinda way out of here', have become the essence of Hendrix for most people. Quite correctly, too, as this radical cover of a Bob Dylan song embodies the Jimi Hendrix Experience – which is an experience in the literal sense as well. Its making was something of a soap opera, with bass player Noel Redding walking out of the sessions while Hendrix's own insecurities meant perpetual disgruntlement and constant overdubbing. The latter's astonishing guitar technique – it features three differently approached solo elements – as well as his ability to get under the skin of a song rather than just reinterpret it, wring every last drop out of the original. All of this turns an already intriguing piece of work into a shocking exercise in extremes.

Hurdy Gurdy Man
Donovan
1968 • Pye

» If you had to sum up late-1960s, post-*Pepper*, hippiefied English pop music in one song, 'Hurdy Gurdy Man' would do it for you. It's all here: from the acoustic guitar and plaintively-sung first couple of lines, to the big drums announcing the searing electric guitar, the sitar, an early synth, phased vocals and lyrics that could be about anything as long as it was trippy. Donovan and producer Mickie Most bring all this together with considerable aplomb, with a slow, contemplative tempo, managing to keep a strong, folkie vibe while being very much of-its-moment pop. It also proved there was much more to Donovan than just a fey Dylan wannabe.

Summertime
Big Brother and the Holding Company featuring Janis Joplin
1968 • Columbia

HUEY MORGAN'S CHOICE ≪ A George Gershwin standard as fabulous as this is difficult to mess up, but when it's one previously covered by Miles Davis, Billie Holliday and Nina Simone, your interpretation has to be special. Big Brother and the Holding Company's achievement was to turn this languid tale of inner-city optimism into a seething, searing blues epic, with featured vocalist Janis Joplin, whose dueling with the guitars is one of her finest studio performances. Theirs is a 'Summertime' of oppressive heat and overcrowded conditions, transforming contentment into frustration and barely repressed anger. Coming over a year after the group had built up an enormous reputation for their live shows, this number recaptured that excitement and served it up for a wider audience.

Badge
Cream
1969 • Polydor

≫ You could probably count on one finger the times you've heard the words 'not long enough' and 'Cream song' in the same sentence, but 'Badge' is a rare and wonderful exception. Written by Eric Clapton with then-Beatle George Harrison to a conventional song construct, it's a masterpiece of gentle blues-rock, flowing seductively from bridge to bridge until it just ends, at two minutes forty-five, meaning your only option is to play it again. For so long, Cream had covered up songwriting deficiencies with virtuoso playing and tunes had tended to ramble, albeit usually enjoyably. Here, within a solid structure that was underpinned by Harrison's subtle guest spot on rhythm guitar, everybody gets an opportunity to show off and we all get something that didn't require much effort to enjoy. It's just a shame that this gem happened so late in the group's life – even before its release on the aptly-titled *Goodbye* album, Cream had split up.

Space Oddity
David Bowie
1969 • Philips

   The song that has kicked off practically every Bowie compilation ever is also the song that kicked off a hit career spanning over 40 years. It opened his second album in a row to be titled *David Bowie*, giving a clue as to how little impact his debut release made.

A lengthy career for Bowie seemed unlikely in the summer of 1969. A pun on the title of Stanley Kubrick's epic movie *2001: A Space Odyssey*, 'Space Oddity' was palmed off by many as a cheap-shot novelty, knocked out to coincide with Apollo 11's launch, the first to put men on the moon. To this end, the BBC opted not to play the song until the moon mission came home safe and sound. The album's producer, Tony Visconti, was so unimpressed he passed the track over to his assistant Gus Dudgeon.

Ironically, it's the assumed associations with Kubrick's baffling blockbuster that proved most appropriate. 'Space Oddity' seemed lyrically ambiguous, leaving listeners to complete the tale for themselves, prompting the sort of discussion and sense of involvement that went way beyond a mere novelty record. What the whole story was actually about became equally open to interpretation: in 1969, hippies and their younger acolytes roamed the earth, many refusing to believe the song's subject matter could be nearly as mundane as a disastrous space mission.

In the context of an album of blatantly influenced material, such multi-layered ambiguity set this apart as an original high point. Musically, too, it was far from cheap. Building from an acoustic guitar and stylophone intro to the climactic 'launch' sequence, then floating off into the blissed out spacewalk finale, it is – partly thanks to session player Rick Wakeman's stirring work on the mellotron – pure musical theatre. And pure Bowie.

Gimme Shelter
The Rolling Stones
1969 • Decca

>> 'A requiem for the 1960s' sums up both this track and *Let It Bleed*, the album it opened. So many people who had been coasting on the decade's sunny optimism, both musical and social, could agree with the description.

Arguably, however, both song and album are as much a requiem for the Rolling Stones as an era-defining creative force rather than a hugely commercially successful band. This was a shame, as 'Gimme Shelter' showed how far the group had come in less than a decade – from imitation to a level of understanding that let their own interpretation, musical and intellectual, develop with integrity. The band had developed from the pouty stage arrogance of 'Let's Spend the Night Together', or the largely addled and mostly awful *Their Satanic Majesties Request* album, to this gorgeously abrasive example of what a contemporary blues band ought to be.

THE MUSIC THAT THRILLED THE WORLD... AND THE KILLING THAT STUNNED IT!

The Rolling Stones
Gimme Shelter

DIRECTED BY DAVID MAYSLES, ALBERT MAYSLES, CHARLOTTE ZWERIN · A MAYSLES FILMS, INC. PRODUCTION
DISTRIBUTED BY 20TH CENTURY-FOX FILM CORPORATION

Keith Richards' dueling guitars are both brooding and predatory, while the harmonica and the piano are so jagged you have to check your ears for signs of blood. As Mick Jagger's singing is slowly submerged in the bass and drum build-up, Merry Clayton's guest vocal – which is anything other than background – carries the song to allow the frontman to be virtually howling before he reins himself back in. Lyrically, 'Gimme Shelter' surpasses even the standards set by its explosive musical content, with lines like, 'It's just a shot away,' and, 'It's just a kiss away,' among the smartest Jagger and Richards ever wrote. The track's title also provided the name for the Stones documentary (see poster, above), which notoriously included footage of the stabbing, at the 1969 Altamont Free Concert, of Meredith Hunter, an 18-year-old man, by Hell's Angel Alan Passaro.

No Fun
The Stooges
1969 • Elektra

Coming out in an environment of prog rock, country rock and LA soft rock, the Stooges' self-titled first album appeared as a particularly violent and ungrateful assault on a scene that by 1969 seemed like a self-congratulatory status quo. 'No Fun', is a textbook example of the album's belligerence: loads of fuzzy distortion; garage rock power-chording; bass and drums doubling up to thump out a beat; and a vocal from 'Iggy Stooge' (as Iggy Pop was then briefly known) which lay somewhere between a whine and a howl, railing about a love lost. But as all-round obnoxious as it appeared at the time, when heard now over forty years later it's not difficult to appreciate how conventional a song it really was. Even down to the narrative, 'No Fun' is just a bit faster and messier than most of the competition, which is why it's stood up so well over time, and why the Stooges were such a clear influence on the Sex Pistols (who would later cover the song).

Time is Tight
Booker T & the MGs
1969 • Stax

STEVE LAMACQ'S CHOICE

The theme tune from Booker T-scored *Up Tight!*, a tense, early blaxploitation thriller, this Hammond-led instrumental should've been subtitled 'Ghetto Chase'. It careers through streets, peeps around corners and lurks in alleys, a melodic bass leading the way, with the organ right on its tail, and the guitar cuts across to provide distraction. 'Time is Tight' shifts though gears so smoothly it feels as if this was something the group tossed out in a rehearsal session. It gives an already atmospheric piece a further lift as Booker T and the MGs enjoy themselves trying to give each other a hard time. There is a documentary film about Stax Records, with footage of the band playing an elongated version of this: if you do nothing else you owe it to yourself to seek it out.

It Mek
Desmond Dekker & the Aces
1969 • Pyramid

A terrific example of how reggae shifted into rock-steady, this had all the soulful tunefulness of the earlier style but a bright, jerky rhythm and an emphasis on the downbeat. It also shows that the sweetening of Jamaican tracks worked if handled with sensitivity. 'It Mek' was cut by producer Leslie Kong in Kingston, with horns overdubbed in London prior to UK release. The horns work so well to emphasize certain beats and fade across the back of the mix that you can't imagine the tune without them. Dekker's quirky, jerky falsetto never lets you forget he was Jamaican, but wasn't so 'yard' that it locked anybody out. It all helped turn him into the island's first bona fide UK pop star.

Fortunate Son
Creedence Clearwater Revival
1969 • Fantasy

  As a true piece of swinging, swampy, Southern-fried, modern-day blues this is something of a classic, even by Creedence's already high standards. Less expected from the boisterous good-times rockers was such a clever anti-Vietnam protest song. Rather than attack America's involvement head on, the group totally understood how their blue-collar audience was largely in favour of the notion of war at that point, and thus approached the subject on a far more prosaic level. The fortunate sons of the title are the offspring of the US's privileged classes who, statistically, were far less likely than working class kids to get called up and sent to south-east Asia. The song eloquently rails not just against the elitism and unfairness of the draft but also the forces' make-up in general. This was something the group knew about, as frontman John Fogerty and drummer Doug Clifford had both served in the military.

Psychedelic Shack
The Temptations
1969 • Tamla Motown

One of Motown's early acknowledgements that young America wasn't quite the same as it was in the 1950s saw the label's shiny sound elbowed aside in favour of screaming guitars, synthesizers and phased drums, with producer Norman Whitfield giving the musicians a bit of freedom. Some of them responded with gusto and a riot of wigged-out funk, but the Temptations were less enthusiastic; as elder statesmen of the label, they were suspicious of anything this new-fangled. They were, however, exactly the right choice to lead a new sound: five distinct, fabulous voices, capable of following direction. It was then that Whitfield began treating them as individual elements within the mix – each singer like a separate instrument – and his vocal arrangements really took off. He alternated leads, faded them across each other and positioned them among the musicians as part of an epic whole, yet still harmonizing recognizably like the Temptations. 'Papa Was a Rolling Stone' wasn't far away.

Thank You (Falettinme Be Mice Elf Agin)

Sly and the Family Stone

1969 • Epic

This standalone single – issued during the 18 months between *Stand!* and *There's a Riot Goin' On* – is one of the group's most important tracks, a powerful staging post between the two halves of their catalogue, or maybe even two sides of their psyche.

Prior to late 1969, Sly and the Family Stone's output had been mostly northern Californian, gently baked hippified optimism, throwing up weed-fuelled melting-pot philosophies built on a largely gospel beat. As Sly says in the documentary *Coming Back for More*: 'I wanted the band to represent as much variety of soul as possible…

I thought that if people could see all these different people having fun on stage then it wouldn't be so hard for people to have a good time.'

It worked too as, without such an approach, who knows when the mainstream might have connected to post-Motown soul music with a social conscience? However, by the time 'Thank You' was recorded, hard drugs, Black Panthers and decadent boredom were part of the Sly Stone equation. Instantly, a less compromising way of thinking shows itself in the music: gone is the gospel basis, and Larry Graham's thumb-popping bass technique makes its studio debut to lead a taut, percussive hard-funk sound, a good while before James Brown or George Clinton were doing it.

But it's in the lyrics that the band's change of pace is most telling. Fast-forward past that hammy, confused opening verse about running from the devil and not staying at parties, to get to the end and lines like, 'Many men are missin' much/ Hatin' what they do,' and, 'Dyin' young is hard to take/Sellin' out is harder'. Perhaps not the tangled paranoia that would drive the *Riot* album, but all the signs are there.

Liquidator
Harry J Allstars
1969 • Harry J Records

>> This early reggae instrumental was supposed to have a vocal, but producer Harry Johnson had the good sense to ditch the original writer's sappy lyrics. Instead he turned Hammond supremo Winston Wright loose to deliver a masterclass in popping, high-stepping organ riffs. This was laid over the most solid of rhythm tracks put down by drummer Carlton Barrett and his bass-playing brother, Aston 'Family Man', Barrett, both later of Upsetters and Wailers fame. A UK top-10 hit, 'Liquidator' inspired the opening of the Staple Singers' song 'I'll Take You There' in 1972 (see page 55), while the original incarnation has lived on via several TV adverts. In addition, the central organ hook and four handclaps have cropped up in football ground chants.

You Did It
Ann Robinson
1969 • All Brothers

>> A long-lost soul gem from Philadelphia soulstress Ann Robinson, 'You Did It' is a perfectly balanced example of late-1960s soul – so much closer to funk than rhythm and blues. Robinson's voice isn't going to blow down any walls; it's confident rather than overwhelming, carrying the kind of inherently swinging melody so associated with the City of Brotherly Love. She's doing it at a canter, too, always staying above the band, which is churning things up behind her. It's the ideal framework for the vocals: chopped up, brass-blasting and easy action, defined by horn riffs and a scratching guitar.

Oh Well (Parts I & II)
Fleetwood Mac
1969 • Reprise

>> One of the best known songs from the original and entirely British line-up of Fleetwood Mac – it's the song with the couplet, 'Don't ask me what I think of you/I might not give the answer that you want me to.' In the 1960s, Fleetwood Mac were all about Peter Green, his guitar playing and his songwriting, and 'Oh Well' is probably his finest moment. 'Part I' is a driving blues number, that revs itself up into an early example of hard rock through Green's nimble-fingered electric guitar work. It then gives way in 'Part II' to a delicate acoustic instrumental take. Here Green supplements his playing with a recorder and cello, and while it stops short of 'Hey nonny no' refrains, it's the blues as viewed from a castle in medieval England.

California Soul
Marlena Shaw
1969 • Cadet

>> In some ways it's strange that a singer with as big and as rich a voice as Marlena Shaw should be so well known for something as ostensibly throwaway as 'California Soul' – it's written by Ashford and Simpson, probably while waiting for the kettle to boil. But Shaw soars above an orchestral arrangement that many vocalists would find overbearing, transforming what could be a flimsy piece of black pop into a soul epic. You no longer register the cheesy lyrics as Shaw grips hold of the song, makes it her own and delivers a far funkier experience than the music behind her, setting up her own internal peaks and troughs and little skips of emotion. It's no wonder this version of 'California Soul' has been borrowed for TV commercials, and is frequently sampled by the likes of DJ Shadow and Gang Starr.

Marrakesh Express
Crosby, Stills & Nash
1969 • Atlantic

<< An absolutely gorgeous piece of hippie cheerfulness, written in the mid-1960s by Graham Nash after a train ride from Casablanca to Marrakesh, but rejected – rather understandably – by his previous band: the variety-show-friendly Hollies. 'Marrakesh Express' tootles along with the rhythm of the train tracks, while the guitars make vaguely Moroccan sounds and the breezy three-part harmonies extoll the joys of forsaking First Class to ride with the people. Such a sunny, life-affirming, fun piece, it's almost frivolous enough to have been made by the Monkees. Meanwhile, Iggy Pop famously dubbed it 'The worst song ever written' – surely an even more encouraging accolade.

Chelsea Morning

Joni Mitchell

1969 • Reprise

>> If there's one thing that unnerves urban types about folk music, it's the unelectrified, unapologetic ruralness of it all. 'Chelsea Morning' continues to serve as re-education. It eulogizes a sunny morning in New York's Chelsea district, so beautiful and at peace, turning it into such a fascinating and magical place it probably had Frank Capra for mayor. Even Manhattan's usually snarling traffic is transformed: 'A song outside my window, and the traffic wrote the words/It came a-reeling up like Christmas bells.' Mitchell's talent as a lyrical colourist has seldom been richer, and her wide vocal range rides some unpredictable acoustic guitar chord changes with an utterly charming airiness. Astonishingly, many dismissed the song, either palming it off as naive or assuming it to be ironic, which shows how much most urbanites know.

Breakfast in Bed

Dusty Springfield

1969 • Atlantic

<< Dusty may have had, far and away, the best R&B voice in the UK, but taking her to Memphis to record an album of soul scorchers with a crack local session band was always going to be a risk, even with Jerry Wexler, Tom Dowd and Arif Mardin producing. But nobody needed to have worried too much. On 'Breakfast in Bed' the backing musicians create a sweep of weepy horn-heavy Southern soul, and sensibly, Dusty doesn't try to compete. For the most part she slips in underneath it with a breathy, restrained reading, building to vocal climaxes then fading away as the tune washes over the listener in waves. It shrewdly lets you appreciate the music as much as the singing, giving the best of both sides of the Atlantic.

THE 1970s

The 1970s brought some streamlining of the ideas that came through the previous decade. Genres continued to meld with increasing sophistication – the likes of Gil Scott-Heron, Gram Parsons and Terry Callier were among the artists mixing up influences: jazz-funk, psychedelic soul, folk-soul, country-rock…and, for the first time outside the US, the rumblings of rap music started to make their influence felt.

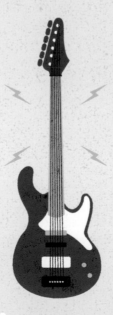

I Wonder
Rodriguez
1970 • Sussex

Although he was never going to get past labelmate Bill Withers in the gently funky acoustic-soul stakes, Sixto Rodriguez had a way about him, as 'I Wonder' shows. Set to a swaying soul background – acoustic guitar, swelling Hammond organ, percolating bass – it's an ingeniously ambiguous song that chastises an errant lover but ends up questioning the ways of the world. His music was so revered in South Africa that when, to much consternation, unfounded rumours of his suicide reached the country, two fans set off to find him and filmed their progress. The ensuing documentary, *Searching for Sugar Man*, won both a BAFTA and an Oscar.

Baby Lemonade
Syd Barrett
1970 • Harvest

With Pink Floyd's Dave Gilmour and Richard Wright playing on and producing Syd's second album *Barrett*, it's probably the closest we'll get to how Pink Floyd might have sounded had Syd stayed. Gilmour and Wright spent a great deal of studio time untangling Syd's ideas, getting them down in cohesive form and embellishing them sympathetically when he was unable to do so. The track 'Baby Lemonade' benefits enormously from this process: the music is as whimsical as you'd have hoped for, and the lyrics are full-on nursery rhyme nonsense: 'Send a cage through the post/Make your name like a ghost/Please, please, baby Lemonade.' Even so, it's subtly teased into an approachable structure and arrangement. Yes, it's Edward Lear for the late 20th century, but it never gets too self-indulgent.

War
Edwin Starr
1970 • Tamla Motown

With its opening shout of, 'War!/Huh!/Yeah!/What is it good for?/Absolutely nothing!', plus a towering psychedelic-soul backing, this is probably the best-known protest song of modern times. It's also an illustration of Motown's struggle to express social comment and embrace the wider world prior to the 1971 release of Marvin Gaye's *What's Going On* album. Written by Motown staffers Norman Whitfield and Barrett Strong, 'War' was originally a track on the Temptations' *Psychedelic Shack* album, and was taken up by anti-Vietnam War protesters who pestered the label to release it as a single. Not wanting to sully the group's slick image with counterculture notions, but not wanting to pass up a sure-fire earner either, Motown re-recorded it with Edwin Starr. Over four decades later, the track still defines Starr's career.

Pressure Drop
The Maytals
1970 • Trojan

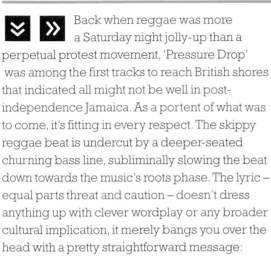 Back when reggae was more a Saturday night jolly-up than a perpetual protest movement, 'Pressure Drop' was among the first tracks to reach British shores that indicated all might not be well in post-independence Jamaica. As a portent of what was to come, it's fitting in every respect. The skippy reggae beat is undercut by a deeper-seated churning bass line, subliminally slowing the beat down towards the music's roots phase. The lyric – equal parts threat and caution – doesn't dress anything up with clever wordplay or any broader cultural implication, it merely bangs you over the head with a pretty straightforward message:

'Pressure gonna drop on you.' Toots Hibbert's urgent gospel hollering acts as a perfect presage.

In spite of such simplicity, this musical warning went unheeded by the Jamaican authorities, just as any innate meaning beyond that irresistible riddim that would have passed most of us by on those idyllic 1970s Saturday nights.

Immigrant Song
Led Zeppelin
1970 • Atlantic

MARK RADCLIFFE'S CHOICE  The powerful chugging opening riff of this tune, capped with Robert Plant's high-pitched wail is the other snatch of Led Zeppelin everybody can sing. An international hit (though not in the UK, where no Zep tracks were issued as singles), 'Immigrant Song' would always have a wide appeal as the bulk of the track is an uncomplicated groove which could easily have found traction in church-hall discos. But this isn't to say it's Led lite as there's a relentless heads-down drive going on, with just enough guitar cleverness thrown in. 'Immigrant Song', which gave the world the phrase, 'hammer of the gods', also introduced all that cod-Viking, Valhalla-esque imagery that's become such a heavy-metal playground.

Who Loves the Sun
The Velvet Underground
1970 • Atlantic

Groove Me
King Floyd
1970 • Atlantic

CERYS MATTHEWS' CHOICE

A masterful example of laid-back early funk that began life as a B-side, until club and radio DJs in New Orleans recognized its potential, and began playing it, pushing it on to become a national hit and eventually a million-seller. In the UK it made its mark in soul clubs as the ideal segue into a reggae session, as its jerky, economical approach to rhythm and the horns sweeping in and out could almost qualify it as Jamaican. King Floyd, who quit his job as a postman when this took off, never had another hit this big, but ended up doing very well out of samples used from the song – LL Cool J, Heavy D and Afrika Bambaataa are among those who have borrowed from it.

When the Velvet Underground signed with Atlantic Records they were ordered to deliver an album 'loaded with hits', which inspired the title *Loaded*. Its opener, 'Who Loves the Sun', is a breezy sing-along with jangly guitars, complete with 'ba-ba-ba-baaa' backing vocals and broken-hearted lyrics. Many a long-term fan was left outraged, believing it not to be 'real' VU. However, if you scratch below the surface of the three previous LPs you will find much of what Lou Reed wrote and the band recorded were solid rock 'n' roll songs in structure and arrangement – just Warholed up a bit. 'Who Loves the Sun' was the Velvets with a mainstream-friendly sheen but without musical compromise.

Message from a Black Man
Derrick Harriott
1970 • Crystal

« Written for the Temptations by Norman Whitfield and Barrett Strong (it's on 1969's *Puzzle People*) and with the hook line, 'No matter how hard you try you can't stop me now', this song quickly became an iconic Black Power statement. Harriott, one of Jamaica's most successful producers and artists, had a long-standing affection for American soul music, thus his take on it is as faithful as it could get without leaving Kingston – swirling organ, wah-wah guitar and close harmonies over a rock-steady beat. He wasn't the only Jamaican to cover the song: with the island's economy gutted eight years after independence, Jamaicans used the track to vent their frustration.

This is Reggae Music
Zap Pow
1970 • Island

⌃ A perfect example of how reggae was more progressive and open to outside influence than many outsiders realized. Zap Pow were a bunch of crack Kingston session musicians who clearly listened to a great deal of funk – and what they did with it was very smart. They slowed down the tempo from reggae of the time, then ushered in wah-wah guitars, phased horns and string-effect synth riffs, but made sure these funky sounds came entirely from a reggae perspective and on top of a properly balanced bass 'n' drum riddim. 'This is Reggae Music' is a far more representative statement than just sprinkling guitars and keyboard on top of existing reggae tracks.

Northern Sky
Nick Drake
1970 • Island

⌃ Although Nick Drake's first album *Five Leaves Left* was, from a sales point of view, hugely under-appreciated, it made sense for the follow-up to continue in the same vein, with just a little refinement. It was a shrewd move, which resulted in *Bryter Layter*. 'Northern Sky' involved John Cale working on the song from demo stage onwards. In partnership with Drake, he drew on his classical music training to add delicate layers of piano, Hammond and celeste to the song's original acoustic framework. The painstakingly constructed layers cleverly flatter Drake's innate abilities, casting light and shade to better display the subtleties of his character. Plagued by clinical depression towards the end of his short life, Drake is just a bit blue and wistful on 'Northern Sky'.

Riders on the Storm
The Doors
1971 • Elektra

↑ Not the most obvious classic featured on *LA Woman*'s tracklisting – that distinction belongs to its title track – 'Riders on the Storm' was the most lizard-like of Jim Morrison's vehicles. The Doors play a sleek, liquid funk distinguished by what they're *not* doing – the bass and drums are far back in the mix, the keyboards only punctuate the driving rhythm with twinkling flourishes, easing out of the way for the occasional flash of a Del Shannon-ish guitar. It's all so brooding and contained that the overdubbed storm effects aren't really necessary, but they do no damage in a spooky soundbed where Morrison can croon his lyrics with louche menace. Whatever the storm refers to, clearly no good is going to come from it.

Whatcha See is Whatcha Get
The Dramatics
1971 • Volt

Double Barrel
Dave and Ansell Collins
1971 • Trojan

» An absolutely gorgeous piece of hippie-pop cheerfulness. Astonishingly, although the roots revolution had been underway for a couple of years, for a few months in 1971 this tune *was* reggae as far as the UK was

concerned. 'Double Barrel' is a lively hammered-out piano riff and creeping organ melody above a jerky, perky, line-dance-friendly riddim. The first-ever recording session for drummer Sly Dunbar (later half of Sly and Robbie), it was completed with whooping self-celebratory vocals from Dave Barker. It got to number one in the UK pop charts; sold 300,000 copies; and is still Britain's best-selling reggae record. When its sales were combined with their similarly-veined second top-10 hit, 'Monkey Spanner', Dave and Ansell Collins became the UK's sixth best-selling singles artists of the year, in between the Sweet and Curved Air.

» A swooping ballad, this song is proof that not all Detroit's vocal groups ended up at Motown (who had let the Dramatics go in the late 1960s). The track has a huge, horn-fed orchestral arrangement, over which each member of the quintet dazzlingly swaps leads and effortlessly harmonizes with unfathomable depth. The song was also used behind the opening credits of *Wattstax*, the documentary of a Stax artists stadium concert, staged in 1972 to commemorate the seventh anniversary of the Watts riots in Los Angeles. It played over images of that event's destruction, which were intercut with the all-black crews building and preparing the stage for the gig. Strong stuff, and a fine example of a love song doubling as social commentary.

What's Going On
Marvin Gaye
1971 • Tamla Motown

The Revolution Will Not Be Televised
Gil Scott-Heron
1971 • Flying Dutchman

 MARY ANNE HOBBS' CHOICE One of the most eloquent, intelligent, poignant social commentaries ever committed to song, proving cathartic not only for the world in general – it kicked off all sorts of conversations among people who previously didn't give a damn – but for Marvin Gaye himself. Just prior to this, as personal tragedies engulfed his life (notably the early death in 1970 of friend and collaborator Tammi Terrell), Gaye had made noises about quitting the shallow and spiritually-bankrupt music business and taking up sports professionally. Quite how football or basketball could be more worthwhile is anybody's guess, but fortunately at the same time, the Four Tops' Obie Benson was determined to make a statement about the authorities' treatment of anti-Vietnam War protesters in Berkeley in 1969, and sought help in finishing a song he'd started. At one stage, Benson had considered taking it to Joan Baez, and also enlisted the help of songwriter Al Cleveland, but when Gaye heard about it (apparently while playing golf) he knew what he ought to be doing.

Gaye completed the work as a plaintive and baffled yet confrontational missive to America. Motown head Berry Gordy hated it, issued a dire warning about career suicide and refused to release it; the singer responded by refusing to record again for the company, with huge potential for embarrassment as he was then still married to Gordy's sister Anna. The label boss relented, and after the single was a massive hit, he greenlit a full album which Gaye recorded in less than two weeks.

 CRAIG CHARLES' CHOICE As funny as it is angry, as rousing as it is resigned, aware that the most effective revolutionaries are those that the masses will stop and listen to, this entertaining rant of a poem is never less than arresting. An attack on apathy and all-consuming consumerism, it's an adroit shift up from a Martin Luther King Jr-era pan-racial, passive way of doing things to a far more self-endorsing approach. It may only obliquely validate direct action by ripping into the by then establishment civil rights leaders like Whitney Young and Roy Wilkins, but the subtext is vivid: 'Don't expect/allow anybody to do it for you.' Just as important is the music behind the orator. The piece is delivered as traditional jazz poetry, but with an entirely contemporary feel thanks to the modern era players involved – Ron Carter (bass), Brian Jackson (piano), Hubert Laws (flute), Pretty Purdie (drums) – who totally understood how funk worked.

Funky Nassau
The Beginning of the End
1971 • Atlantic

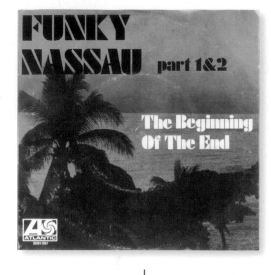

>> One of the most infectious, irresistible funk tunes ever captured on vinyl, 'Funky Nassau' made such a splash because, in what was a relatively straightforward dancefloor world, it was funk, but not as we knew it. It had all the right ingredients – pumping bass and drums; crisp guitar licks; razor-sharp horn riffs; and a semi-chanted vocal of largely self-celebratory nonsense. However, because The Beginning of the End were from the Bahamas – hence the title – they mixed it up differently. Faster than most of its US counterparts, the musical accents give a subtle hint of a one drop and the percussion injects true island flavour. As enduring as it was endearing, it crops up on compilations all the time and will be a mainstay of any old-school funk night, although even back in the early 1970s nobody could name another track on the album they put out.

Stay with Me
The Faces
1971 • Warner Bros.

LIZ KERSHAW'S CHOICE << In a list of songs young men used to sing when they were drunk, this could well have been number two (number one on such a list would obviously be another Rod Stewart anthem: 'Maggie May'). Quite understandably too: it's a cleverly constructed raucous sea shanty of a rocker, seductively chorded and arranged for maximum audience participation. Disregard the double-time intro – as most disco DJs would – and it's a smart, no-nonsense rock 'n' roll number, grabbing listeners with a driving, churning central riff. Although such an approach could have seemed backward-looking in the early 1970s, fuzz tone sounds help to keep it sounding contemporary, while there's still plenty of space for a guitar solo. As for the misogynistic lyrics, it was a time when TV's Jason King was regarded as the pinnacle of sophistication, and although it's no excuse, such unpleasantness was considered socially acceptable back then.

LIZ KERSHAW'S SELECTION

(See Liz's song choices on pages 31, 44, 76, 82, 100, 142, 148, 155, 171, 209 and 229.)

Musicianship, passion – that's what is important to me…that's basically it. The songs I've chosen for this book are very emotive, they just make you want to jump up and down. Passion and great musicians, and dirty guitars…and sweaty drummers. I love drums, I always listen to the drums and I love the bass lines in songs as well…it's all about pounding beats and dirty guitars…

A lot of it comes down to having a personal connection with music. The Faces was the first gig I was ever allowed to go to, which is why I've chosen them. Although I don't like misogynistic crap, and I don't like it from them either.

Before 6 Music, there wasn't a radio station for me as a listener or a DJ, 'cos BBC Radio 1 and 2 didn't play bands that I actually went to see or that filled festivals. And so I was quite vocal about demanding, 'We need a radio station for the bands we actually love and go and see'. And then 6 Music came along and of course I was delighted to be asked to present on it.

'MUSICIANSHIP, PASSION — THAT'S WHAT IS IMPORTANT TO ME… THE SONGS I'VE CHOSEN FOR THIS BOOK ARE VERY EMOTIVE, THEY JUST MAKE YOU WANT TO JUMP UP AND DOWN.'

When I was a DJ on BBC Radio 1 there were records I could only play at night because they were objectionable to the daytime audience, according to management: too hard, not easy enough on the ear. So when 6 Music came along, suddenly we could play those records, real rock 'n' rollers, all day long. The rock 'n' roll ethos is like a mindset, it's like a way of life, it's sticking it to the man, it's not unquestionably bowing to authority. And that's why we have it, but you never had that same attitude on Radio 1 or Radio 2 in those days.

And another thing: it's a bit like never conforming and growing up – why spend your money on new curtains when you could go on a road trip and see your favourite band?

Why do people get together at Glastonbury every year? It's not just for the music – it's because they live in a suburb of Wigan and they have to go to work nine to five, and once a year they can get together with like-minded people. And on 6 Music you can do that every day of the week.

Jeepster
T. Rex
1971 • Fly

>> Never mind the psychedelic folk, the guff about wizards or the sparkly hippy poetry, Marc Bolan was really just a lad from Hackney who knew what it meant to have a good time on a Saturday night. What was remarkable was how he managed to give T. Rex's Mud-style glam an elfin credibility. 'Jeepster' is a track that pretty much sums this up – a straight-ahead boogie, pumped out with verve and precision; hooks that even the most inebriated could still dance to; and catchy lyrics in the chorus. Simple and effective – Bolan always looked like he was having so much fun that everybody felt compelled to join in, and young fans like Johnny Marr (who bought this single, aged eight) were inspired to become musicians themselves.

Express Yourself
Charles Wright & the Watts 103rd Street Rhythm Band
1971 • Warner Bros.

This band made a name for itself in funk clubs through their ability to stretch a compelling tune out seemingly indefinitely, and 'Express Yourself' is no exception. The bass, drums and scratching rhythm guitar lock down a beat with such metronomic precision it allows the horns, vocals and lead guitar to stay loose. Yet whatever ideas the players wanted to go off and explore, they knew the groove would be exactly where they left it. There's an 'Express Yourself (Part II)' as well, which makes Part I seem hyper-disciplined in comparison, as the band break it down into a call and response that's not easy to understand, but is as funky as hell.

Strawberry Letter 23
Shuggie Otis
1971 • Epic

<< The Brothers Johnson had a disco hit in 1977 with a funked-up cover of this song; the original from six years earlier, however, gave a far gentler reading and was, in many ways, a more suitable take. Shuggie Otis, the son of R&B bandleader Johnny, had a penchant for mild, vaguely psychedelic black rock, of which this is a suitably paisley clad example. Although he had such luminaries as Wilton Felder, Ainsley Dunbar and George Duke playing on his *Freedom Flight* album, 'Strawberry Letter' placed Otis and his acoustic guitar centre stage, cramming with colour an amiable, softly trippy love song, '…rainbows and waterfalls run through my mind…', that never entirely forgets its soul roots.

I Am the Black Gold of the Sun
Rotary Connection
1971 • Chess

⏶ There hasn't been nearly enough psychedelic soul handed down for posterity; you know, the all-natural, barefoot, bright-eyed optimistic, pop-friendly soul music – the sort of fare that made *Hair*, then went on to make the world a happier, more loving place. Thus it's a good job the Chicago-based Rotary Connection is still remembered all these years later. A multi-racial band including a very young Minnie Riperton, they were part of group founder Marshall Chess' bold experiment to move away from conventional blues, soul and rock. 'I Am the Black Gold of the Sun' remains probably their finest hour, a massive show tune of mid-tempo jazz-tinged soul lite. With a host of cheery, optimistic voices and a message about self-empowerment, it's so big and overwhelmingly friendly you can't help having fun to this track.

All the Young Dudes
Mott the Hoople
1972 • Columbia

MARC RILEY'S CHOICE ⏶ Even at the time of its release, this song's writer, David Bowie, gave interviews explaining how the song wasn't a celebration of any titular young dudes, or intended as some sort of glam rock anthem. And you could see why he felt the need: Mott the Hoople's breakthrough single got to number three in the UK and the 'all the young dudes, follow the news' lines had become something of a sloppy disco sing-along. From a more sober standpoint, some 40 years later, it's astonishing anybody could mistake this for anything other than a clear portent of impending doom; it's practically 'Rock 'n' Roll Suicide Part II'. There's a death-march tempo, an electric guitar that drags it down even further, and a stark acoustic guitar, while Ian Hunter's vocal has a poignant air of resignation about it. It comes together in such a gripping study of youthful pessimism that a fallout shelter seems like a good idea.

Vicious
Lou Reed
1972 • RCA

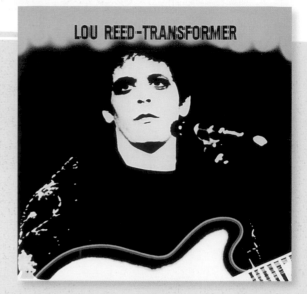

Even if not entirely accurate, you will want to believe the following story simply because things like this happen so rarely in the modern music business: Lou Reed leaves the Velvet Underground, makes a solo album of sub-VU wretchedness and his nascent solo career is all but written off. Enter David Bowie and Mick Ronson who, by way of a thank you for all the Velvets' influence, take Reed into London's Trident Studios and produce a follow-up album, *Transformer*, which would more or less come to define Reed's future.

It wasn't that much of a gamble. Bowie and Ronson, flying high on the breakthrough of Ziggy Stardust could do no wrong. London's original glam-rock scene, legendarily open-minded with its mixture of mildly pervy sex, oblique drug

references and sartorial idiosyncrasy, was essentially a more disciplined and knowing Velvet Underground.

However, the album still needed something to make listeners sit up and listen. 'Vicious', a straight rock 'n' roller, does exactly that. Cleverly, while channeling the kind of power chords favoured by the Velvets, Ronson's taut guitar riffs make the song structure cleaner and more secure, meaning all sorts of slurred, sleazy asides have space to make an impression, stopping the music from getting too respectable and poppy.

Reed's open-to-interpretation lyrics work perfectly with such careful arrangements, as they don't really distract from a deceptively imaginative piece of music, but at the same time the words will give you plenty to speculate on, if that's your idea of a good time. For what it's worth, the fans' favourite interpretation back then was that it was pure sarcasm, a diatribe against an ex-lover who was far from vicious: 'You want to hit me with a stick/But all I've got is a guitar pick.'

Freddie's Dead
Curtis Mayfield
1972 • Curtom

 A tune from the blaxploitation classic *Superfly*, that works as a recurring instrumental theme in the film but required additional words for the album track and single release. At the time, like the film itself, 'Freddie's Dead' was attacked for apparently glorifying the drug trade, but anybody who believed this had clearly not listened to much Curtis Mayfield. The lyrics made references, oblique and otherwise, to the circumstances that had created the doomed junkie of the title, then backed them up with the most ingeniously constructed 'mournful funk' (could that be an actual category?). The bass synth and wah-wah guitar power the track along, but behind both lies a bleak string section which cleverly grounds any excitement, and which renders the funk to sound desolate rather than uplifting. All the while Curtis' falsetto soars above it with as much pleading as foreboding.

Skylarking
Horace Andy
1972 • Studio One

 A few years back, Horace Andy revealed the secret behind Jamaica's Studio One label's astonishing success: when the label owner Coxsone Dodd founded his own recording studio in the early 1960s, his were the only premises in Kingston where musicians were allowed to smoke weed. In many ways the seductive 'Skylarking' bears out this claim – the beat is precisely chopped out early reggae, but the horns drag across the back of it, giving the music a woozy, slightly-blurred-at-the-edges quality. Meanwhile, Andy's falsetto is so airy it drifts across the landscape, giving out a stern warning to delinquent youths, and outlining the consequences for their antisocial behaviour.

Dancing Girl
Terry Callier
1972 • Cadet

As the 1960s became the 1970s, thanks to an explosion of small black-owned radio stations, African-American music beyond jazz was starting to define itself, and folk-soul was a big part of the funk revolution. Terry Callier was part of a fraternity that included Bill Withers and childhood friend Curtis Mayfield. They used soul roots, folk methods and jazz ideas to make music that was gently urging, which could be quietly or obliquely militant. 'Dancing Girl' was one of the style's undoubted masterpieces, a nine-minute epic that starts as a delicate but slightly bleak number, which slowly swells as the arrangement builds to a full orchestration. Along the way, the listener has been guided on a tour of the pain, joy, desperation and hope to be found on the ghetto's streets.

Cravo e Canela
Milton Nascimento
1972 • EMI

GILLES PETERSON'S CHOICE ›› Back when jazz-funk was still called jazz-fusion, it had far fewer dancefloor considerations, and it was all about the playing and expanding musicians' parameters. Many of its practitioners in the US – Chick Corea, George Duke, Al Di Meola and so on – looked further south to incorporate Latin ideas, with Brazil's rich musical tapestry proving particularly attractive. Here, Brazilian guitarist and songwriter Milton Nascimento, whose background in samba and contemporary jazz was adopted by US musicians to add a little authentic colour to their fusions, moves the other way. 'Cravo e Canela' shows off a very modern samba, percussion-rich, airy and relaxed, overlaid with keyboards and synths. Glorious jazz-funk, with no usurping of Nascimento's Brazilian roots.

Roadrunner
Jonathan Richman and the Modern Lovers
1972 • Beserkley

‹‹ In so many ways 'Roadrunner' is the perfect 'post-rock 'n' roll' rock 'n' roll song: it's about the gloriously pointless teenage experience of driving around at night with the radio blasting, just because you can. But it doesn't just tell of the experience, it fairly accurately recreates it, in a brightly coloured, totally uncomplicated, dancing arrangement – it's mostly just two chords – which gives substance to the spunky, stupid optimism of youth. What makes it especially glorious is the lack of any edge or a dark side: what you hear is what you get. Remarkable that anything so sunny could be the missing link between the Velvet Underground and the Sex Pistols. All the more remarkable, then, that in 2013, it was further distinguished when a state representative campaigned to have it named as Massachusetts' official state song.

The Needle and the Damage Done
Neil Young
1972 • Reprise

>> Anti-drug songs don't come much more unnerving than this. Accompanied by his acoustic guitar, Neil Young plaintively recalls how heroin ripped through the music world he knew, laying waste to people he loved. Rather than rail against drug use in a Father-knows-best fashion, which is always faintly ludicrous coming from any rock star, he unflinchingly talks about the damage the drug wreaked and the sadness it caused. Never morose or self-pitying, it's simply resigned and so personal it only just stops the right side of being uncomfortable. In what is a compliment to Young's communication skills, 'The Needle and the Damage Done' is thankfully only two minutes long.

Back Stabbers
The O'Jays
1972 • Philadelphia International

<< As the 1960s rolled into the 1970s, against a background of the Vietnam War and Watergate, it seemed the underlying emotion in protest soul music was paranoia. Formerly a vocal quintet, but reduced to a trio by 1972, the O'Jays' breakthrough moment was a study in suspicion. Written by McFadden and Whitehead, it features one of soul's greatest couplets: 'What can I do to get on the right track?/I wish they'd take some of these knives out my back.' 'Back Stabbers' deals with distrust on an entirely parochial level – when you're not looking, expect your friends to try it on with your wife. A Gamble and Huff production, it showcases a guitar leading an unsettling rhythm section, hyperactive congas adding an air of shiftiness and sweeping strings keeping everybody on their toes. With the urgency of the O'Jays' harmonizing, this is edginess of the highest order.

Virginia Plain
Roxy Music
1972 • Island

Roxy Music's first single came out a couple of months after their self-titled debut album, so although they'd made something of an impact, it was daytime radio that introduced the group to the rank-and-file UK pop buyer, who took to them immediately. Quite rightly too, as at that point, mainstream music was in near disarray, with the singles charts clogged up with un-evolved soul, soft rock, the hod-carrying end of glam, novelty items, and Wings.

Here was a song that intelligently played the trends of the early 1970s off against pop music's far more basic requirements, all within a framework of entirely accessible sophistication. 'Virginia Plain' had enough art, in Eno's electronics and Andy Mackay's oboe (an *oboe!*); enough glam in their whole presentation; and, crucially, enough rock in Phil Manzanera's guitar. Bass player Rik Kenton's no-frills anchoring of the whole thing meant it was

disco-friendly, yet the willfully opaque lyrics meant there was enough to make the song a popular subject for discussion. However, the deciding factor and the most attractive element of the song's first *Top of the Pops* appearance – and of the band in general – was Bryan Ferry. As a former working class lad he seemed to know not just what went into most people's everyday soundtrack, but into their look too, delivering a dress code and haircut people could realistically aspire to. Meanwhile, after years of androgyny and apparent bisexuality-as-career-choice, he portrayed a glitzy, unapologetic heterosexuality. But the biggest plus point of 'Virginia Plain' was Ferry's louche-sounding, uncomplicated croon, a style of singing practically every fan felt confident enough to approximate, no matter how ill-advisedly.

CRAIG CHARLES' SELECTION

(See Craig's song choices on pages 8, 9, 18, 22, 43, 55, 70, 79, 158, 226 and 258.)

A musician can transcend the music he's playing by the attitude he strikes, if you know what I mean. So some guys who aren't particularly great musicians can come across brilliantly by the music they decide to play and the way they decide to play it.

That said, beats are really important to me. I like music that gives you a wiggle, you know, to get a wiggle on to…and I like rawness, I like real drums, real bass, real guitars…I like the whole thing. A lot of people are into 1980s music and stuff like that, but to me that's a real cold decade, musically, because it was so much to do with machines and synths and drum machines and stuff like that. Which I think, when you listen to it now, really dates that music to that particular decade.

You get both attitude and great beats in funk music. A lot of the riffs are quite simple in funk and soul music, y'know…The bass riffs, although they've got a groove on are, in fact, quite simple. You marry that to the drums and you've got a tight rhythm section if the drummer and the bass player know what they're doing.

They don't have to be doing anything that difficult to make it sound so syncopated, make it sound so cool. And a lot of the riffs from the horn sections are fairly simple. It's fairly difficult to master the 'wacka-wacka-wacka-wacka' on the guitar, but the rest of it is fairly simple. What's always stunned me, what I've found stunning, is the excellence of the vocalists in funk and soul music. Think about it, the thing about funk and soul music is because it's so simple you can't get away with a bad vocalist. You need somebody who can really bang it out and that's the only thing that keeps it all together.

At 6 Music there's no interference from any of the bosses or the suits, no one's ever come in to my studio and told me you've got play this or you've got to play that. They don't know what I'm going to play until I rock up on a Saturday and bang it out. That is the ultimate freedom. Sometimes I don't know what I'm going to play until the middle of the show. We try and keep it as an organic thing, we've got a template that we might work on during the week of what we might do on a Saturday, but sometimes that changes from the first record. If something's happened to me on a Friday night, then that all goes out the window and I'll build a different show live on air because we've got the Trunk of Funk section there and we can go anywhere we want. And we often do. To have that freedom, to be that organic when you're doing a radio show to take away playlists and stuff like that is a tremendous freedom and a total pleasure.

> 'I LIKE RAWNESS, I LIKE REAL DRUMS, REAL BASS, REAL GUITARS…I LIKE THE WHOLE THING.'

ROCK & POP

BILL WITHERS

Think (About It)
Lyn Collins
1972 • People/Mojo

Use Me
Bill Withers
1972 • Sussex

When it comes to consistently excellent soul songwriting, Bill Withers has few peers. Indeed many of his songs are better known when covered by others: 'Ain't No Sunshine', 'Who Is He?' or, indeed, this one. Sometimes such covers, which have assumed all manner of soul sub-genres, have unfairly overshadowed Withers' original versions, but none can better his warm, welcoming way with a song. 'Use Me' shows off what Withers did best: up-tempo funk with the melody carried by his rich voice, allowing for minimal backing – sometimes it's just drums. This gives so much space between the instruments it makes an acoustic, almost folky feel, resulting in a very modern sound that was instantly intimate and somehow organic.

James Brown's decision to finally allow a light to shine on those around him – among them Fred Wesley, the JBs and indeed Lyn Collins – was one of the smartest moves he could have made. Funky as the Godfather of Soul's singles were, they could be numbingly limited in their approach – everything was a rhythm – and while this was great fun on the dancefloor, they weren't doing a huge amount to advance the music or Brown himself. Somebody like the powerfully melodic Lyn Collins was ideal for solo potential, as her voice was big enough not to be overwhelmed by the massed riffing going on behind her, and could turn this beat-fest into a superb single without sacrificing any intrinsic funk.

I'll Take You There
The Staple Singers
1972 • Stax

>> Right from the introduction, apparently filched from Harry J's reggae classic 'Liquidator' (see page 33), the gentle, laid-back funk of 'I'll Take You There' is the perfect intersection of soul and gospel. The easy-action, spacious Muscle Shoals backing track is built around a bass line that supports the electric piano and horns almost in rotation, meaning nothing collides, and even the brief guitar solo has its own window. It's a perfect soundbed for the trio's tight gospel arrangements, and a song of such sunny, uplifting optimism. As soul music became increasingly politically concerned and tended to protest about what was going wrong, this – a US number one – became an anthem of forward-looking hope for just about everybody who cared to listen.

Roforofo Fight
Fela Kuti
1972 • Barclay/Wrasse/MCA-Universal

CRAIG CHARLES' CHOICE << Even those of us who were immersed in American funk, who understood the value of ten-plus minutes of groove, were sometimes at a loss when it came to the work of Nigerian maverick Fela Kuti – you knew you *ought* to like it but was it really worth the effort? 'Roforofo Fight', however, connected straightaway. Owing as much to James Brown as it did to afrobeat, it lays down a monstrously funky groove built on a relentless drumbeat and an equally reliable bass. That backing provides the densest foundation for a cascading and anarchic saxophone-led brass section, seemingly ad-libbed vocals and a popping electric piano. Weighing in at just over a quarter of an hour, it's not for the faint-hearted, but it is dictionary definition jazz-funk.

Get Up, Stand Up
The Wailers
1973 • Island

Part of *Burnin'*, the most representative collection of Wailers songs following their time recording with Lee Perry, 'Get Up, Stand Up' enjoyed particular significance beyond both that album's and the group's lifespan. It became a regular closing number of frontman Bob Marley's stage sets, and indeed closed the group's final-ever show with Marley in 1980 (at the Stanley Theater, Pittsburgh, Pennsylvania). Both Peter Tosh and percussionist Bunny Wailer had left the Wailers in the mid-1970s, but would record solo versions, too.

Written by Marley and Tosh, this blunt, uncompromising call to arms casts the Wailers as revolutionaries by any means necessary – more Trenchtown pragmatists than global spiritualists. As such, the song continues to stand as the most

broadly-acceptable reminder thereof, serving as an articulate if hardnosed *ying* to the more happy-clappy *yang* of such later sentiments like 'One Love' and 'Legalize It'. Just as importantly, the tune is a lasting souvenir of the precision and power of the Wailers as a self-contained group, with full status afforded to the Barrett brothers (on bass and drums) and Wire Lindo on keyboards.

What also stands out on this song is how much the group have learned from the overdubbing and tempo-tampering that so distorted their previous album. Rather than attempt to disguise reggae as

rock, they assume a wider outlook by adding their own guitar twiddles and Clavinet flourishes within an unambiguous Jamaican framework. Meanwhile, prodigious rhythmic skills chop out a beat so crisp it can support all manner of sub-riddim without confusing the novice. As the vocal trio's tight harmonizing harks back to impressions of their tenement-yard days, it gives the song a real depth. Finally, when Peter takes over for a verse, you remember what a talent he was and wonder what would have happened if the threesome had stayed together.

Gypsy
Chubby Checker
1973 • 20th Century

» Come the early 1970s, Chubby Checker could no longer trade profitably as the man who invented the twist, and so a decade after his trademark hits, he underwent a bizarre reinvention and became a psychedelic rocker and hardcore rhythm and blueser. 'Gypsy' is one for the former category, a breakneck, fuzz-drenched, acid-flavoured B-side of bluesy, early heavy metal. It gives prominence to a explosive, take-no-prisoners drummer and Checker's obvious Jimi Hendrix aspirations – not based so much on guitar-playing prowess but on the general intense feel of the production. Even if it wasn't by Chubby Checker, 'Gypsy' would still be worth the price of admission, but if you're really seeking novelty value, flip the single over and play its A-side, 'Reggae My Way', which is every bit as terrifying as the title might suggest.

Finders Keepers
Chairmen of the Board
1973 • Invictus

« When the prolific writing and production trio Holland-Dozier-Holland quit Motown in 1967, one of their issues with the company was a lack of creative control within its famed production line. Yet remarkably, the cornerstone of their new label, Invictus, would be a vocal trio assembled as identikit Motown in every respect, except, maybe, lead singer General Johnson's titanic afro. Named Chairmen of the Board, the group had a long run of hits from 1970 but, by 'Finders Keepers', the label had evolved Invictus' sound into something far funkier. The trio hollers through the track with deft harmonizing and real urgency, with backing provided by a cement-mixer blend of low-register electric Clavinet and stabbing horns. The producers even permit a solo trombone on a couple of occasions – and that would never have been allowed at their previous employers.

Higher Ground
Stevie Wonder
1973 • Tamla Motown

   Coming in the middle of Stevie Wonder's golden four-year, five-album period (a rush of developmental creativity bettered only by the Beatles' roll of 1963–7, from *Please Please Me* to *Sgt Pepper*), the *Innervisions* album has often been viewed as its era's peak: a set offering a range of social documentation including issues such as urban deprivation, drugs and racism.

By this point, protest and community commentary among the dance anthems and love songs was almost regulation as part of funk's canon. Less predictable was the message of hope and optimism that was set out by 'Higher Ground'. Set to the deceptively simple backing of a Moog bass and a Clavinet riff, uncomplicated enough for anybody to follow, yet with enough depth to satisfy the more discerning listener, the song is a series of straightforward exhortations. The vibe is very Martin Luther King Jr-ish in that the message of everyday positivity largely encourages good people, across the board, to keep on doing what they're doing and the reward will come: 'Teachers keep on teachin'…Lovers keep on lovin'/Believers keep on believin''. Yet there are warnings that others could do a lot better: 'Powers keep on lyin'/While your people keep on dyin'…' and a request that 'Sleepers just stop sleepin'.'

It's a balance that few could pull off without sounding mawkish or simple-minded but by then, such was Stevie Wonder's standing in both the music world and the real world, that he succeeds. When Wonder surrenders clever lyric writing to a humanitarian desire to make the world a better place it has genuine buoyancy. When he sang, 'Gonna keep on tryin'/'Til I reach my highest ground… Don't let nobody bring you down', few were able to resist.

Give Me Love (Give Me Peace on Earth)
George Harrison
1973 • Apple

>> One of the best (and best received) solo efforts by a former Beatle, George's tranquil country-tinged soft rocker seems far closer to 'the Quiet One's' apparent personality than the lusher Phil Spector co-production of his triple album, *All Things Must Pass*. Harrison's five-piece unit strums up a folky, gently-undulating rhythm, over which he plays some beautiful slide guitar solos. His singing is equally serene on this simple, clever song, one that seems to be blending the spiritual with the materialistic and with his personal quest for making the world a better place. On original release, 'Give Me Love' knocked Paul McCartney's single 'My Love' off the top of the US charts, simultaneously placing ex-Beatles at numbers one and two.

I Believe in Miracles
The Jackson Sisters
1973 • Prophesy

<< A huge orchestral production sounding like a psychedelic disco, this track from the five Jackson sisters from South Central Los Angeles is reminiscent of late-1960s theatrical soul. On original release, it almost sank without a trace, but eventually made its mark in the late 1980s, gaining currency on London's rare-groove scene.

Keep On Truckin'
Eddie Kendricks
1973 • Motown

⌄ Eddie Kendricks was an original Temptation, the falsetto lead in the group and responsible for many of their early vocal arrangements, but he left acrimoniously in 1971, just before their series of vast Norman Whitfield-instigated epics like 'Papa Was a Rollin' Stone'. This was Kendricks' answer to those sonic mini-movies, which, in one crucial respect, made an even greater impact: it was a club tune first and foremost, aimed at making people dance rather than the product of desk-induced drama. Here we find a thumping beat made road-trippy with a rolling Clavinet riff and supplemented with a huge orchestral arrangement that, on the eight-minute version, often drops out to leave just percussion or drums. All the while, Kendricks' voice swoops around it.

Return of the Grievous Angel
Gram Parsons
1973 • Reprise

The title track of an album that housed the best Gram Parsons material since the Flying Burrito Brothers' *Gilded Palace of Sin* in 1969, this became something of an elegy; Parsons fatally overdosed between its completion and its release. Dominated by guitar picking, pedal steel guitar and fiddle, 'Return of the Grievous Angel' is nearer country than rock – and all the better for it, giving the casual observer an easy way into modern country without having to buy a pick-up truck. It walks that thin line between being resigned and morose with a touch of humour, thanks to the duetting with Emmylou Harris, whose bruised-angel tones work wonderfully with Parsons' weary-but-a-touch-mischievous cynicism. There's a wry grin hovering over lines like, 'Twenty thousand roads I went down/And they all lead me straight back home to you', that elevates it above so much standard honky-tonk fare.

African Dub
Joe Gibbs
1973 • Joe Gibbs Music

GIDEON COE'S CHOICE The Mighty Two, alias producer Joe Gibbs and engineer Errol Thompson, released a series of increasingly inventive dub albums under the name *African Dub: All-Mighty,* and this is the first track from the first volume. Somewhat underrated in mainstream terms, Thompson was a mixing-desk alchemist who ranked alongside Lee Perry and King Tubby. With this song he spins the backing track to the Techniques' rock-steady classic 'Love is Not a Gamble' into slowed-down rootsy gold. Using hardly any effects, Thompson X-rays the tune, deconstructing it by stripping it to its bare essentials, then reintroducing its original components as slightly reverbed riffs, allowing us to forensically examine what makes a killer track. Nothing particularly spectacular, but carried out with such a sure touch it's totally absorbing – not least for the almost subliminal but constant tambourine way back in the mix.

GIDEON COE'S SELECTION

(See Gideon's song choices on pages 60, 144, 145, 164, 174, 176, 216, 253 and 293.)

Since I've been at 6 Music I've had my ears opened to Jamaican and African music, that I knew very little about before. That shows what 6 Music has done for me and hopefully what it does for listeners.

Sonically, Jamaican dub from the 1970s was as important to music all over the world as anything that's happened in the past 60 years – Joe Gibbs, King Tubby, Lee Perry…

As well as keeping up with the new releases, 6 Music has to keep a watch on the reissues too, so we can bring music from the past to listeners, reacquainting, reminding and introducing people to music.

Super Furry Animals were adventurous. They were always underrated because they were great pop songwriters, and although they had influences – every artist does – they were doing their own thing; perhaps because they didn't come from somewhere that had an accepted scene.

Jon Hopkins' song 'Immunity' is a striking record, a beautiful piece of music. The whole album is great. It's got King Creosote – Kenny Anderson – singing on it and that's like having Gene Hackman in a movie – it makes what's already good great.

There's a connection between that and the Joe Gibbs track, because both have an awareness of space within a tune and will work with it, stretching the sound. They're aware of the melody too, but will never overfill it or clutter it up. I'm sure Jon Hopkins has listened to the last two Talk Talk albums, but I'll bet he's listened to a lot of dub tunes as well.

There's not really one thing I look for in a record, all the records I listen to have different things I like in them – melody, harmony, rhythm put together with sonic beauty – and that can happen in any style. Somebody said to me the other day that I was playing too many noisy records, but that's just how it goes sometimes on 6 Music – because you've got the freedom you might find you've been playing a lot of beautiful records so you want to shake it up with something unpleasant!

> 'ALL THE RECORDS I LISTEN TO HAVE DIFFERENT THINGS I LIKE IN THEM — MELODY, HARMONY, RHYTHM PUT TOGETHER WITH SONIC BEAUTY — AND THAT CAN HAPPEN IN ANY STYLE.'

The Payback
James Brown
1973 • Polydor

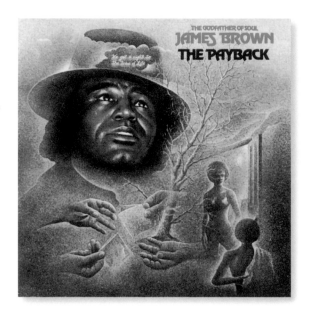

Less then 15 seconds into 'The Payback' you know exactly what you're letting yourself in for: a thumping bass line, metronomic drum, churning wah-wah guitar, a James Brown yell, sugary backing singers – and horns that creep into the mix to skewer it through with a counter rhythm. This is early-1970s funk of the absolute highest order, a culmination of what the Godfather of Soul and his band the JBs had been looking for since the second half of the 1960s, when the former 'Mr Dynamite' became 'Soul Brother No. One'.

Astonishing as it may seem now, such early 1970s masterworks as 'Talkin' Loud and Sayin' Nothing', 'Super Bad' and 'Make It Funky' were little more than warm-ups for an album comprised largely of extended, intensified, barely embellished

grooves, of which this single was the title track, and possibly the funkiest. The double album was recorded as the soundtrack for the blaxploitation film *Hell Up in Harlem*, the mostly forgettable follow up to *Black Caesar* (a classic of the genre, and also Brown-scored). However, the *Harlem* set was rejected by the movie's producer, leaving Brown to release it in its own right.

Hell Up in Harlem was to be Brown's third soundtrack, by which time in any case he understood that film scores didn't have to conform to traditional pop song rules. This gave him and the JBs the freedom to build their grooves as moods rather than tightly structured musical narratives. Essentially, he decided to deliver what he'd been aiming at for years – the James Brown live experience recorded under studio conditions.

'The Payback' track epitomizes just such a liberated approach, as it constructs a dense and relentless rhythmic attack, in which every single instrument (Brown's vocals included) makes a powerful contribution. Of course, this sort of thing only makes sense if it goes on for over five minutes, and at seven-and-a-half, 'The Payback' becomes the essence of James Brown, and the essence of funk.

Personality Crisis
New York Dolls
1973 • Mercury

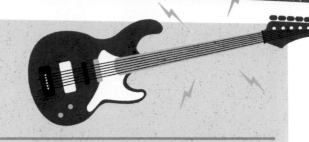

If anybody needed a bridge from the Rolling Stones to the Sex Pistols, this would be it: no frills, tightly packed blues-based rock 'n' roll; shouted, insulting lyrics; and vocals that are more enthusiastic than anything else. Less self-consciously arty than the Velvet Underground, and with more conventional songs than the Stooges, the Dolls elevated early-1970s metal to a higher plane. They did this by stripping it of its excesses that verged on cabaret, yet not losing sight of its essentials – the gloriously dense boogie-woogie piano is a case in point here. Interestingly, the readers of the highly influential US rock magazine *Creem* voted them the best *and* worst band of 1973, but songs like 'Personality Crisis' gave them a lasting influence far beyond their necessarily brief lifespan.

Money
Pink Floyd
1973 • Harvest

>> Quite rightly massively acclaimed, *The Dark Side of the Moon* album could be a challenging listen at times. 'Money', however, that opened its second side, was an accessible track and (in some territories but not Britain) a hit single. It showed everybody exactly how good Pink Floyd could be. In essence it's a simple blues tune, but even while the subtly clever playing is anything but simple, the arrangement (often in complex 7/4 time) never loses sight of the song's essence. You don't need to spend too long listening to realize how carefully crafted it is. Although it was recorded in a garden shed and with homemade sound effects including paper being ripped and coins clinking, the sound is never anything less than sophisticated. And, as is key to all the greatest performances, the band sound like they were thoroughly absorbed in what they were doing – which arguably happened less and less on subsequent Floyd records.

Mind Games
John Lennon
1973 • Apple

≫ Like fellow former Beatle George Harrison, John Lennon chose 1973 as the year he dispensed with the services of producer Phil Spector, and opted for self-production. The *Mind Games* album from which this is the title track very much played it safe – in fact, if its creator was anybody other than John Lennon, you might even question the confidence involved. The song itself is a stuttering mid-tempo number, with the kind of keyboard orchestrations reminiscent of the earlier Plastic Ono Band output. Supplemented with a slide guitar, it had an instantly familiar sound and easily slipped into our consciousness. As do the sentiments of the lyric, concerning itself with peace and love, and how to achieve such things with the power of the collective thought. At the time of its release, the track's reception was lukewarm, with Lennon viewed as merely marking time, but over the ensuing years it's become valued as epitomizing pretty much everything that was good about his solo output.

I Feel Sanctified
The Commodores
1974 • Motown

>> Remarkably, for a group that became internationally renowned for some of soul's cheesiest ballads, the Commodores began life as a pretty sweaty funk band – and yes, this was while they had Lionel Richie out front. 'I Feel Sanctified' is from their first album, *Machine Gun*, which pitched them as Motown's answer to the self-contained New York acts, and they hold their own with aplomb. A rubber bass and gut-level Clavinet are knitted together with pin-point horn lines – arranged by Richie – and an earthy vocal celebrating the sanctification brought about by the love of a good woman. It showed Motown could comfortably stand up against competition from New York like Kool and the Gang and BT Express, and doubtless helped to pave the way for the label's future, with it signing Rick James a few years later.

It's Better to Have (And Don't Need)
Don Covay
1974 • Mercury

<< >> During the 1950s and 1960s, Don Covay bounced around the music business with little more than patchy success as a singer, but had considerable success as an R&B and rock 'n' roll songwriter for the likes of Aretha Franklin, Solomon Burke, Chubby Checker, Wilson Pickett and Gladys Knight, who all had hits with his compositions. Then in the early 1970s, his earthy vocal style and gutsy soul arrangements found favour on funk-oriented radio stations looking to add some depth to their programming. 'It's Better To Have' went further than that: a sizeable hit in the US, the skippy pace, wailing guitar, stacked vocals and relentless tumbling riff gave it an extended life on Northern Soul dancefloors.

Mr Soft
Cockney Rebel
1974 • EMI

>> In the mid-1970s, few bands were more likely to provoke a foaming rage in the music press than Cockney Rebel – or, as they were becoming, Steve Harley & Cockney Rebel. Therein lay the problem: Harley's alarmingly self-assured opinion of himself versus the group's innovative, violin-led psycho-pop that most people wanted to like. 'Mr Soft', from the group's second album *The Psychomodo*, follows a typical horror-show theme of a circus gone bad, weaving a skillfully spooky soundscape peopled by sonic visions of sideshow freaks and scary clowns. The song is built around a welcoming oompah beat, and a familiar calliope circus riff, but it's all a bit off-key, and gradually you realize this big top is a dark and frightening place – even before the entrance of Harley's eerie, mannered vocals.

Fire
The Ohio Players
1974 • Mercury

<< As Funkadelic's labelmates on the small, mostly free-thinking Westbound Records, the Ohio Players made a trio of sexually-charged albums with wild (for back then) S&M themed covers. By 1974's *Fire*, their second LP for a mainstream record company, they were proving they could still throw down nasty, slippery funk, but were now making their X-rated points through innuendo. This, its title track, simply sizzled with its wailing siren opening, working a less-is-more theme, building on a springy bass line and distant horn riffs, with occasional guitar or keyboard shadings; but it's only during the couple of instrumental breaks where the players really come to life. Which means it's down to the vocals to carry so much of this, and their apparently chaotic arrangements do a perfect job of creating a sense of sleaze and celebration.

Tell Me Something Good
Rufus
1974 • ABC

>> Rufus had started out as an egalitarian group, with Chaka Khan as merely their singer. However as soon as she took to the stage or the studio microphone nobody noticed anybody else. It took a tune like 'Tell Me Something Good' to ram that point home, as it wasn't written by the group – in a moment of staggering generosity, this sure-fire hit was given to them by Stevie Wonder. As a result, the track transcended their previous limitations. The backing is solid funk-by-numbers, given a lift by the vocoderish effects and big bass synth, but the record is really all about the vocals, and Chaka Khan gets stuck in: sensuous, playful and downright lascivious, she takes the song to places the band's self-composed numbers had probably not even considered.

Pretzel Logic
Steely Dan
1974 • ABC

>> A tremendous example of Steely Dan's ability to transfer their liquefied-jazz sensibilities to a relatively-disciplined, radio-friendly format, without sacrificing the gorgeous looseness that had made their previous work so attractive. 'Pretzel Logic' is supremely elegant jazz-rock in which Dan founders Donald Fagen and Walter Becker set up a fascinating conversation between, respectively, electric piano and lead guitar. Not that this is a two-handed affair; bass player Wilton Felder – comparisons with the Crusaders are entirely valid – lays down a solid structure for Fagen and Becker, and the rest of the players, including a restrained brass section, fall in and out of the mix, adding colour around the edges and almost absentmindedly coming together for the occasional peak. Tight as it undoubtedly is, it sounds effortless.

Autobahn
Kraftwerk
1974 • Philips

Not the sort of thing most people want to be told, but to genuinely *get* 'Autobahn', go for the full version which occupied the whole first side of the album. Kraftwerk's international breakthrough is mundanity served up as art – a kind of musical L S Lowry, with or without bleak industrial references – and the three-minute single edit will let you off the hook much too easily, long before it even risks being humdrum.

In its complete 22-minute version, though, this motorway commute as entertainment has ample time to settle into a comfortable kind of tedium, before introducing aural effects like vague changes of scenery, flicking through radio stations, and rising and falling volumes of traffic. This is an electronic symphony, meaning it not only sounds melodically exquisite, but also is sufficiently intriguing to make you want to keep your foot on the pedal, so to speak.

The backing swooshes along with a road-noise rhythm, while the players delve into their prog-rock bag of tricks like toccatas and twiddles, dropping them into the mix to form riffs and counter rhythms. Along with several more sweeping but equally repetitive sub-themes, they shift from movement to movement. Appropriately, after the best part of half an hour, the song just sort of peters out – the only climax you might apply to a motorway drive doesn't bear thinking about.

Following several years of dismal MC5-ish *rock sans frontières*, Kraftwerk's decision to celebrate rather than attack the commonplace, via electronic instrumentation, was a far more radical statement. *Autobahn*, their fourth album, found them and producer Conny Plank immersed in learning their craft, and less likely to fall back on clichés.

This Town Ain't Big Enough for Both of Us
Sparks
1974 • Island

Before Sparks recorded the *Kimono My House* album this track came from, brothers Ron and Russell Mael had moved from California to England, where they found an altogether more encouraging environment: glam rock. Working with UK musicians and producer Muff Winwood (the duo had wanted Roy Wood but he was unavailable), they were much more focused and could allow their sense of the ridiculous to flourish. 'This Town' owes a debt to Roxy Music and Queen (who had once opened for Sparks at a London show), but the combination of synth-pop sensibilities with huge, theatrical flourishes and a movie-cliché lyric are all their own. A piece of frantic whimsy that fitted so perfectly into mid-1970s British pop that many didn't realise its creators were American. But then again that could just have been because Sparks understood irony.

September Gurls
Big Star
1974 • Ardent

As the 1970s got properly underway, while the poppiest artists continued to regard the album as a collection of singles, most musicians outside pop used the format to stretch out and experiment in some way or other. Big Star from Memphis, Tennessee, were something of an anomaly in rock circles, in that they were excellent songwriters and more than competent performers, yet were happy to make the best singles they could and, when they had enough of them, put them together on an album. 'September Gurls', taken from *Radio City*, is a gutsy, guitar-driven pop song with tinges of R&B and an insane lyric about September gurls and December boys, plus a full-on acoustic guitar and plaintive vocal. It's a neatly built bridge between Brill Building New York pop and West Coast folkier rock, perfectly presented in two-and-three-quarter minutes.

Take Me to the River
Al Green
1974 • Hi

« After five albums in three years, a period when 'Tired of Being Alone' had made him a mainstream success story, Al Green, his producer Willie Mitchell and the Memphis players knew exactly what they ought to be doing. Luckily for us, instead of becoming complacent, this pushed them to explore beyond the edges of what had become known as the Hi sound. The arrangement on 'Take Me to the River' is not nearly as overwhelming as on many of Green's previous hits, as the rhythm section sets a faster-than-expected tempo, with the horns laying down a melody while the familiar organ is throttled back. In spite of strings brushing through the back of the mix, there's plenty of room for Green to show off some lyrical and vocal dexterity with a gospel-tinged reading of the tale of a woman that done him wrong.

P-Funk (Wants to Get Funked Up)
Parliament
1975 • Casablanca

 CRAIG CHARLES' CHOICE » The song 'P-Funk', from the *Mothership Connection* album, initiated a whole concept, spawning a sprawling funk soap opera of half-a-dozen albums and one of the biggest stage shows yet undertaken by an African-American group. Although Parliament's previous album, *Chocolate City*, had kicked the theme off – black people in unexpected situations – 'P-Funk' was a more overt introduction to proceedings, musically as well as lyrically. While a softly funky backbeat and bass line swells, the horn section, keyboard and voices dart in and out until the drop comes, and everything joins up to forcefully make your funk the P-Funk. All the while, ringmaster George Clinton pushes things forwards with seemingly stream-of-conscious street lyrics, promising to return your regular radio to you, 'as soon as you are grooved'.

Gloria
The Patti Smith Group
1975 • Arista

>> ∨ In the UK's popular music scene of 1975, a female artist usually meant Helen Reddy, Olivia Newton-John, Marie Osmond or, for the rebel in you, Patti Labelle. Suddenly, seemingly from nowhere, Patti Smith's *Horses* album churned up the big-haired landscape.

Leading the charge was 'Gloria', a semi-spoken piece introduced by a lone piano and a sultry, 'Jesus died for somebody's sins but not mine.' Cleverly layered arrangements build the simple three-chord structure to an overwhelming musical momentum. But the most arresting aspect came from the transformation of Van Morrison and Them's comparatively chirpy love song into a belligerently passionate hymn to lesbian sex – startling for 1975. It was only at the halfway mark and the familiar 'G-L-O-R-I-A' chorus when you could be absolutely certain you were in the same song.

Neither the only, nor even the first, known song that Patti Smith trashed so comprehensively (her reinvention of 'Hey Joe' was earlier still), but it was the first that many of us heard, and in attitude alone, Smith became a crucial punk catalyst.

Back in the Night
Dr Feelgood
1975 • United Artists

>> By the mid-1970s, no-nonsense rock 'n' roll was becoming the rebellion of choice against the rising tides of prog noodlings and twiddly synths. Dr Feelgood were part of the pub rock scene, a genre so named not merely because it was (originally) played in pubs, but also because it embodied dimpled pint glass, roll-up smoking London taproom culture in general. That the group came from Canvey Island – an unglamorous, anachronistic seaside resort off the Essex coast – fitted the vibe perfectly, but their music was always far more uplifting than these settings might suggest. This was good-time, rollicking, riff-heavy Saturday night stuff, and 'Back in the Night' isn't ashamed to borrow from the Mud/Sweet end of glam to chop out a groove with a doubled-up bass and rhythm guitar. An effects-laden lead rips across the top, and the lyrics tell of how work can get in the way of having a good time. It was probably mixed through a Ford Cortina dashboard speaker.

Supernatural Thing
Ben E. King
1975 • Atlantic

<< After huge success with the Drifters and as a solo artist in the late 1950s and early 1960s, the following decade wasn't particularly kind to Ben E. King. He was from the wrong side of the street-funk watershed, and therefore no matter what pimp-ish suits and hats he was dressed up in the kids would still see him as representing middle-aged nostalgia. Really, though, instead of acres of velvet, all he needed was the right song, and 'Supernatural Thing' was it. Cowritten by Gwen 'Ain't Nothing Going On but the Rent' Guthrie, it was a supremely laid-back, spare, mid-tempo loop of organ and bass, stitched together with rolling congas. King himself eased in and out of the beat, making it his own without disturbing the record's very modern, very funk sound.

Shining Star
Earth, Wind & Fire
1975 • Columbia

From what many would say was the group's best album, 'Shining Star' contains almost everything you'd want from Earth, Wind & Fire, but without a great big cosmic pyramid getting in the way. It's infectiously optimistic, with lines like: 'You're a shining star/No matter who you are'. A killer bass line to anchor the groove and a scratching guitar on top of that, plus a horn section drilled to within an inch of its life – and any other holes are filled in with percussion or lead guitar. Ultimately, though, it's the vocal arrangements that lure you in: individual, tightly harmonized and ultimately acapella, they work the sentiments, and the choruses of the lyric leave a listener in no doubt: they really can be all they can be.

Foot Stompin' Music
Hamilton Bohannon
1975 • Dakar

A title that has nothing to fear under the Trades Descriptions Act, this was one of a series of thumping disco records made by drummer and percussionist Hamilton Bohannon. Initially Stevie Wonder's drummer, then Motown's touring bandleader, he quit for a solo career in the early 1970s. At the time his single-minded approach to a groove went down far better outside his US homeland; like his previous single, 'South African Man', 'Foot Stomping Music' was a sizeable club and chart hit in the UK. Slightly more sophisticated than its predecessors, this was disco-dedicated, but the beat was held down by a guitar and organ as much as by the obligatory drums, and while it had a melody, this was pumped out as rhythmic snatches rather than as a bona fide tune.

Movin'
Brass Construction
1975 • United Artists

 Brooklyn funk group Brass Construction's track 'Movin'' was a tune of such epic proportions in London clubs in the Summer of 1976 (the long and very hot one), that if a DJ dropped the huge opening chord towards the end of another tune, the dancefloor would all but stop in anticipation of what was to come. Producer Jeff Lane and arranger Randy Muller had constructed a dangerously fat funk sound by packing layers inside the rhythm track so densely you couldn't hear the bottom of it, yet it remained flexible enough to embrace its environment. Brass hooks and weirdly melodic keyboard lines formed staging posts as they weaved in and out, while the semi-chanted vocals ticked things over; but it was really only ever about that phenomenal beat.

Low Rider
War
1975 • United Artists

 As a Los Angeles funk band, at a time when New York was far and away the Good Groove capital, War and their cool, jazzy, Latin-tinged sounds were usually explained away as being 'laid-back' or 'sunny' or 'Californian' (as if the latter was a good thing in itself). In truth, they were a tough bunch of characters from the streets of Long Beach, South Central and East LA. 'Low Rider' explores that side of them: tense, churning funk, topped off with hyperactive timbales and percussion that was more LA Chicano than anything from south of the border. Taking low-riding car culture as a metaphor for the multi-culti ghetto life, that several of the band members had grown up in, resulted in probably the definitive song of their back catalogue.

HUEY MORGAN'S SELECTION

(See Huey's song choices on pages 10, 27, 38, 57, 77, 124, 125 and 188.)

The tracks I've chosen are a music lover's selection. I'm still a fan of music, always will be, listening for the next cool band. I think it's important to love music if you're in the music business.

One of the reasons I chose 'That Old Black Magic' was because it was my wedding song for our first dance. I've always loved Louis Prima because it's like the punk rock of its day! That tune in particular really struck me because it's just an amazing track.

With all these tracks there's a story behind every song. Like for example, 'Voices in My Head' by The Police – I'd be in the Latin Quarter, I'd be home on leave from the Marines and we'd go out to these clubs and they'd throw that one in there and it was cool because, as much as people love to stick it to Sting, it was one of those songs that moved people – everybody loved that track, it had something in there. The bass line is fucking slammin'…The Police were marketed as a reggae-esque boy band, but they were excellent musicians. And for a three piece you could hear those guys going for it.

There's a sense of joy and wonder in all the songs I've chosen. When you listen to Brick doing 'Dazz', they're having fun. 'Gypsy' by Chubby Checker, he's out of his mind, but he's having fun in a record that he disavows to this day. It's almost

> 'I'M STILL A FAN OF MUSIC, ALWAYS WILL BE. THERE'S A SENSE OF JOY AND WONDER IN ALL THE SONGS I'VE CHOSEN.'

like a drum 'n' bass beat with crazy stuff going on and it was on this album called *Chequered*. And he put it out in like in the early 1970s and he wasn't happy with it, but his label said you gotta put out a record and I love it, quite frankly.

I look at the Janis Joplin cover of 'Summertime', that's a song that in the first ten seconds of her singing, it's like she's got you by the heart. When she bends up to that note you don't know if she's going to hit it. You really don't know and she just bends into it and you're like, 'Woah! She got it.'

And I put that in there like I put in Sixto Rodriguez: he should be as big as Bob Dylan. He put out two records while Bob Dylan did a whole bunch of stuff, but on those two records every song he recorded was very, very good: like, epic good. I picked that one because I thought the bass line was of the era but also funky.

And Fatback, of course, that's like my jam. And 'Remedy' by the Black Crowes was my favourite song by them because I think it caught them at their best.

When people say, 'I really like your radio show', I'm like, 'Thank you', and I take it as a compliment because it's my personal selection. When you just get down to it, it's 'Here's a song, have a listen.' That's what we're there for: DJs are there to kinda curate people's afternoons or their midnight hours.

New Rose
The Damned
1976 • Stiff

  It was appropriate that the Damned cut the UK's first punk single. While their contribution to punk rock has been somewhat submerged beneath, for example, the Sex Pistols' powers of self-promotion and the Clash's revolutionary stance, they represented the spirit of punk as a fresh musical situation. They wanted to rock their crowds, and had the skills to do exactly that. On 'New Rose' drummer Rat Scabies brings an explosive drum pattern that stays the course hurling the piece forwards; Captain Sensible, on bass, doesn't just keep up, he riffs; while on top lies the crunching chords of Brian James, who wrote this and so much of their early stuff. Producer Nick Lowe stacks this dynamic, hard-driving power pop, and Dave Vanian's stagey vocals give this love song – about the tingly excitement of meeting a new girl – just enough camp value. It's what really lay at the heart of so much punk: very good musicians, putting a new and exciting spin on traditional pop music.

Natty Rebel
U-Roy
1976 • Polydor

Real old-school toasting from the old-school master and pioneer of the form – rather than ride a specially constructed riddim or even an instrumental version, on 'Natty Rebel', U-Roy does it just how he did it on the sound systems ten years earlier. He works within the existing track, with echoing vocals reacting to what the singers are doing, commenting on it and connecting it to the everyday lives of both himself and his audience. This was a challenging job, but works so well here because U-Roy has a spontaneous sense of timing and a touch so light he rides the track without interfering with its original dynamic. Most importantly, he doesn't lose the roots flavour of his lyrics but his diction is so clear you can understand everything he says. Toasting this skilful can only enhance a track.

Dazz
Brick
1976 • Bang

◀◀ 'Dazz' is an abbreviation of 'disco jazz' and that sums up what Atlanta-based outfit Brick brought to the party. They did it rather cleverly too. It starts off as a decent disco-type groove with some wailing sax thrown in and an on-going chant of 'Dazz dance disco jazz'. Once that's softened the dancers up, at around the two-and-a-half minute mark, things get jazzier: a hyperactive flute comes in, the sax steps it up a gear, the bass takes a turn as a poppin' slappin' lead instrument and some intriguing echoes can be heard from the back of the mix. After a couple of minutes of this, it's back to the disco groove to finish things off.

Blitzkrieg Bop
The Ramones
1976 • Sire

▶▶ The most important ingredient in this record is Craig Leon, a pop producer who eventually put his classical-music aspirations to good use, working with the Royal Philharmonic Orchestra and Pavarotti, among others. Before that he was a pop producer for the likes of Blondie and, at the very start of his career, the Ramones. Here he puts a great deal of effort, technique and microphone placement into getting this to sound like it does. OK, it still only took a week to record the whole of their first album, but without his attention to detail, that rabble-rousing 'Hey ho, let's go' and the crunching chords that swirl around it would never have sounded so live and direct. The whole point of 'Blitzkrieg Bop' was to give the Ramones maximum impact – the speed, the absurdity and the adolescent catharsis of their helter-skelter live show all had to be captured in the grooves. It was, and American rock was never the same again.

I Want More
Can
1976 • Virgin

>> As the original figureheads of seemingly mainstream-shunning, minimalist Krautrock, Can caused some commotion with 'I Want More', a tune best described as art disco, and their first and only top-30 hit in the UK. But those throwing up their hands in horror missed the point: because the band was experimental rock, therefore they did what they liked and as long as it was from a Can point of view it was valid. This from an album that dabbles in reggae! Although clearly a first cousin of Sparks or Roxy Music, 'I Want More' opts for a Teutonic approach, meaning rigidly ordered riffs and beats more or less marching you through, until some lovely chiming melodies thaw some of the cold in its second half.

So It Goes
Nick Lowe
1976 • Stiff

>> The first single on the iconic Stiff Records was, if legend is to be believed, recorded in an afternoon for less than £50, involving only Nick Lowe and a drummer. If that really is the case, 'So It Goes' is a triumph of resourcefulness over resources and easy to see why the label appointed Lowe as its in-house producer. As such he was responsible for a trademark Stiff vibe that gussied up the live-music sound of so many small London venues and presented it for a wider audience. 'So It Goes' is a textbook example. A big expansive guitar sound that never overwhelms you, but rather carries you along through a subtly shaded landscape so you know you've been rocked, it still didn't detract from the wryly funny essence of Lowe's song: the lyrics comment on the arbitrary nature of life and death, with the phrase 'So it goes' borrowed from Kurt Vonnegut's 1969 novel, *Slaughterhouse-Five*, which is repeated each time someone dies in the book.

I Wish
Stevie Wonder
1976 • Motown

CRAIG CHARLES' CHOICE « »

Given this is a track from *Songs in the Key of Life*, a double album so fussed over that its release was postponed or delayed several times over two years, it's a spectacularly spontaneous, casually joyful affair. 'I Wish' has all the qualities of later Stevie Wonder and none of what could so often get on your nerves, and it struck gold, hitting the number one slot on the Billboard Hot 100 in the US. Its funky foundation is an ever-present upbeat bass-synth riff, fleshed out with a few well-spaced upper-register twiddles while horns shift it to the peaks and crescendos that give it a showy sense of event. The personalized lyric, a romp through the childhood of Little Stevie, gives the song an immediacy often lacking in his more considered narratives. It's everything 'Ebony and Ivory' isn't.

Station to Station
David Bowie
1976 • RCA

MARC RILEY'S CHOICE » If the *Station to Station* album acted as a near-precise mid-point between the cod-Philly sound of Bowie's previous *Young Americans* and the synth-driven Euromiserablism of his subsequent *Low*, this elongated title track finds him gazing across the Atlantic towards Europe and Kraftwerk before he starts the journey. It's his homage to 'Autobahn' (see page 68) and a nod to Norman Whitfield as a hangover from his soul-boy musings in its defined sections and sense of drama. Bowie claims he was so buried in cocaine during the recording of *Station to Station* he can't remember anything, which is a genius triple whammy of spin. Firstly, it creates a rock'n'roll legend; secondly, it creates no legend at all, saying make up what you want (and many writers have); finally, it would have absolved Bowie of responsibility had the change of direction been badly received. In fact it was embraced as a return from what he called the 'plastic soul' of *Young Americans,* and a return to something more meaningful, somehow more Bowie.

SHAUN KEAVENY'S SELECTION

(See Shaun's song choices on pages 58, 91, 124, 153, 256 and 288.)

I think in all those instances, with the possible exception of The Cure which is a little more doom laden and introspective, there's a great joy and abandonment. If you're talking about Stevie Wonder or that particular Ian Dury track, there's a great joy to it. And in particular, broadcasting at the time we do, in the mornings, we're always looking for that. Sometimes life's not offering it up to you at that moment – it's a ridiculous time in the morning and you're exhausted, possibly pissed off and you've run out of sugar, you've got nothing but a stale piece of toast before you for the foreseeable future, you're looking for some uplift. And the music's the place to get it most often on our show.

What do I look for in a record? We're the entry point for 6 Music [at breakfast time], we have to be the most accessible, so we're the least challenging, the friendliest and the cuddliest. Even when we're listening to new music for Record of the Week, or when you've listened to recommendations from other people of old music you've not come across before, it's always the same thing you're looking for. I guess there's a feeling that there's got to be something within it that is a bit transcendental…You can get in a brand new artist that is 22 years old or you can get it in Bobby Womack, that sort of feeling…that an old soul has created this music, and that it's communicating something really resonant

> 'WHAT DO I LOOK FOR IN A RECORD?...I GUESS THERE'S A FEELING THAT THERE'S GOT TO BE SOMETHING WITHIN IT THAT IS A BIT TRANSCENDENTAL...'

about the human experience. I'm being hyper-pretentious now, but some stuff you can put on and go: 'Yeah…there's a nice melody to that, y'know, that's catchy'; but with the really great stuff there's something else there that's really… 'I couldn't have done that', there's that feeling as well. It's like, 'The bastard! How the hell did they come up with that?' It's a feeling of specialness that only certain people have that can get to you. That's what I'm looking for.

I don't think many acts have got the capability to pump out album after album of brilliant transcendental inspirational music that gives you that sense of wonder, but there are some. Most weeks you'll see one piece of music that gives you that sense that it's still out there. It's still possible, because for an old fart like me there's always that discussion of, 'Oh, it's not quite as good as it used to be, with the Beatles and the Velvet Underground and all that', but there's enough great stuff out there year on year to make me keep the faith, really.

If I had to, at gunpoint, chose a genre that spoke most readily to me, it would be 'guitar based/song based'. That's a very wide sort of area, not even a genre, but from the blues through to West Coast California to modern indie music, those sorts of touchstones are where I find most of my inspiration. And being a failed rock star myself, I always hark back to that and it was always really important stuff to me.

The Blank Generation
Richard Hell and the Voidoids
1976 • Sire

By the time he got to recording his first album, of which this is the title track, Richard Hell had been around the New York punk block a few times, and was experienced enough – he was previously a member of Television and the Heartbreakers – and old enough (nearly 30) to know there needed to be substance behind the posturing. The music on 'Blank Generation' is sharp-edged, tense and never gets too comfortable. This song is a twitchy, asymmetrical dialogue between the two guitars – but by avoiding overt aggression it becomes an intriguing conversation to try and be part of, rather than a rant to be endured. Likewise Hell's lyrics and vocals are unafraid of letting his widely cultured slip-show, here he draws reference to the beat culture of 20 years earlier, while an obviously well-read background give his lyrics a, well, *lyrical* quality which was lacking in many of his peers.

Police and Thieves
Junior Murvin
1976 • Island

Lee Perry's Black Ark studio was roots reggae's apex, and nobody else approached the musical and vibesical summit he sat upon in the second half of the 1970s. Perry combined knackered recording equipment – giving that warm, soft sound – with a fantastic imagination and a philosophy of record making that treated the vocal as another instrument – similar to how Norman Whitfield employed the Temptations. And in Perry's establishment, singers and musicians were encouraged to hang out, swap ideas and mess around until something happened: like 'Police and Thieves'. It developed organically out of the band jamming, then Junior Murvin, who already had a lyric written, was sitting about in the yard and joined in. Perry the producer liked what he heard, and set to work on it.

King Tubbys Meets Rockers Uptown
Augustus Pablo
1976 • Mango/Island

 DON LETTS' CHOICE The title track from a set of instrumentals and semi-instrumentals, for which Pablo – notably the only person ever allowed to smoke weed in King Tubby's studio – took to the mix master. His bigger, more dramatic approach to dubbing perfectly complemented his own more introverted, upper-register productions. This track is a remix of Jacob Miller's song 'Baby I Love You So', in which Tubby leaves Pablo's skittering feel intact, even adding to it with echo, but takes out a lot of the mid range to beef up the bottom end and turn it into an exhilarating exercise in extremes. And to think Island were going to put this out as the B-side to the 'Baby I Love You So' single release, until somebody who actually went to sound system dances suggested otherwise.

Whole Wide World
Wreckless Eric
1977 • Stiff

 LIZ KERSHAW'S CHOICE One of the more inspired promotional items Stiff Records sent to journalists, in the hope of having them listen to their music with a favourable ear, was the Wreckless Eric Brick. These standard red house bricks with the artist's name painted on one side became a fixture on so many desks, as the hollow on the top became an ashtray that seldom needed emptying. There was nothing too subtle about new-wave rock 'n' roller Eric, either – 'Whole Wide World' is underpinned by just two chords, his voice doesn't even have that wide a range and the crescendo is as noisy as you like. Yet such was Eric's enthusiasm for his task, and there was so little difference between him and his audience, that he and his music were instantly likeable.

I Feel Love
Donna Summer
1977 • Casablanca

Prior to 'I Feel Love', most disco records were lushly orchestrated, using *actual* orchestras to give them a big, full, velvet-lined sound. Munich-based Italian producer Giorgio Moroder wanted to create the same sort of effect, by utilizing already-popular electronic instrumentation. Using only a Moog synthesizer he crafted music of great depth and phased melodic subtlety, with an unremitting double-time beat, and Donna Summer's ethereal voice of calm floating just above it. 'I Feel Love' was a huge international hit because it was a) unusual; and, b) a very, very good disco tune, but it also triggered a change of course for disco, as producers started to imitate its shinier, more hard-edged sound. This, of course, saved the cost of hiring that orchestra.

Two Sevens Clash
Culture
1977 • Joe Gibbs Music

>> 'Two Sevens Clash' is perhaps better known for what it stood for than for what it actually was. It foretold of a catastrophe of biblical proportions to be unleashed on the Earth on 7 July 1977 (a date when four sevens clashed), sweeping away wickedness like Noah's flood. As well as that, the song, and its parent album, was one of the highlights of roots reggae music in terms of both sound and narrative. Produced by Joe Gibbs and Errol Thompson, 'Two Sevens' is supremely tuneful with a sparkling array of higher-register melodies floating through a gutsy, insistent riddim, using all manner of modern sounds and instrumentation on a subtle dub technique. Essential too is the trio's singing – a beautiful, light three-part harmony, never portentous or angry, and celebrating righteousness as much as it was issuing a warning. Incidentally, on the day in question in 1977, Jamaica experienced record levels of absenteeism from schools and work places – the only unusual thing that happened.

Marquee Moon
Television
1977 • Elektra

<< When New York's Television were sold to the UK as a punk band it was to a fair bit of consternation – punk was considered noisy, often stupid and usually angry about something, yet 'Marquee Moon' had two shimmering guitars (expertly played by Tom Verlaine and Richard Lloyd) talking to each other across a delicately poised rhythm section, careful vocals and was an unusual ten minutes long. Using the gift of hindsight, it jettisoned what might have become stale in favour of fresh ideas, and so moved punk smartly along. It's intelligent, textured and impassioned modern rock that showed how not to be scared of a guitar solo and encouraged you to take a punk attitude anywhere you liked. Effectively, post-punk started here.

(Get A) Grip (On Yourself)
The Stranglers
1977 • EMI

>> When the Stranglers hit the punk scene in 1977, it was to great suspicion from the music press and other bands. As well as an approach to music closer to US acts like the Ramones and Patti Smith than the Sex Pistols or the Clash, they were older than their British peers and had more eclectic musical backgrounds, varying from classical to jazz to blues. Their debut single, 'Grip', explains the mistrust – while it has a certain belligerent energy, it's melodic, especially in the bass line; the lyrics are thoughtful; and thanks to the lively Dave Greenfield, it includes *keyboards*. Although this did not endear them to the Keepers of the Punk Flame, it would give the group a sucessful career, and a springboard into other styles of music.

This Perfect Day
The Saints
1977 • Harvest

>> On the surface, the Saints (made up of singer-songwriter Chris Bailey, drummer Ivor Hay and guitarist-songwriter Ed Kuepper) were hardcore punks from Australia, but listened to more closely, they were audio poster boys for what punk had already rapidly evolved into. As the next wave of bands emerged on the scene, the genre's limitations became glaringly obvious – so new acts started to push the medium in other directions. Made in the summer of 1977, barely 18 months on from the Ramones' first album, 'This Perfect Day' has all the hallmarks of the previous wave – breakneck pace, buzz-saw guitar sound, hollered vocals – but the structure is closer to blues-based rock, and the group bring an understated underlying melody to it.

Do Anything You Wanna Do
Eddie and the Hot Rods
1977 • Island

>> Part of the wave of Essex acts that included Dr Feelgood and its frontman Wilko Johnson, Eddie and the Hot Rods made a smart move quickening the tempo of their Canvey Island mix of rock and R&B. They were too intrinsically conformist to be punk, but with so much contemporary rock shifting in the same direction, their gravitation to the power pop of 'Do Anything' ticked all the right boxes. They were good enough musicians to make it work, too. Dense, noisy but cleverly layered, the end result brings out the qualities they brought to pub rock, but with a bit more muscle.

Could Heaven Ever Be Like This

Idris Muhammad
1977 • Kudu

  When veteran jazz drummer Idris Muhammad unleashed this chunky eight minutes of disco funk there was a predictable gnashing of purist teeth – which might have made sense had he disgraced himself. Far from it as things turned out; he recruited some top-level contemporary fusion players – the Brecker brothers and Jon Faddis on horns, guitarist Hiram Bullock, and so on – and built 'Could Heaven Ever Be Like This' from the ground up, with his buoyant drum patterns as a foundation. Horns and guitar swap licks, and the keyboards occasionally chip in, as it chases itself around the groove. It's a thumping jazz-funk epic that keeps things seductively soft with a brief vocal that the drummer had sense enough not to attempt himself.

Don't Dictate
Penetration
1977 • Virgin

Play Penetration back after all these years, and you realize exactly how few women were in punk bands to begin with, let alone ones that have lived on (musically speaking) beyond their bands. Pauline Murray of Penetration had one of the most striking voices of practically any genre at the time – wheeling above the music, plaintive and fearless but never obnoxious. Consequently, she made far more of an impact than anything more strident, and, as a bonus, she could carry a tune. 'Don't Dictate' finds Murray and Penetration at their late-punk best: exuberant, energetic but always in control, as they career around in a mix of windmilling chords and pulsating drums.

Frankie Teardrop
Suicide
1977 • Red Star

Punk attitude meets Kraftwerk, pointing the way to the gloomier end of synth-pop and more than a few of Bowie's Berlin musings, 'Frankie Teardrop' is ten minutes of the most harrowing outpourings ever to be classified as popular music. Against an unsettling throb of a drum machine, laced with discordant synth noodling, vocalist Alan Vega deadpans a detailed commentary of a young factory worker and father losing his grip on life, coming home to shoot his wife and baby then kill himself. It doesn't stop there either – the 'music' and an accompanying screaming follows him into perdition. As an unflinching exercise in extreme social commentary it has few peers, but when author Nick Hornby described it as a record you'd listen to only once it's not difficult to see his point.

Lust for Life
Iggy Pop
1977 • RCA

>> While Iggy's previous Bowie collaboration recorded in Berlin, *The Idiot*, sounded little more than Bowie-by-proxy, the *Lust for Life* album seemed far more of a joint effort. The title track lives up to its name: Iggy celebrates getting his heroin habit under control and learns how to negotiate the obstacles life will put in your way: 'I'm just a modern guy/Of course I've had it in the ear before/'Cause of a lust for life, a lust for life.' It's all delivered with a confident, exuberant swagger you could dry washing with, and updates the wiry but often loosely structured power of his earlier recordings with the Stooges to something more immediate and sophisticated.

The driving force behind this rediscovered strut (*The Idiot* was a far more delicate affair) lies with the Sales brothers, Hunt and Tony (drums and bass, respectively), who arrived in Berlin from Detroit. Whether or not the siblings from Iggy's old neighbourhood inspired him, the geographical connection couldn't be more pronounced than on this track. Although there are keyboard and guitar parts involved, it's the Sales rhythm section that carries this tune all the way, with a drum-driven riff picked straight out of Motown's Funk Brothers' playbook (as heard in The Supremes' 'You Can't Hurry Love'). The track is a taut rock 'n' roll force of nature that steams ahead for almost a whole minute before Iggy comes in, by which time it has built up such a tsunami of vibrant optimism it's swept all who have heard it along in its wake. Not for nothing has this song been so widely covered: it's cropped up in situations as varied as the movie *Trainspotting*'s opening sequence, commercials for Gap and Royal Caribbean Cruise Line, and even the kids' cartoon *Rugrats*.

JAMES STIRLING'S SELECTION

(See James' song choices on pages 28, 83, 115, 210 and 280.)

There is just a handful of radio stations with fiercely loyal audiences and BBC Radio 6 Music is one of them. Occasionally those who haven't come across the station ask what it is. The simple answer is that, along with our audience, we celebrate the spirit of alternative music from the 1960s to the present. That sentence is brought to life through the music in this book and for me, these five tracks and artists form a crucial part of our story.

I vividly remember the surprise and excitement in the 6 Music office when David Bowie slipped out 'Where Are We Now?' in January 2013. That anyone – let alone someone of his stature – could record and release an album in total secrecy in an era of constant gossip and camera phones is astonishing. He is one of those rare unifying artists and 'Space Oddity' – the first of his entries in the book – still resonates. Regular producer Tony Visconti passed on the record, claiming it was a cheap shot at the moon landing, but in truth it was a warm-up for much of the Bowie magic that was to follow.

With his legendary DJ sets, Don Letts had the honour of introducing Culture's *Two Sevens Clash* to the punks at The Roxy in Covent Garden. It helped the Clash find their sound. It featured heavily on John Peel's Radio 1 show – despite criticism from a few voices who said there was no place for reggae on the BBC.

It's fair to say that Joy Division is one of the foundation stones of 6 Music. They remind me of the Velvet Underground in that their considerable influence overshadowed their record sales. One cannot overestimate the importance of this band – and their record label Factory – in the development of independent music. Factory Records were virtually the dictionary definition of alternative spirit and Joy Division, followed by New Order, have an incredible legacy. 'Transmission's '…dance, dance, dance, dance, dance, to the radio …' mantra will always sound perfect on 6 Music.

In truth, any of the eleven tracks on the Stone Roses' debut album could have featured in this book. But 'I Am the Resurrection' stands out for the sheer joy of its unifying chorus and instrumental climax.

As you would expect, Radiohead have a close connection with 6 Music. Most of the members have hosted shows at some point, tracks across their eight albums feature prominently in our schedules and various side projects are met with much interest from our audience. *OK Computer* was a blockbuster follow-up to *The Bends* but there aren't many radio stations that would play all six-and-a-half minutes of 'Paranoid Android' in their Breakfast Show. Happily we do.

The National are dear to our audience, who both voted 'Bloodbuzz Ohio' into the top 5 of 6 Music's greatest hits and recognized the band as having given one of the stand-out performances at the 6 Music Festival in 2014.

'THERE IS A JUST A HANDFUL OF RADIO STATIONS WITH FIERCELY LOYAL AUDIENCES AND BBC RADIO 6 MUSIC IS ONE OF THEM.'

Complete Control
The Clash
1977 • CBS

STEVE LAMACQ'S CHOICE » There's a laughable irony, and more than a touch of cynicism, when a song about the evils of big record companies is released by a big record company like CBS. On the other hand, without the big record company's machine then the kind of carping heard on 'Complete Control' wouldn't have reached so many people – the system being used to strike a blow against the system. But leaving aside any questionable integrity, this is a Clash punk anthem to rank alongside 'White Riot' and 'London Calling'. Just as the Clash's stage performances and presentation of themselves in the media was, underneath it all, far more conventional than many of their peers, so there were shrewd musical sensibilities at work behind the raw-throated yelling. Within a conventional verse/chorus structure, the two guitars play across each other, neatly offering depth, before the rockabilly guitar break shatters the tension brilliantly, and allows them to build it up again. So many elements here made it easy for the uninitiated to get a grip on the track, and these were the very same things that gave it such longevity. The song's masterstroke, though, was to engage errant Jamaican dub genius Lee Perry as producer, only to remove pretty much all of his contribution once he'd gone.

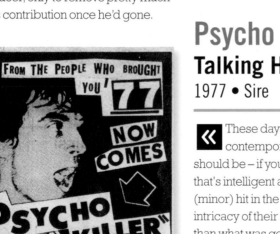

Psycho Killer
Talking Heads
1977 • Sire

« These days it's difficult to avoid Talking Heads as so much contemporary rock clearly references them. And so it should be – if you're going to 'borrow' then do so from a band that's intelligent and open-minded. 'Psycho Killer' was their first (minor) hit in the US, and immediately shows that the depth and intricacy of their arrangements and ideas was so much greater than what was going around them at the time, never mind the modern-day pretenders. It blends rock, soul and 1960s pop into a series of sharply twisting time shifts, jagged-edged bridges and stream-of-consciousness lyrics, hung together through an understanding of: a) what the public actually wanted from new wave music; and, b) exactly how far they could push such a bond.

American Girl
Tom Petty and the Heartbreakers
1977 • Shelter

>> In the 1970s, what with garage-band punk, art rock clever-cleverness and deliberately chilly synth-pop, there were vast swathes of land between Los Angeles and New York in danger of being forgotten by US music. Or they were until what became known as heartland rock established itself. A more grounded descendant of the preciously new wave of LA folk-rock, heartland rock's song structures were straightforward, the instrumentation comprised of conventional guitars, bass and drums, and the subject matter was of blue collar America and its trials, tribulations and triumphs. Tom Petty and his Florida band the Heartbreakers were leaders of the genre, adding a contemporary bluster to the countrified middle-American car-radio fodder, and immediately finding an audience. 'American Girl' has a familiar, jangly, Byrdsian feel, but with far more energy and urgency, and tells an ambiguous tale of apparent disappointment as one more aspect of mundanity that's easy to empathize with. Almost 40 years later, it's still an American radio regular.

Young Savage
Ultravox!
1977 • Island

<< 'Young Savage' reflected a band in transition. Ultravox! were messing about with new ideas as they looked to shift themselves from being the last glam band in town towards something slightly more contemporary. Interestingly, they went for a punk attitude and approach, but with vastly upgraded electronic instrumentation and ended up with a gloriously hilarious set of songs (the *Ha! Ha! Ha!* album) that exuberantly covered all manner of things from sexual depravity to the world's problems. 'Young Savage' was a single released just before the album, and a sound taking shape: the chilly synthesizers are starting to emerge through crisp thrash chords and vocalist John Foxx's snarling John Lydon impression. Far more enjoyable than the group's mild-mannered hits with Midge Ure that were to come in the 1980s.

Wake Up and Make Love with Me
Ian Dury and the Blockheads
1977 • Stiff

» When Ian Dury's band the Blockheads really got going they could unleash an astonishingly effective blend of pub rock and jazz-funk, of which 'Wake Up' is a real stormer. The pounding 4/4 beat is craftily augmented with all manner of keyboard, guitar and percussion inventions – some very jazzy, some proper cockney – and the players know exactly when to show off. It's as lively as it is enthralling and although it shouldn't be, it's exactly right for Dury's low-key and highly original episodes of London and life's humdrum. This story concerns itself with waking up with an erection and trying to rouse his partner using, among other things, the power of his mind.

Alison
Elvis Costello
1977 • Stiff

« 'Alison' has a purity that not only shows off Elvis Costello's musical intelligence and perception, but also allows the dexterity and sensitivity of his lyrical wordplay to be fully appreciated. What could be bitter or syrupy as he muses on an ex-lover becomes a provocative and intriguing double entendre: is he, as a better man, making a bid to win back a former flame; or is he about to kill her? As he leaves it up to us, the ladies and gentlemen of the jury, to decide, it's sold to us against a delicate guitar-led country-soul background, wholly appropriate for the subject matter. It wasn't that Costello necessarily had more in his musical locker than so many of his late-1970s new-wave contemporaries; it's just that he wasn't afraid to borrow elements from his wide range of influences and present them to a more mainstream audience.

Pretty Vacant
The Sex Pistols
1977 • Virgin

It's appropriate the Pistols' third single was the one that finally landed them *Top of the Pops* exposure, as it demonstrated just how well drummer Paul Cook and guitarist Steve Jones could play. And with the original bassist Glen Matlock now replaced by non-musician Sid Vicious, Jones ended up playing the bass as well.

'Pretty Vacant' also shows how well the musicians (including Matlock who cowrote the song) understood the writing of three-minute rock 'n' roll numbers, which then benefited immeasurably from producer Chris Thomas, who had learned his trade on Beatles, Pink Floyd and Roxy Music recordings. Take off the lyric, and this was as tight and compact a modern rocker as you could hope for, starting off with a lead-guitar line before the crunching riffs take over. Its power-chording reminds you how much the Pistols listened to the Stooges, MC5 and the Ramones, and how much in turn the likes of Iron Maiden, Girlschool and Saxon listened to them.

: NEW SINGLE OUT THIS SATURDAY ON VIRGIN RECORDS VS184 :

Their musical competency, overlooked at the time, remains the reason why the Sex Pistols' sound was so influential and so enduring. It was such a shame it took so relatively long for their records to come out, especially as punk was practically mainstream. Furthermore, the UK media had painted the group as all that was wrong with western civilization for so long that they'd gone from being convincing, self-anointed situationists, who spearheaded and defined what was probably Great Britain's last major cultural shift, to pantomime villains. In truth, their swapping Glen Matlock for Sid Vicious had more or less condemned them to cartoon status. Cook and Jones always said they got together primarily to make music, and on this evidence it's a pity they didn't stick around to make more of it.

In the City
The Jam
1977 • Polydor

The Jam's first single is as good an introduction as anybody – either the group or the public – could have asked for. Given the raw power of their playing it's difficult to believe that there are only three of them, but it's that vintage art of power-pop musical stacking – also displayed by the Who, Motorhead and Cream – that fills every space, but with bits so precise and interesting nothing sounds clogged up. Never less than rousing; always more than two-dimensional.

While this gave the group real presence, what set them apart was a lyrical and ideological approach that bonded with their teenage and 20-something audience through a delicately balanced blend of angst and ambition. It wasn't just about everything being shit, it was about them being the generation that were actually going to change it. This kind of upwardly mobile anguish reflected suburban roots, giving The Jam an appealing honesty, which combined with their being obviously and proudly (without being bigotedly) English, offering up a huge potential audience.

Gary Gilmore's Eyes
The Adverts
1977 • Anchor

>> Back in 1977, when the British tabloid press was desperate to liven up Middle England's breakfast with (yet) another 'Punk Rock Depravity Exclusive!', punk rock itself was seldom slow to recognize a PR opportunity, often while having a bit of a laugh at the same time. Here was one such song, a hilariously ludicrous number based on newspaper reports that soon-to-be-executed American murderer Gary Gilmore wanted his eyes to be used for transplant purposes. In this narrative the recipient got taken over by the killer's ocular organs and went berserk, inevitably enough to provoke a Fleet Street frenzy in which words like 'depraved' and 'degenerate' loomed large. None of which should detract from the quality of the record. At the glammier end of punk, and as one of the movement's hardest working and most popular live acts, the Adverts had honed a taut, bouncy sound that was well aware of how to connect to a broad cross-section of the public. Consequently, 'Gary Gilmore's Eyes' would reach the top 20 in the UK.

Uptown Top Ranking
Althea & Donna
1977 • Lightning

<< To many non-Jamaican newcomers to roots reggae in the late 1970s, Althea & Donna were an anathema – this was reggae, but not as we knew it: no one was suffering and it sounded more like pop music than anything that could be called cultural. But in reality, Althea & Donna were the imported tip of an iceberg that saw many more lovers' rock-pop-reggae records being sold in the UK than major label roots releases. This was reggae as its own mainstream, a pop music mirroring the same sort of Saturday night shenanigans enjoyed all over the world. Althea & Donna themselves were uptown girls, and the song was a fresh take on Alton Ellis' classic rock-steady tune, 'I Am Still in Love with You'. In the UK, it knocked 'Mull of Kintyre' by Wings off the number one spot.

Science Friction
XTC
1977 • Virgin

>> 'Science Friction', the debut single from Swindon band XTC, both offers irrefutable evidence that they should have been major stars, and also provides clues as to why they weren't more popular (despite a long career nonetheless). XTC came from the New York Dolls end of punk, but anglicized it to a degree by flirting with UK art rock's synth leanings, then adding influences of contemporary glam. When they started out there was an approachability to their nuttiness. This track fluently shows off musical ideas, hooks are casually tossed out, and catchy lead lines frame Andy Partridge yelping about aliens. It packs so much in that it can be a little too clever and distanced for the casual listener, but it's worth the extra effort and is also loads of fun.

Flash Light
Parliament
1977 • Casablanca

<< In the saga of P-Funk, 'Flash Light' was intended as the climax to the stage extravaganza, as a soundtrack to the unfunky killjoy Sir Nose being bathed in the beam of the flashlight and unable to stop himself dancing. As such it needed to be something of a funk sensation, even by Parliament standards. Remarkably, it achieved this by dropping Bootsy Collins from bass guitar (he switches to drums on this track) and giving a part specially written for Collins to the keyboard player, the conservatory-trained Bernie Worrell. Worrell adopted the bass maestro's riff on three Moog synthesizers, and when he stacked them on top of each other, one of the biggest, most-sampled bass lines known to mankind was born.

One Nation Under a Groove
Funkadelic
1978 • Warner Bros.

After a decade of dark, druggy weirdness that, in its own dark, druggy way, was America's conscience from a perspective few social commentators could even contemplate, Funkadelic were on daytime radio with their first ever hit. This was a tune with a killer dancefloor groove, a sing-along vocal hook and with the group's coded sociopolitical messages pitched dangerously close to 'feel good'.

For long-term Funkadelic fans, more familiar with borderline scary albums like *Maggot Brain*, *America Eats Its Young* and *Cosmic Slop*, this new direction didn't make sense, and they had a point. 'One Nation Under a Groove' was conceived as a song by Parliament, Funkadelic's sunnier, funnier alter ego band, as another chapter in their ongoing funk opera. The new track's bass synth

and handclaps were certainly more reminiscent of Parliament, but George Clinton (leader of both groups) quite rightly realized this could be the biggest hit any P-Funk band had ever had, and wanted to give it to Funkadelic, as they were the collective's founding fathers.

Instead of adding horns, Clinton carried the melody via vocal arrangements so fragmented and mobile at times it's a wonder they don't trip over themselves. Yet, against a persistent groove, the vocals meshed perfectly with the lead guitar work of Mike Hampton, who at just 21, was producing probably his finest P-Funk moment. As for the tune itself, it was a rare occasion when the finest elements of both hemispheres of George Clinton's world met on an equal footing, and brought out the best in each.

What Do I Get?
Buzzcocks
1978 • United Artists

 CHRIS HAWKINS' CHOICE This was the single punk rock was invented for, as everything about it is absolutely perfect: ascending chord progression, buzz-saw sound, pounding bass, manic rolling drum patterns and Pete Shelley's anguished but self-aware vocal over the top. 'What Do I Get?' is an adrenaline-fuelled rush of youthful, hormone-loaded energy that grabs you and sweeps you along with it in a way you can't ignore. And it does it with such consummate ease because there's a real actual pop song in here – with verses, choruses, a bridge and even a lyric about unrequited love – only played much faster and with much more gusto.

Damaged Goods
Gang of Four
1978 • Fast Product

  Leeds band Gang of Four trod a path hardly attempted by anyone else at the time, one that allowed them to approach the new wave of R&B, so prominent in London and Essex, from a punk perspective rather than from a traditional soul point of view. Really, this was a logical progression as the pub rock scene had a real 'by the people for the people' ethic about it, presumably held back because soul music's inherent orderliness and generally shiny presentations were assumed to be worlds away from punk. Thank goodness Gang of Four proved that wrong. 'Damaged Goods' is powered by their big-shouldered, metronomic drummer Hugo Burnham and smoothly liquid bass player Dave Allen, giving Andy Gill plenty of support for his staccato scratching guitar work. A superb example of real punk-funk.

Rock Lobster
The B-52's
1978 • Island

'Rock Lobster', coming when it did among punk protest or new wave art cool, could have easily got it so wrong and just sounded ridiculous. As it was, the B-52's fusion of surf pop, rock 'n' roll and pre-pop-culture pop music sounded quirky and intelligent, was so avant garde it out-arted art rock, and was – in its way – more genuinely punk than so much accepted punk at the time. Most importantly, though, it had a refreshingly bonkers sense of humour (the chorus is a repeated chant of 'rock lobster'). Camp as a row of tents, the group worked because they were no tribute band; instead they were serious contemporary musicians with a mischievous streak, but who had found a style that encouraged that sense of fun. Combined with their own take on punk, funk and new wave, they came up with a stew that made all the nostalgic moves, but was still instantly familiar. 'Rock Lobster' was credited by John Lennon as the song that prompted to get him back in the recording studio after a five-year hiatus to raise his son.

Moving
Kate Bush
1978 • EMI

« Kate Bush was just 19 years old and a recording debutante when, somehow, she was able to talk a major label into allowing 20 seconds of whale song at the start of her first-ever album, *The Kick Inside*. You just knew she was going to make something of herself, and the rest of 'Moving' is an excellent early example of what that something might be. An astonishingly mature love song for a teenager to write and perform, the floaty music that bubbles up from rococo piano flourishes into the quasi-orchestral, while her voice zigzags around her dazzling multi-octave range with giddying shifts in tone and tempo. While this tune was nothing less than outstanding, in another surprising record company decision, it was a single in Japan – with 'Wuthering Heights' on its B-side.

Shot by Both Sides
Magazine
1978 • Virgin

» As good as Buzzcocks were – and they were very good – Howard Devoto's decision to quit after only one EP and found Magazine instead was an incredibly worthwhile move. As 'Shot by Both Sides' (cowritten with ex-Buzzcocks collaborator Pete Shelley) demonstrates, Magazine had all the energy and focus of Devoto's previous group, but he felt less restricted, and the group as a whole could open up what they were doing to a plethora of subtle touches and themes to round out the music. We get splashes of surf guitar, keyboard waves and masses of reverb that help to spin this debut single into the realm of thoughtful, grown-up music, that was becoming an increasingly popular destination as more and more punks came of age.

Up Against the Wall
Tom Robinson Band
1978 • EMI

« Although as fiercely sociopolitical as so many of their contemporaries, the Tom Robinson Band came to represent a bit of light relief. Their power rock had an intriguing texture; see, for instance, keyboard player Mark Ambler, who had learned his craft from jazz legend Stan Tracey, and whose contribution to Robinson's group had a bouncy verve to it, as he subtly filled the space behind the riffs with colour. Mostly, though, they succeeded because their tales of everyday London life had some wit to them and, like 'Up Against the Wall', were more a call to arms – to actually *do* something – rather than simply complain about their lives.

Another Girl, Another Planet
The Only Ones
1978 • CBS

LIZ KERSHAW'S CHOICE » If you had to name one song that comprehensively out-performed the band who recorded it, the chances are you'd say 'Another Girl, Another Planet'. From a group that had more of a classic rock than punk rock background, it's a masterpiece of modern psychedelia – chiming guitars, plenty of fuzz, tumbling drums, loony lyrics delivered apparently off the cuff – and even the sleeve was flowered up. Loved by practically everybody that heard it, on first release, it didn't get near the charts on first release, but it would take on a life of its own which far outlasted the band. Belatedly a minor hit in New Zealand in 1981, it finally charted in the UK in 1992 after being included on a new wave compilation album called *Sound of the Suburbs*. Irish radio stalwart Dave Fanning adopted it as a theme song; Vodaphone used it in an advert in 2006; and it's been covered by, among others, the Replacements, Blink-182 and Belle and Sebastian.

Being Boiled
The Human League
1978 • Fast Product

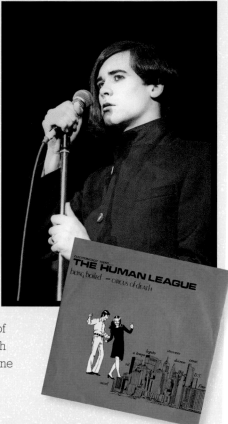

>> The Human League's first release, recorded three years before Joanne and Susanne joined for their run of hit singles and albums, this is pure electronic experimentation. More interestingly, though, as it's approached from a disco-soul rather than a rock point of view, it anticipates many sensibilities of what would become bona fide electro a few years later.

Beyond Phil Oakey's barely intelligible, sub-Bowie vocals, the most important thing here is the rhythm, which has built itself up with enough presence and empty space to support the riffs and phrases that prompt interior melodic allusions. It's crisp, complex and sinewy enough to appeal to breakdancers across the board. This is the sort of sound the early hip-hoppers would soon be searching for and isn't that far removed from the foundations of dubstep. It makes you wonder what founder members Ian Craig Marsh and Martyn Ware (who would leave to form Heaven 17) might have done if they'd stayed the course with the Human League, or if hip-hop in the UK had been more aware of what was happening on its own doorstep.

I Can't Stand My Baby
The Rezillos
1978 • Sire

<< Another striking female voice in British punk was Fay Fife of the Rezillos, made all the more so by the fact it was so obviously Scottish, as opposed to cockney, mockney or mid-Atlantic. The group as a whole was memorable, partly because they had a sense of humour – something else punk wasn't overblessed with – and this one about brattish behaviour (and how uncool it is) is a case in point. It's a supremely hyperactive two-and-a-half minutes of late model punk, with a passing nod to US garage rock and the more energetic end of 1960s pop, and that's knowing enough to be able to subvert its own melody by compressing it into buzz-saw riffing.

Ready Steady Go
Generation X
1978 • Chrysalis

>> Although from a punk background – they were the first band to play the Covent Garden venue, the Roxy, and three members of the line-up had been in punk band Chelsea – Gen X always had their eye on a wider world. To this end, and thanks to crisp, clean productions and their gifted lead guitarist Bob Andrews, they were the conduit between glam and the more back-combed aspect of post-punk heavy metal. 'Ready Steady Go', partly a tribute to the TV pop show of the 1960s, is certainly fast and spirited enough to be classed as part of the new wave, and Billy Idol's vocals retain a standard punk cadence, but when it dissolves into a guitar solo it's obvious the band has other ideas. Unfortunately those other ideas would ultimately lead to the band members going their separate ways in 1980, when the struggle to decide what path their music should take became irreconcilable.

(You Gotta Walk And) Don't Look Back
Peter Tosh featuring Mick Jagger
1978 • Rolling Stones Records/EMI

<< As the baritone voice in the original Wailers' harmonizing, then as a charismatic solo artist, an excellent songwriter, a nifty guitarist and as a frequently entertainingly angry orator, Peter Tosh had built himself a solid worldwide audience. To whom it came as a surprise when a Motown cover as downright cheesy as this had his name on it – but Tosh had always had pop sensibilities, and it was a bone of contention that he hadn't hit the same heights as his former bandmate Bob Marley. Under those circumstances a duet with Mick Jagger, with a keyboard-centric perky backing is understandable.

Tropical Hot Dog Night
Captain Beefheart and the Magic Band
1978 • Warner Bros.

 Captain Beefheart does disco, or at least about as close to disco as Captain Beefheart could possibly get. If his previous two or three albums had seemed unnecessarily bewildering, 'Tropical Hot Dog Night' is an inspired exercise in twisted jazz-funk. Beefheart is assisted by a line-up including trombone, marimba, synthesizer and accordion, and a solid 4/4 beat permits all sorts of riffing, dueling and soloing to explore individual and collective themes, even if it's often no more than a repeated leitmotif. Meanwhile, Beefheart's wonderfully lyrical howl treats us to couplets such as, 'Like two flamingoes in a fruit fight/I don't wanna know 'bout wrong or right.' But could you dance to it? Well, yes, you could, but you'd need to be at least as demented as the track itself.

Public Image
Public Image Ltd
1978 • Virgin

Had the Sex Pistols not become caricatures of punk, ex-frontman John Lydon's Public Image Ltd is probably how they should have evolved. There's a certain irony there as Lydon was chiefly responsible for such representation. Lydon set PiL up to explore punk's boundaries, and their debut single 'Public Image' is a smart, high-intensity rocker, not scared to flaunt its musicianship – guitarist Keith Levene once roadied for Yes and had an affection for prog rock – or studio ideas through Jah Wobble's reverbed bass. These touches give it a greater power, hurling Lydon's letter of resignation, 'You never listened to a word I said/ You only see me for the clothes I wear', at his former bandmates and ex-manager Malcolm McLaren with his usual entertaining venom.

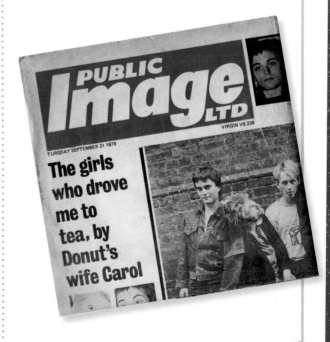

Hong Kong Garden
Siouxsie and the Banshees
1978 • Polydor

  A song written about a Chinese takeaway in suburban Kent that kicks off with rinky-dink oriental-type music, doesn't appear too appetizing. But 'Hong Kong Garden' (the name of said takeaway) soon redeems itself with music so totally engaging it is almost impossible not to like this bizarre song. Steve Lillywhite's first hit as a producer, the song features the brightest, most scintillating guitar hook, clean and speedy and creating a modern but vaguely Far Eastern vibe without being remotely patronizing at all. That same guitar hook sits on top of a drum sound so fat it can leave sufficient space for the riffing.

Warm Leatherette
The Normal
1978 • Mute

» Recorded two years before Grace Jones made the song famous, the original version of 'Warm Leatherette' is – astonishingly for anybody who hasn't heard it – far, far odder. The single that launched Mute Records – the Normal was the *nom de studio* of Mute founder Daniel Miller – it was a reaction to Miller's belief that making punk music was far too complicated and involved much too much effort. As an alternative, he spent £100 on a synthesizer, plonked away at it with one or two fingers and droned his lyrics over the top. It's a kind of urban-oriented, budget version of Kraftwerk's 'Autobahn' (see page 68), all about driving through a forbidding cityscape and, just possibly, crashing; a vision so determinedly strange that the squelches and bleeping remain worryingly seductive.

"the normal"

Prodigal Son
Steel Pulse
1978 • Island

>> As a reggae album in the late 1970s, Steel Pulse's *Handsworth Revolution* was a revelation. Jamaican reggae was almost exclusively a singles medium, and much of UK reggae had followed suit, yet here was an entirely credible roots reggae album that had had been conceived and recorded as such – with a centric theme and a content balance, rather than as a collection of singles. It was the first high-profile example of British reggae's uniqueness, inasmuch as its practitioners formed self-contained groups and wrote reggae songs in the image of the pop and rock they heard all around them. 'Prodigal Son', for instance, is crafted out of very contemporary sounds, including a bass synth and plenty of guitar. While the arrangement remains like a reggae record, the song itself has the structure and timing of a pop song, yet neither its words nor its music subverts a roots message. Thus it wasn't hard to fit it on to a daytime radio playlist and the album went top 10 in the UK almost immediately.

Take Me I'm Yours
Squeeze
1978 • A&M

>> One of only two songs on Squeeze's debut album that wasn't produced by the Velvet Underground's John Cale. As a result, 'Take Me I'm Yours' was one of only two songs on the album that remotely reflected their live performances. The song has a uniquely London, Saturday night sound that assumes so many elements of a pub jukebox – soul, rock 'n' roll, disco, R&B – all captured in a crisp, lively knees-up that has far more going on that its outward simplicity might imply. It's the sound of a group that knew exactly what it was doing, and had performed and recorded long enough to understand their appeal. It would become their first top-20 hit in the UK.

Alternative Ulster
Stiff Little Fingers
1978 • Rough Trade

>> Given that so much high-profile punk was middle class former art students complaining about their lives, it's hardly surprising that a band from a genuinely tough background – Belfast in the 1970s – should deliver material of such comparatively illuminating depth and breadth. 'Alternative Ulster' is a thoughtful contemporary rebel song, urging their audience to make life better by making the changes themselves, regardless of, 'the Army on your street/And the RUC dog of repression barking at your feet' It's more than just thrash, too, with the sneakily melodic power pop driven by the skill and invention of Brian Faloon, probably the best drummer punk produced. The song would appear on their 1979 album, *Inflammable Material*, which was originally scheduled for release on Island Records, but when the label declined to release the finished LP, it became the first-ever album release (and a hit to boot) on the newly formed independent label Rough Trade.

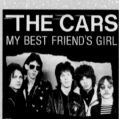

My Best Friend's Girl
The Cars
1978 • Elektra

⌃ ⌄ Although fabulously radio-friendly, the Boston band's early single 'My Best Friend's Girl' could've ended up as just another adult-oriented, MOR, gently rockin' tale of longing; hugely commercial but largely insipid. But it was recorded in London, with producer Roy Thomas Baker, who didn't sacrifice any potential widespread appeal, but instead enhanced it: the Cars brought contemporary new-wave noodling to the mainstream, and subtly updated what already existed. It set a late 1970s template for not only the Cars but also for many of their peers in US rock too, and so this fusion of synth sounds and gentler guitar rock would herald the 1980s with minimum fuss. And the hoedown-type licks halfway through? That would be Roy Thomas Baker again. He was Queen's producer, after all.

Teenage Kicks
The Undertones
1978 • Sire

To many, the mere idea of 'pop punk' was an abomination, but switch the two words around and 'punk pop' is surely what the movement should have been moving towards – the beautiful subversion of the kids making music for themselves rather than for grown-ups, and singing about exactly what mattered to them, no matter how dreary that might seem at first.

Enter the Undertones, four teenagers from Derry, in Northern Ireland, whose raucous two-and-a-half-minute rock songs had all the DIY ethic and spikiness of the Clash or the Pistols, but which concerned themselves with things like heartbreak, falling in love, getting spots, first dates… Never mind The Troubles, here's what teenagers *really* worried about, and 'Teenage Kicks' even made reference to parents going out and leaving the house unsupervised. This anthem to (most likely unrequited) lust, delivered exactly what the title promised, but did it with full awareness of what made a good pop song: some drumbeats to get things going, irresistible hooks, a simple melody anybody could follow, catchy lyrics and a warbling singer who didn't sound much different to his audience. Yes it was still pop music, but as dictionary definition punk, it empowered a section of music buyers who may have previously felt excluded simply because they weren't yet angry enough.

Such sedition, coupled with the immediacy of the music, meant that 'Teenage Kicks' remained John Peel's favourite-ever record, from its first release (on the independent Good Vibrations label), right up until his passing in 2004. You couldn't really ask for greater acclaim.

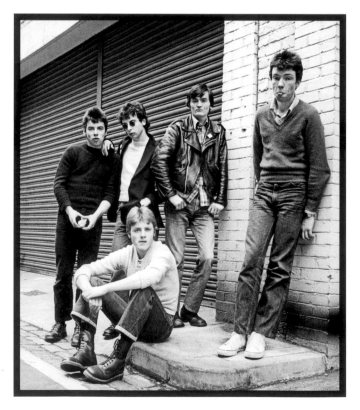

Outdoor Miner
Wire
1978 • Harvest

 Wire had the good sense to step off the punk carousel in the nick of time, developing their sensibilities into something far artier and synth-rinsed than the foreshortened, guitar-driven crunch of their first album, *Pink Flag*. 'Outdoor Miner', however, is far from typical of the debut album's successor, *Chairs Missing*. Within the album's carefully prepared and delicately arranged thrust – some of which bordered on the contrived – this sunny, nutty and fresh-faced optimism is so relaxed it verges on the throwaway.

Far from it. Such a simple, cocksure framework lets the jangly guitars and piano tumble around on top of each other in complete safety, showing off the intrinsic musicianship, while the cascading vocal harmonies give a jaunty lift to the usual London tones. Beneath that, though, the crisp edges of production give all this Byrdsiness a very British feel. It's a song the showier end of future Britpop – Elastica, Suede and so on – would have listened to keenly.

The Sound of the Suburbs
The Members
1979 • Virgin

>> 'The Sound of the Suburbs' was produced by Steve Lillywhite, who always had a way with a drum sound, so it certainly didn't do the Members any harm that their drummer at the time was his brother; but even without such a boost they were probably the most musically savvy of any band coming out of the back end of punk (so to speak). 'The Sound of the Suburbs' lets you know immediately there's more about this band, as a lovely melodic bass line dips underneath a guitar that is pure pop in its twangy insistence, giving the hard drive of the rhythm another dimension. Even the lyrics have an irony to them, and they lift this narrative of the humdrum to a place where observing the mundanity of suburbia is actually quite funny.

Rapper's Delight
The Sugarhill Gang
1979 • Sugarhill

It seems remarkable now that before this became a breakout hit (number three in the UK), nobody outside of New York or half a dozen frighteningly hip Londoners had any idea what rap was. A mere 35 years later, the genre has reinvented itself so often and to such a degree that a 15-year-old rap fan now would be hard-pushed to associate 'Rapper's Delight' with what they currently listen to. With a loop borrowed from Chic's 'Good Times', and with its cheesy, sing-song vocals and music supplied by a backing band, 'Rapper's Delight' remains gloriously self-celebratory. It's pure DIY house-party music, but is probably best described as 'quaint', which is probably the last thing any self-respecting hip-hopper wants to hear.

10.15 Saturday Night
The Cure
1979 • Fiction

The Cure are perhaps the best example of demonstrating where punk went next, and one of their earliest songs shows that off to perfection. So much of what the group did came from a punk aesthetic but with a much less self-consciously punk outlook. It's partly why their later work was so difficult to pin down, as they really did disregard convention and did what they liked. '10.15 Saturday Night' takes an ultra-simplified musical approach: a guitar riff and bass line that aspire to be basic, plus drums that probably broke stones in another life; yet such simplicity hangs together as the ideal framework for a primal guitar line that makes it all make sense. Add to this Robert Smith's vocals, and lyrics which celebrate the commonplace in a fashion forever unique to English culture, and the result is an engagingly simple marriage of punk and pop.

Babylon's Burning
The Ruts
1979 • Virgin

 It was such a good idea to write a song about how the regular world's own fears were destroying it from within, and then set it to music that seems to be built atop a surf-guitar take on the *Batman* TV theme. It means the whole thing has an appropriate sense of urgency and mild paranoia, carried through by the chopping bass that periodically argues with a central guitar riff, and adds to the air of panic in the streets that the song conveys with consummate ease. 'Babylon's Burning' underlined that the Ruts had the musical intelligence to match their socially aware integrity.

Tusk
Fleetwood Mac
1979 • Warner Bros.

The title track of the first album to cost over a million dollars to make and the first to be recorded in the new-fangled digital format, this was never going to stand or fall on the strength of the song alone. It's virtually impossible to listen to *Tusk* (the single or the double album) without concentrating on its lavish production, but as you check out its cleverness, you are pulled into a madly audacious musical world. There's such a precision to the separation and subsequent mix of the instruments that immerses you in a 360-degree tune with elements of a medieval banquet, or a circus, or some sort of wild multi-faceted carnival. It's a thrilling ride, and was definitely worth what was, at the time, an exorbitant cost of admission; the *Tusk* album retailed at almost $16, the sort of money you would have expected to spend on a small car in 1979.

FLEETWOOD MAC

California Über Alles
Dead Kennedys
1979 • Fast Product/Optional Music

>> The Dead Kennedys can be credited with both kick-starting the San Francisco punk scene and giving their musical contemporaries in Los Angeles a sharp slap around the head. Such an accolade could not have been bestowed on a more deserving bunch, as the Dead Kennedys were possibly the most *punk* punk band the US ever produced – indeed they could have more than held their own in the hurly-burly nihilism of the British scene. Their music borrowed from just about every style they had ever come across, and was compiled at express-train speed with an accompanying production so flimsy it was almost clinging on by its fingertips. It was the perfect setting for their incisive, unrestrained, often hilarious or witheringly sarcastic polemics denouncing anybody and anything that was working against the common good. On 'California Über Alles', the main target is California governor and presidential hopeful Jerry Brown, while hippiefied fascism is also under attack.

Are 'Friends' Electric?
Tubeway Army
1979 • Beggars Banquet

>> The legitimizing of the synth as a part of pop music really didn't start until Gary Numan's Tubeway Army rescued the instrument from icy art rock and prog rock, and reclaimed the usually chilly form as borderline cuddly. In spite of Numan's android stage persona and remote vocals, set against swirling synth lines, drum-machine beats and no obvious hooks, 'Are "Friends" Electric?' undercut itself with a conventional kit drummer and bass guitarist. It gave the impression of a brittle antithesis to punk, but had enough identifiable sounds for the nonbelievers to latch onto. The song went to number one in the UK, returning, in part, to the top of the charts some 15 years later when a sample of it became the basis for the Sugababes' hit 'Freak Like Me'.

Memphis Tennessee
Silicon Teens
1979 • Mute

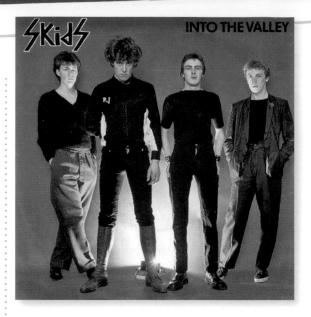

Another early project from Mute Records founder Daniel Miller, the four-piece group Silicon Teens turned out to be Miller himself, an inexpensive synthesizer, plus some stand-ins to do whatever press was required to promote the album *Music for Parties*. It wasn't what you might call a hoax, more a bit of a laugh. The same could be said of the music which was, mostly, a series of covers of pop and rock favourites from the 1950s and 1960s dinked out on the tinny synth, and with Miller's untutored vocals on top. Here the Chuck Berry rock 'n' roll classic is given this DIY treatment and comes across like a modern-day version of somebody knocking out a tune on the dining-room piano at a family gathering. *Music for Parties*, it seems.

Into the Valley
Skids
1979 • Virgin

When Richard Jobson and Stuart Adamson were both in the Skids, and Jobson had yet to become overly arty, the band epitomized the degree to which punk had opened up the mainstream music business. They came into music too late to be true punks, but they benefitted hugely from the attitude that anyone could try and make music – a philosophy that had permeated the mainstream during the previous couple of years. Hailing from Dunfermline in Scotland, they were a musically literate guitar band that, a few years previously, would have ended up playing prog or heavy metal, but used this new freedom to craft a singularly Caledonian kind of rock (this track introduces the bagpipe guitar sound Adamson made famous with his next group, Big Country). This, 'Into the Valley', was their most successful song, and their sole top-10 hit. For a music scene that had been battered with either London or New York bands for what seemed like ages, the Skids more open sound came as a breath of fresh air.

Boys Don't Cry
The Cure
1979 • Fiction

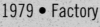

The truly entertaining thing about the Cure was, until you heard the song, you never quite knew which Cure might turn up: the gloomy Goths; the perky pop kids; the fey art rockers. A musical dressing-up box, all approached with an eccentricity that appeared to please nobody but themselves, it usually made their releases intriguing at the very least. 'Boys Don't Cry', one of their earliest singles, finds them in sunny, jangly guitar mode, breezily knocking out a deceptively layered piece that, surprisingly cheerfully, details the regrets, despairs and bottling up of emotions that come in the aftermath of a break up. Hardly the usual approach to such subject matter, but as per the norm, the band seemed to enjoy it.

Transmission
Joy Division
1979 • Factory

 JAMES STIRLING'S CHOICE Although 'Love Will Tear Us Apart' is the Joy Division track most people can name, and is widely hailed as the song that defines them, it's an earlier single that finds the band at its peak. While in some quarters its vibe might be perceived as uncharacteristically cheerful – 'dance, dance, dance, dance, dance, to the radio' – it's somehow much more 'Joy Division' than much of their output. This is because 'Transmission' is wilful in a way that initially may be tricky to deal with, but will never disappoint you once you realize what's going on. The whole thing seems to owe less to the post-punk era than it does to the more functional end of art rock as it evolved towards dance music. Plus it's blatantly Bowie-influenced.

Joy Division never gave any assistance to the casual observer or the innocent bystander – you either signed up and came in or moved on, sharpish – and 'Transmission' doesn't go out of its way to encourage lovers of their previous album, *Unknown Pleasures*, presenting itself as one of the most simplistic productions in their catalogue. As was so often the case, Peter Hook's bass guitar takes what melody there is into a series of throbbing progressions: the guitar counterpoint ends up blasting a riff that reverberates through the mix, while an indistinct but swelling synth washes through. There may be only two chords in the song, but producer Martin Hannett helps to highlight them with an intensity that powers the song rhythmically forwards, meaning the metronomic drumming doesn't have to do too much. Then comes Ian Curtis' monotone baritone urging us that things might well turn out okay if we all just, 'dance, dance, dance, dance, dance, to the radio'. Not exactly obvious Joy Division, which is what makes it exactly that.

NEMONE'S SELECTION

(See Nemone's song choices on pages 104, 160, 259, 281, 286 and 292.)

I would describe myself as an emotional listener to music. For some of my favourite tunes I'm much less aware of the lyrics and content – it is the atmosphere of the music in a track that initially grabs me. The selection of songs I've chosen are a bunch of my favourites, which on first listen may seem sparse and simple but they just give you so much. It felt great to revisit songs I hadn't listened to for a while, to really think what it is I like about them and why it is that they mean so much to me.

In the beginning, one of the propositions for 6 Music was as a repository for the Peel sessions – we had so much material and nowhere to play it. Around the time 6 Music started there wasn't a lot of old music being played on many stations, and there weren't many places you could hear tracks from the 1970s, 80s and 90s on a more left-field tip. Obviously you would hear tracks from those years on Radio 2, but not with the alternative spirit that 6 has. 6 was very much conceived with that kind of ethos.

I was always attracted to music. I collected records from an early age, cassettes and vinyl, and then started playing musical instruments more on the classical side. I had classical training as a flautist, and I picked up the saxophone from being able to play the flute; their keying is not dissimilar. Later I was playing sax in a funk band with the guys from Groove Armada.

Nobody from my family had any connection to the

> 'I WOULD DESCRIBE MYSELF AS AN EMOTIONAL LISTENER TO MUSIC...IT IS THE ATMOSPHERE OF THE MUSIC IN A TRACK THAT INITIALLY GRABS ME.'

music industry or anything like that, but I grew up around a bunch of guys who were deejaying and I loved it; I loved the music and realized I wanted to do it. There weren't many women deejaying when I started, not as many as there are these days. I collected vinyl, I had the tunes but I needed that push to get me to actually do it. It was deejaying at college in Manchester where I got that push. Then when I first walked into a radio station in Manchester I just sighed, 'Aww, this feels like home!' That was KISS back in the 1990s.

I bought records I felt a connection to and every record I've ever bought falls into that category. Sometimes it was because I wanted a closer listen and the track would sound better listened to on headphones; it would be easier to hear the intricacy of the music. Or there are the records that move me on first listen – which is certainly the case with the Joe Goddard track. That is exactly the sort of record that, had I heard it as a listener and gone, 'What is that? I want to own it!', that I would've hunted down and then played on repeat.

Electronic music is very close to my heart: I grew up listening to it. My dad had Jean Michel Jarre and OMD in his vinyl collection. The heartbeat of a track for me is the bass line, the 808. I love electronic music, but I'm not tied to a genre. It's not the genre that a tune belongs to, it's the individual track. I listen to hundreds of records every week and it can be something really left-field that sticks out for me. I have to have a connection with it.

The Prince
Madness
1979 • 2-Tone

Madness' first single and almost everything you need to know about them in two-and-a-half minutes: a healthy disregard for convention, exuberance, cleverness, comedy, an obvious love for what they're doing and a deep affection for Jamaican music of the 1960s and early 1970s. All that's missing are the baggy trousers, and they were only a year away.

'The Prince' is just one of three of the group's tributes honouring ska legend Prince Buster (even their name came from a Buster song), but rather than earnestly copy ska or rock-steady, they use reggae-tinged structures as a launch pad for their own inimitable North London style of musical tomfoolery. A shrewd move, as all manner of punchy riffs, sounds and ideas are piled on, hinting at a versatility that would prove they were no one-drop wannabes. Like Suggs sings, 'This may not be uptown Jamaica but we promise you a treat.'

Dance Stance
Dexy's Midnight Runners
1979 • Oddball

>> It was a big step for Kevin Rowland to eschew what was happening in the British music business, disband his punk band the Killjoys and make a vintage soul album. And then go for it in such a wholehearted, horn heavy, hang-the-expense manner. But that's where tracks like 'Dance Stance' succeed – Dexy's Midnight Runners were so committed to what they hoped to achieve it's almost impossible to be churlish, no matter how pretentious the lyrics. Their first single, 'Dance Stance' (titled 'Burn It Down' on their subsequent album) worked beautifully because it had all the slickness of classic 1960s soul, a big brass section and a thumping beat, but Rowland's vocals were so incongruous – strangled and angry, not soulfully lush – that it was never intimidating and had the rough DIY edge punk had made part of UK pop.

On My Radio
The Selecter
1979 • 2-Tone

>> Right from the beginning – 'On My Radio' was their debut single – the Selecter had two qualities which set them apart from the punk ska of the time: Neol Davies' songwriting and Pauline Black's voice. Davies' songs never simply aped punk or ska, and instead assimilated all sorts of influences. 'On My Radio', for instance, is a bouncy pop-reggae number in essence, but also loaded with Queen references, a spiky Stax-ey organ and a mad drum break in the middle. Soaring above all of this was Black's soprano – one of the finest and most distinctive of the era – giving the song a genuinely soulful dimension.

Chelsea Girl
Simple Minds
1979 • Zoom

>> Especially in their early days, Simple Minds had a way of fusing different elements of late 1970s rock that anticipated the 1980s. Their second single, 'Chelsea Girl', takes bits of Queen, bits of Bowie and quite a lot of Roxy Music to make it their own. It has such a clever balance between delicately tinkling keyboards and crunching power chords it can even shepherd a violin into the mix without sounding affected. Stitched together by Jim Kerr's urgent vocals, the whole thing successfully builds into something both arty and epic.

I Fought the Law
The Clash
1979 • CBS

» A song that has become such an integral part of the Clash's story, even 35 years later not everybody realizes that 'I Fought the Law' was a cover. Previously a hit for mild-mannered rock 'n' rollers the Bobby Fuller Four in 1966, Mick Jones and Joe Strummer had heard it on a vintage jukebox in a San Francisco recording studio. Apart from 'Police and Thieves' – and even that had been more an homage than a cover version – 'I Fought the Law' was the first song the group recorded that they didn't write themselves. Debuting on *The Cost of Living* EP in between the albums *Give 'Em Enough Rope* and *London Calling*, it represents a crucial bridge between the two, and is fairly faithful to the original, albeit in a supercharged, Clash-like style. It marked the start of them ushering in other influences and showing off their musicianship and arrangement skills, and would continue into the *London Calling* era, elevating the band above so much of their environment, and resulting in a fabulously well-rounded punk rock album.

Human Fly
The Cramps
1979 • Illegal/IRS

« Surf punk meets Hammer horror meets urban rockabilly in a New York garage, by way of Los Angeles. As paid-up members of the CBGBs/Max's Kansas City set, the Cramps' sound and style were a tour around American trash culture of the previous two decades. Never gimmicky or patronizing, either, their reference points – regardless of their hyper hip surroundings – kept close to that thin line separating trash from the regular consumerism of those times. Hence they were seldom out of reach for most of us and Cramps records always had sufficient sleaze to make them just dangerous enough. 'Human Fly' is a creeping, nasty, R&B-based monster, drenched with fuzz and reverb, and with the kind of huge sound and mad sci-fi lyrics that became their trademark.

Man Kind (You a Sinner)
Misty in Roots
1979 • People Unite

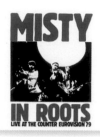

Compared to Aswad and Steel Pulse – the other British bands largely responsible for bringing roots reggae to a mainstream audience – west London's Misty in Roots had a lower profile, but their contribution was no less important. They forged the strongest links with punks and the new wave of revolutionaries such as the Anti-Nazi League and Rock Against Racism, while their more or less constant gigging in small venues and colleges made them very accessible. It showed in their output too: a tight, crisp reggae, very pop-rock oriented in arrangement – and sounds like their trademark billowing keyboards. This live track, 'Man Kind (You a Sinner', shows how they could provide a genuine reggae experience without ever being insular or introverted.

Zerox
Adam and the Ants
1979 • Do It

Recorded and released as a single by an early incarnation of Adam and the Ants (managed by Malcolm McLaren) the year before Adam and a later line-up became teen idols, 'Zerox' was later added to the 1983 reissue of their 1979 debut album *Dirk Wears White Sox*. It shows where the group would have been headed had its lead singer not been so impatient for success. 'Zerox' is a sprightly, messy fusion of glam, disco and post-punk guitar-rock ideas that was performed with the sort of organic dynamism that was part of punk's legacy, but which would be missing from so much of the hit material from mark two of the Ants.

Tears of a Clown
The Beat
1979 • 2-Tone

The Beat (or, in North America, the English Beat) seemed more focused and self-aware than their punk-ska contemporaries. Taking the Miracles' Motown classic as their first single was a shrewd move, providing precisely the right introduction for them. Not only was it a song good enough to survive a cover using such a sharply accelerated tempo but, being such a vintage tune, it also enabled the group to add another dimension by flirting with ska's R&B and soul roots, and meant they didn't have to worry about sounding 'authentic'. Not that they needed to worry about that thanks to the inclusion in their line-up of veteran Jamaican saxman, Saxa. He had been part of the original ska scene, and his strong, confident blowing helped seamlessly marry the two halves of punk and ska.

Money in My Pocket
Dennis Brown
1979 • Lightning

Whereas Bob Marley was universally respected, Dennis Brown was loved by the reggae community throughout the 1970s and 1980s – and the crisp lovers' rock of 'Money in My Pocket' is a prime example of why. Quite apart from his beautiful lilting tenor voice, Brown may have been one of the genre's international stars but his outlook remained completely parochial, making records primarily for the sound systems. His subject matter tended to be equally contained, as his lyrics tended to deal with affairs of the heart or localized social politics: 'Money in my pocket but I just can't get no love' struck a chord with women everywhere. The Jamaican people and the wider reggae audience felt he always belonged to them and had never turned his attentions elsewhere.

Kid
The Pretenders
1979 • Sire

Although as much a part of the new wave as, say, Blondie or Talking Heads, and quite capable of expressing a scowling and snarling punk attitude, the Pretenders were at their most effective on superficially conventional pop songs like 'Kid'. The song is a beautifully textured mid-tempo piece of rock, led by guitarist James Honeyman-Scott in a not-quite-jangling style, and isn't scared to layer on the effects. This gives it a unique chiming depth of field that contrasts with the solos and their casually stretched notes. It's these overlapping levels in production that keep up an easy, natural momentum, and provide just the right degree of gentleness to cushion but never envelop Chrissie Hynde's aching voice, which transforms a perfectly nice tune into something far more interesting.

THE 1980s

The decade of excess, the 1980s were never going to be remembered for subtlety. These were the years when the heavyweights of alternative music – rap and heavy metal – collided in the form of the Beastie Boys; hip-hop had what many believe its finest hour at the hands of Public Enemy; alt-rock went experimental with the Pixies; and Prince sang of the world's ills with soulful urgency.

A Forest
The Cure
1980 • Fiction

» In the blinding light of later albums *Faith* and *Pornography*, *Seventeen Seconds* gets a bit overlooked. Except for this song, that is. Sensibly resisting record company overtures to make it more suitable for daytime radio, 'A Forest' is a masterpiece of desolation without being meaninglessly unoccupied. It's got all the new-wave mannerisms – up-tempo beat, repetitive phrases – then softens the edges of the instrumentation and separates it so you can almost hear the wind blowing through the mix. This shifts the focus subtly but most effectively, meaning Robert Smith's eerie, distant vocals somehow make the track as a whole sound emptier.

Messages
Orchestral Manoeuvres in the Dark
1980 • Dindisc/Virgin

« The original album version of 'Messages' was a moodier reading of the song, nestling within the 'sadness' end of the emotional spectrum, in keeping with the synth duo's ultra new wave, almost anti-pop-star, presentation of themselves. While few people found it problematic as an album track, it wasn't ideal single material, so the duo re-recorded it. They plumped it up, adding a lush, swelling background with crisply cut-up riffs pushed further out front, and delivered much greater depth by creating a more forceful emotional quality. In turn, this seemed to prompt a reaction rather than resignation out of Andy McCluskey's lead vocals, giving the tune an angry and poignant sting. It gave OMD the first of many top-20 hits in the UK.

Backstrokin'
Fatback
1980 • Polydor

» Back in the early 1970s, the Fatback Band as a physical presence were literally huge – big horn section, percussionists, a couple of guitarists – and were one of the founders of the New York street-funk scene defining the good times, paaarty notion of the sound. By the time 'Backstrokin'' came out, the economics of keeping a big band fed had taken its toll, and they'd even downsized their name simply to Fatback, but thanks to an innate understanding of what made a record swing, they had lost little momentum. 'Backstrokin'' proves how they could still do it with synthesizers; while the sounds looked forwards, the riffing and the chant vocals were pure old-school funk.

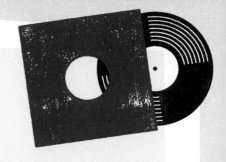

Coming Up
Paul McCartney
1980 • Parlophone

 Literally pure Paul, as he played all the instruments on this track, adding instrumentation to a drum machine track as the mood took him; indeed, he said in an interview at the time that he had no idea where it might end up. Where it ended up was pure Paul too – the finished article was so perky and up-tempo, he even gives a smiley thumbs-up in the video. That was the refreshing thing about 'Coming Up' in 1980. Here was a bloke who used to be in the biggest group ever, and remained a brilliant musician, yet here he was just larking about with a simple cheery song *and* playing all the parts in the video, just for a laugh. Interestingly, given McCartney's autonomy on the studio version, the same song would top the US charts with a live version performed by him and a full band.

Voices Inside My Head
The Police
1980 • A&M

HUEY MORGAN'S CHOICE ›› Part of the trio's *Zenyatta Mondatta* album, their most musically interesting and adroit work, this wonderful piece of taut, small-band instrumental funk demonstrates another side of their capabilities. Built on an insistent bass riff and nagging guitar, it lives up to its title with vocals limited to distant background refrains. The instrumentation and pacing is so restless and edgy it becomes an exercise in agitated paranoia, where almost everything sounds like it's out to get you. This exercise can only be properly achieved with playing that is absolutely on the one, and The Police are relentlessly tight here. Perhaps more importantly they understand how, in these circumstances, less is more, and they never clutter the clear lines of the track.

Rapture
Blondie
1980 • Chrysalis

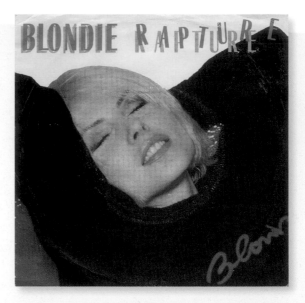

>> ⌄ If ever a record split British music critics' opinion it was this. Back in 1980, when most of the rock mainstream was still assuming hip-hop to have a short shelf life and little value, for new wave poster children like Blondie to dip a toe in bordered on treason. There was the exploitation lobby, haranguing anybody who would listen about downtown trendies appropriating uptown culture. While other commentators lauded the group for bringing rap to a wider audience, just as many simply thought it was lame.

Almost all of this misses the point. The New York new wave scene was always more open-minded than its Brit counterpart, and as a result noticeably more multi-culti – as was a fair amount of early hip-hop. Blondie's *Autoamerican* album experimented playfully with all kinds of US musical culture from the group's own perspective, and if the results were mildly self-indulgent, some deserved success came, most notably on 'Rapture'. Sure, Debbie Harry was rapping, but she wasn't setting herself up as a rapper. The tune and its video did far more than put rap in the charts, it introduced hip-hop as a rounded and interesting state of affairs, but did so obliquely and artily rather than lecture the listener. And as for it being lame, it fits so snugly with other rap records of the time: 'Rapper's Delight', 'Monster Jam', 'That's the Joint', 'The Breaks'; half sung, half rapped, backed by a live band and featuring nonsense lyrics about having a good time.

Blondie clearly had respect for the genre and had worked hard at it. But too many were fixated with the rap section and ignored the first couple of minutes – a true monster of a disco-funk tune that embellishes driving bass and drums with a plethora of interesting touches: horn riffs, bells, handclaps, squawking bird noises and guitar flourishes. The end result shows complete understanding of how a groove ought to work.

Totally Wired
The Fall
1980 • Rough Trade

>> Anybody who was surprised by the Stone Roses or Happy Mondays had clearly never listened to the Fall, especially not in this kind of cheerfully loony, wonderfully obdurate approach. Mark E Smith's many incarnations of the group may not have been propelled to stardom via a Madchester movement – and probably wouldn't have joined such a movement anyway. Instead they set a tone for the subsequent wave, in attitude if not exactly in sound. Their approach was precise, if usually berserk rockabilly, clever enough to blend in a host of other musical ideas and motifs, all of which kept everything and everybody on their toes. All the while, Mark E Smith acts as ringmaster to this subversive circus, barking out lyrics; in this case, unsurprisingly, about being totally wired.

Could You Be Loved
Bob Marley and the Wailers
1980 • Island

DON LETTS' CHOICE << The very disappointing *Uprising* album – the last released during Bob Marley's lifetime – was all a bit Wailers-by-numbers, though it had two bright spots. One was the acoustic 'Redemption Song', while the other, 'Could You Be Loved', showed awareness of the wider world by taking a disco direction. Built on a relentless 4/4 beat and a chugging Clavinet, its masterstroke was for it to still sound like, essentially, a Bob Marley reggae tune but it was an obvious shoe-in to American nightclubs and black radio stations – and it was to Marley's huge frustration that black America just wasn't so interested in what he did. At least it reached the top 10 in the US dance music and soul charts, but it would have been interesting to see how much further Marley could have taken things, had it not been for his early, untimely death in 1981.

Treason
The Teardrop Explodes
1980 • Mercury

« Most of the Teardrops' debut album *Kilimanjaro* was produced by managers Bill Drummond and David Balfe (under the name of The Chameleons), but for the single 'Treason', Madness producers Clive Langer and Alan Winstanley were drafted in. 'Treason' has a less bombastic feel to it – there's no horn section – and it seems a more faithful representation of Cope and co. Admittedly, the guitar and keyboards by themselves create an impressively big sound, but not so overbearing it inhibits the group's whimsical qualities. The echo on Cope's voice, the tumbling chord progressions, the Hammond-ish keyboard signatures, and odd lyrics like, 'Mirror hopping days of coarse reaction/Oh, it's very hard to fight', give it a clever 1960s feel, translating into an agreeable modern form of psychedelia.

Whip It
Devo
1980 • Virgin/Warner Bros.

» If ever a rock group managed to bridge the 1970s and the 1980s it was Devo, and, thankfully, they did so with wit and mischief. Take 'Whip It' and its video: robotically phased, conventional drums and lead guitar, flowerpot hats, cowboy-scene inserts reminiscent of *Bonanza*, and a man in cycling gear wielding a bullwhip. With Robert Margouleff – the man who set up Stevie Wonder's synthesizers – on production duties, and the song making a satirical point about life in the US, it could have taken itself very seriously. Instead, it chooses to dub itself 'whiptease', kicks off with a lively lead line appropriated from Roy Orbison's 'Oh, Pretty Woman', adds jerky, dance-friendly Moog riffing then tops it all off with some synthesized whip cracking. A wonderfully boisterous approach to art as rock.

CHRIS HAWKINS' SELECTION

(See Chris' song choices on pages 97, 134, 166, 173, 230 and 241.)

Our audience reacts most when we play old songs, the ones that trigger a memory, that hold nostalgia for them; yes, it's exciting to hear a new band from Sheffield, but play 'Saturdays Kids' by the Jam and the love for a track like that on texts and social media is remarkable.

Bands often write their best material when they're young-ish and generally free of the constraints of record companies breathing down their necks. They're more likely to be able to create, organically, what they set out to do and it's far more likely that something special emerges.

The Manchester scene was so different to the London scene. I genuinely believe it's because the weather's so bad that kids didn't have much else to do. Because they were indoors all the time they'd pick up instruments like guitars or start banging something and that's why so many great bands were born in that city and with that similar gloomy feel about them – and the cynicism about what they were writing about. Not only was the place pretty grim, but they were stuck indoors writing about this grim place.

The songs I've chosen largely encompass my time at 6 Music, from the launch day in London's Broadcasting House to the present day, now doing my show at MediaCity in Salford. They're the songs that tell my

'I'M AN UNASHAMED SUCKER FOR A GREAT CATCHY POP SONG, SO IT WOULD BE THE HOOK THAT'S MOST IMPORTANT IN A TRACK FOR ME.'

6 Music story. I was 25 when I started working at 6 Music, so these are the songs that have soundtracked my 20s and 30s: most of my adult life. If I wasn't around when those songs came out it doesn't matter – they sound as good now as when I first heard them, and I would guess as good as they did when they first came out.

I'm just an unashamed sucker for a great catchy pop song, so it would be the hook that's most important in a track for me, I think. I'm very much tune first, lyrics second, and it takes me quite a long time to get to the lyrics of a song, if I'm honest. If there's anything new, there'll be a lyric that stands out. Arctic Monkeys do that brilliantly – he's an amazing songwriter, Alex Turner. I think that his lyrics *properly* stand out, but where lyrics are not so high in the mix, or as prominent as they are in an Arctic Monkeys song – speaking about contemporary tunes – it's got to have something hooky and catchy. That's what I most want to hear in something new.

Yes, I like a soppy singer-songwriter, male or female, and I appreciate those tunes, particularly at the early time of day I'm on the air – it's exactly what's needed, something really soft and delivered gently, and on a rainy cold Monday morning, that's what's needed. But for me, if I'm listening to new music, what excites me greatly is hooky indie pop.

New Life
Depeche Mode
1981 • Mute

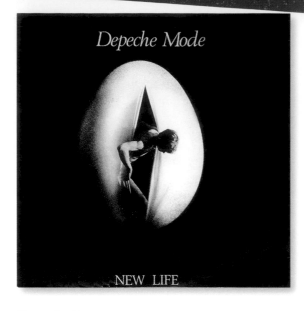

>> Depeche Mode's breakthrough single is a jaunty, bouncy number, using their electronics to create springy, repetitive uncomplicated phrases. At the time, it placed them well to the fore of the synth-pop wave as it evolved out of art rock, and it now seems altogether removed from the rather serious souls the band would evolve into. This is down to original songwriter Vince Clarke and his gift for crafting catchy melodies out of the bare minimum of a soundscape. Clarke wrote 'New Life' and nearly all of the group's debut album *Speak and Spell*, departing directly after its release to continue his adventures in synth-pop, firstly with Yazoo, then with Erasure.

Bedsitter
Soft Cell
1981 • Some Bizarre

<< Although 'Bedsitter' went top 10 on release, in time its status has been overshadowed by Soft Cell's previous single, the juggernaut that was their take on Gloria Jones' song 'Tainted Love' (see page 16), which is a little unfair. This icy, vaguely menacing tune is another chapter of disappointment and disillusion, as documented on the *Non-Stop Erotic Cabaret* album's overview of the seedier side of London clubbing. It was subject matter that split opinion on the duo: exploitative; insightful; pretentious; not sexy enough; too rude.

Underneath their controversial veneer, though, was a perceptive musical nous that shifted synth-pop into an altogether darker and more textured area without alienating a wider audience.

(We Don't Need This) Fascist Groove Thang
Heaven 17
1981 • BEF/Virgin

>> Former Human Leaguers Martyn Ware and Ian Craig Marsh walked a couple of fine lines when they formed Heaven 17. Firstly the electronics of *Penthouse and Pavement*, their first album, clearly owed a debt to later-model Kraftwerk, but managed to keep on the right side of mainstream daytime radio. On its lively opening track, debut single 'Fascist Groove Thang' in particular, their anti-racist and anti-fascist ideas were aimed at the pop kids who would be dancing to them in the discos, an approach which, in many respects, was far more revolutionary than ranting against Mrs Thatcher. Yet radio play at the time was thin on the ground; the BBC banned it on the grounds that the lyric's references to Ronald Reagan may have been libellous.

Pretty in Pink
The Psychedelic Furs
1981 • CBS

>> The song, which partly inspired the 1986 John Hughes film of that name, is from an album (*Talk Talk Talk*) produced by Steve Lillywhite, where lots of big musical statements slot together with plaintive lyricism about teenage love and lust. It's an interesting juxtaposition, because while the arrangements don't sound overbearing, these adolescent dramas are still taken as seriously as the protagonists of them would desire. 'Pretty in Pink' is a case in point; it sounds like a big belting soul tune, with crashing guitars and the sax blowing up a storm, but the song itself seems to occupy familiar territory – yearning for an unattainable girl.

131

Genius of Love
Tom Tom Club
1981 • Island

《 》 The New York new wave was always far more eclectic than its London counterpart, and would absorb all sorts of influences, elevating what was essentially contemporary rock 'n' roll into a wide range of areas. Hip-hop was rarely far away – the two styles came together in warehouse clubs and graffiti art – and 'Genius of Love' shows Chris Frantz and Tina Weymouth's Talking Heads side-project adopting early rap's styles, cadences and daft sense of fun. This gem clearly never thought of itself as actual hip-hop but was happy to adapt what bits of it made most sense. It's not exploitative or disrespectful or culturally colonizing, it's more playful than anything and a very good example of what can be achieved in music when all the neighbours get along with each other.

Southern Freeez
Freeez
1981 • Beggars Banquet

GILLES PETERSON'S CHOICE 》 A common complaint about jazz-funk in general was that it was too fiddly, that there was too much intricate playing for its own sake, and while 'Southern Freeez' has its indulgently fussy moments it's predominantly an exercise in simplicity. A straightforward chugging beat draped with layered keyboards taking clean sweeps across the rhythm and a largely uncomplicated guitar make an easy-to-follow dance track – indeed, the 'Southern Freeez' was a London dance. Freeez's musicianship was as good as that of their peers, but they would later work with electro hip-hop production wizard Arthur Baker on their massive club hit, 'I.O.U.', which was about as minimalist as you could get and still be exciting.

GILLES PETERSON'S SELECTION

(See Gilles' song choices on pages 13, 49, 50, 132, 181, 199, 200 and 251.)

It's quite abstract to have Wayne Shorter all the way through to Skream, but there is a direct connection in the sense of my life as a DJ. I was brought up on jazz and soul, and the basis of my record collection and of what I've done on the radio – and in clubs – is to make sure that I could introduce that kind of music to an audience in an environment where people wouldn't switch off.

I was on pirate radio for quite a few years, then I had a show on BBC Radio London called *Mad on Jazz*. I was 18, 19 then, and in the space of three weeks I interviewed three people who I never would have interviewed if I hadn't been on the BBC: Wayne Shorter, Jalal from the Last Poets, and Mark Murphy the jazz singer. All three were coming out of jazz, but out of very different places. The thing about Wayne Shorter for me, as this naive young boy from South London suddenly spending two hours in a studio – just him and me – I still can't believe he had the time to spend with somebody who knew so little. And I was really amazed by the fact that he shared that time with me. And the same with Jalal, and Mark Murphy. Those three people at that stage in my life gave me…I dunno, I almost felt like I was responsible to maintain and to make the connection. I always felt that I had a responsibility to make sure that I never forgot and that people didn't forget about this music. And I think that as time goes on, the music becomes even more significant. To me, a record like 'Speak No Evil' or 'Witch Hunt' by

'THE FRESHNESS OF A TUNE ATTRACTS ME, YOU KNOW, THE ALL-ROUND QUALITY OF A TUNE, BECAUSE THAT'S RARE!'

Wayne Shorter represents an era in music that is totally timeless and actually grows with time in terms of its effect.

When I first heard the Skream track at Plastic People, it was being played by the owner Ade – when it got a bit too commercial in his club, he used to get on the decks and just twist it. He'd play some sort of free jazz, then he'd play some very obscure record from the Ivory Coast, and then I remember him dropping Skream, 'Midnight Request Line', and I'm like, 'My God! This is just unbelievable how you're placing it.'

Something like Terry Callier is more of a radio song. But the whole thing for me is being able to push the limits of what is applicable in club culture, and connect that to what I do on the radio.

The freshness of a tune attracts me, you know, the all-round quality of a tune, because that's rare! Fundamentally what really gets me when I first listen to the hundreds of tracks I hear every week, I think it's the finesse and the subtle differences in production. Because music is what I spend most of my time doing I've got a refined taste – not because I'm gifted but because I'm still in it, I can't get out of it! So when there's a subtle difference in a track, I can hear it; I hear it when something's got that little spark, that it's properly unique, rather than being a copy of something else.

That's what gets me going, when I feel there's that little something new in it, that tiny little percentage that people who might not be so 'in it' might not catch at first.

Ghost Town
The Specials
1981 • 2-Tone

CHRIS HAWKINS' CHOICE

Something of a theme song for the United Kingdom during the Thatcher years, 'Ghost Town' summed up the urban decay, industrial decline and casual violence that had come to define so much of British life. Quite rightly, it made its points eloquently and without compromise, and with its point of view (simple disappointment rather than anger) it had a much greater empathy factor: more or less everybody could feel Jerry Dammers' pain.

As the last single from the original Specials line up – there was considerable internal tension during the song's recording – it was the best music they ever made, a woozy masterclass of minor chords and ska attitude seemingly off-key but in truth perfectly pitched. A number one hit in the UK, nobody was too surprised when all three of the country's biggest weekly music papers (*NME*, *Melody Maker* and *Sounds*) voted it single of the year.

Sponji Reggae
Black Uhuru
1981 • Island

« The sturdiest bridge between the soft-edged, more organic-sounding roots reggae and the hard-surfaced dancehall came from the work that Sly Dunbar (drums) and Robbie Shakespeare (bass) did with Black Uhuru. One of Jamaica's finest rhythm sections, Sly and Robbie's playing and production also marked them out as the most outward-looking. At a time when reggae was almost entirely insular, they embraced overseas styles – disco, Philly and hip-hop in particular – and explored modern technology as an opportunity rather than with suspicion. Theirs was a simple strategy – take a traditional roots-reggae harmony trio, fellow Jamaicans Black Uhuru, produce roots reggae music for them, but play it on modern computerized instruments, and use dub ideas and arrangements, but with contemporary sounds. Songs like 'Sponji Reggae' dragged Jamaican music out of the 1970s without alienating the existing roots audience.

Atomic Dog
George Clinton
1982 • Capitol

» As P-Funk ran out of ideas or got hogtied in various legal disputes, George Clinton redefined the collective for a series of 'solo' albums. Although these could be a bit sketchy, they produced some remarkable moments, one of which was 'Atomic Dog'. Using mostly computerized sounds, but programmed by actual instrument-playing musicians, it's a whirlwind of spontaneity of the sort P-Funk did better than anybody else. In a single session, Clinton improvised the lyrics, and semi-rapped them over a rhythm track played backwards, later adding harmonized backing vocals and a few keyboard lead lines. Unbelievably funky, it's now one of hip-hop's most popular sample sources – adopted by Snoop, Public Enemy, Ice Cube, Herbie Hancock, Tupac, the Fresh Prince – and it knocked Michael Jackson's 'Billie Jean' off the number one spot in the US R&B charts.

The Message
Grandmaster Flash and the Furious Five
1982 • Sugarhill

'The Message' was eulogized as rap's first political single. It wasn't, but it was the first of that type to reach a wide audience for several reasons. Firstly, it was social comment instead of political diatribe, and the notion of 'ghetto sufferation', albeit with a 'don't push me 'cause I'm close to the edge' footnote, was far more mainstream and palatable than, say, Brother D's 'How We Gonna Make the Black Nation Rise' (1980), which can probably lay claim to being rap's first political single.

Sugarhill Records had, by 1982, established itself as rap's most pop-friendly label, and therefore far more likely to be listened to by reviewers and radio producers. And, most importantly, 'The Message' sounded completely fresh. Much has been made of it advancing hip-hop's focus from pure party fare to having something to say, but equally significant was the shift it prompted in hip-hop hierarchy through manipulation of the music. This wasn't primarily a record for dancing, with the rappers occupying a position of glorified hype men, simply enhancing the rhythm and exhorting the crowd.

As the first rap record with a backing track exclusively made up of synth loops (most likely a Prophet 5) and a drum machine instead of either a backing band or turntable pyrotechnics, the track's balance was altered far more effectively. Slow, brooding and noirish, it was jagged enough to provoke dystopian inner-city visions, hook-laden enough to stick in your head, but was sufficiently restrained to never overwhelm the vocals. It meant the lyrics should be listened to rather than just heard, and as Melle Mel (the only member of the Furious Five, including Flash himself, to actually appear on the record) took centre stage, suddenly the rapper was what counted and hip-hop, as a form, was much easier for rock's traditionalists to understand.

Rip It Up
Orange Juice
1982 • Polydor

>> As blue-eyed funkateers, Orange Juice had a sense of purpose about them so often missing from their early-1980s counterparts; a purpose explained by superior songwriting, and supported by a production that understood how to balance a big sound with a straightforward beat. 'Rip It Up' was the band at their zenith: a rubberized bass synth and a Chic-style guitar hook kick off an infectious handclap-heavy funk demon so self-aware that even Edwyn Collins' vocal refrain of 'rip it up and start again' becomes a riff in its own right.

Planet Rock
Afrika Bambaataa and the Soul Sonic Force
1982 • Tommy Boy

<< If you opened the dictionary at 'electro' the chances are you'd be looking at a picture of 'Planet Rock' — or if you had a really futuristic dictionary, a *sonic* picture of the track. Produced by early hip-hop and breakbeat pioneer Arthur Baker, the people who actually performed on the record are almost irrelevant, as it was a producer's record, made at a time when the style was so new its rules and musical covenants were yet to be established. Against a persistent, sparse beat, and governed only by his innate sense of timing and musical drama, Baker added material from a variety of sources: vocoder vocals, electronic SFX, a theme from *For a Few Dollars More* and snatches of Kraftwerk–inspired melodies. None of these submerged the beat. 'Planet Rock' is an immense piece of work, the seminal track that all electro would be compared to.

Talk Talk
Talk Talk
1982 • EMI

>> As one of the new wave bands that made an impact in the early 1980s, the first incarnation of Talk Talk was always pleasant enough, but seldom sounded much greater than the sum of its parts. And those 'parts' were pretty much those of their contemporaries – anticipating mid-period Eurythmics and with a strong bias towards Duran Duran; indeed their debut album and this track was actually produced by Duran Duran producer Colin Thurston. Occasionally, though, as on 'Talk Talk' itself, Talk Talk would win the day with their largely likeable gaucheness and unashamed way in which they flaunted their influences. 'Talk Talk' approaches its task with such enthusiasm and carefree spirit that you can't help but get on board.

Party Fears Two
The Associates
1982 • Associates/Beggars Banquet

What was absolutely brilliant about the Associates was they very publicly lived in the sort of excess-ridden, absurdist and subversive way you'd assume all new romantic figureheads should. In their case, excess wasn't just sartorial. During the recording of 1982's *Sulk* album, they spent a ridiculous amount of record company advance money living in a London hotel – with a separate room for singer Billy Mackenzie's whippets. They went way beyond the regulation indulgences of early 1980s rock 'n' roll, filling drums with water to see what they would sound like and ordering guitars to be specially made out of chocolate for a *Top of the Pops* appearance. Out of all that came some very good soul-pop, of which 'Party Fears Two' is a crisp and bouncy synth-driven example, with an unforgettable piano hook.

Shipbuilding
Robert Wyatt
1982 • Rough Trade

>> Here's a song with music, lyrics and vocals that engage together so perfectly it's difficult to imagine any of them beginning life without the others in mind, but how 'Shipbuilding' turned out is far from how it was intended. Written by producer and former Deaf School guitarist Clive Langer for Robert Wyatt, Langer was so dissatisfied with his own lyrics that he asked Elvis Costello for input. For a time, the intention was not to involve Wyatt – the song would be sung by four other different vocalists on an EP – and it was only after Costello finished writing that he became re-involved. Which was all worth it as this beautiful, wistful, acoustically-backed song – about the incongruity of needing a war (namely the Falklands) to save nations' shipyards while would-be workers from those same areas are being blown up – remains one of the most intelligent, insightful protest songs ever made.

Carnation
The Jam
1982 • Polydor

<< >> The Jam's final album, *The Gift*, was a disjointed affair that caused strained relations within the trio, partly due to Paul Weller's growing interest in soul and Northern soul. That change of direction is not reflected on the largely overlooked 'Carnation'; instead of drawing on American influences, it harked back to the group's English rock traditions of post-mod mod – the Kinks, the Small Faces, the Move and so on. And as such it's what the Jam always did very well when they were getting in touch with their less angry side: breezy guitar pop with a bit more guts and more than a hint of psychedelia.

Night Nurse

Gregory Isaacs
1982 • African Museum/Island

>> 'Night Nurse' shows off every reason why Gregory Isaacs should have crossed over to trouble the charts on a far more regular basis. It's a slow and dreamy lovers' rock tune, put together by the Roots Radics, a Kingston session crew who were taking huge steps towards a digital style without changing their essential arrangements, so it was very contemporary in sound. Gregory's vocal effortlessly floats over the top of this, crooning a continuation of his 'Lonely Lover' theme – how his redemption will only be found in the love of a good woman – with a vulnerability and helplessness that would melt the stoniest heart. Perfect early 1980s fodder, but as the singer's drug habit and generally cantankerous demeanour introduced a whole new level of 'difficult to deal with', mainstream success never happened for him.

Ghosts

Japan
1982 • Virgin

>> Revisiting the early-1980s singles charts today seems like stepping through the back of the wardrobe, into a musical Narnia of eclecticism, distinguished by interesting ideas and full-on nuttiness. 'Ghosts' is all of the above. By 1982, the last year of Japan's life as a group, they had all but abandoned their new wave/new romantic beginnings and evolved into a synthesized version of Japan the country. The doomy 'Ghosts' lacks a conventional rhythm section or even a beat – instead David Sylvian croons over a bleak echoing soundscape that approximates Japanese chamber music. It's enlivened – if that's the word – with a few minor chords drifting through an arrangement with no conventional narrative, and after four-and-a-half minutes it just stops. A bold choice for a single in any era, this reached number five in the UK.

MARY ANNE HOBBS' SELECTION

(See Mary Anne's song choices on pages 26, 43, 120, 150, 172, 195, 196, 213, 219, 230, 287, 294 and 295.)

I guess it's quite an eccentric selection of songs to pull together, and that'll be the influence of my hero John Peel.

As a kid I grew up listening to Peel, under my blankets in the dead of night on a tiny transistor radio. John didn't have affinity to genre of any kind. His love of music was instinctive. Does it thrill you? Does it touch the very core of your soul, or not?

There's definitely a sense of poetry that will attract me to a piece of music. Poetry comes closest to the type of expression that music can make. There's a purely emotional dimension which is almost impossible to express in any other creative form, be that fine art or film, or a chapter from a book. That's what will attract me to a piece of music in the first instance, and certainly a piece of music that will travel across decades with me.

To give one specific example, the Nils Frahm track I've chosen 'Says', is extraordinary. It sounds like he has captured the complex textures of what love could be

'JOHN [PEEL] DIDN'T HAVE AFFINITY TO GENRE OF ANY KIND. HIS LOVE OF MUSIC WAS INSTINCTIVE. DOES IT THRILL YOU? DOES IT TOUCH THE VERY CORE OF YOUR SOUL, OR NOT?'

and transposed them into sound. That track has really resonated with 6 Music listeners. Nils has been in touch to say that as a consequence of the passion that I have shown for his work and the platform I've given him, it's changed the trajectory of his career and the way in which audiences are connecting with him as an artist.

I believe that radio can change people's lives. It might be as simple as just lifting someone's day. Or it could be more profound, in my case for example, helping build a career for an artist as radical as James Blake. I was the first to play his music on the radio, and he's has gone on to have a Top 10 album and win the Mercury Music Prize.

The musicians, the broadcasters, and the 6 Music audience; we form a circle. When we meet to share a radio programme together there's a tangible sense of communion. These are the most precious moment of my life, and they have a kind of magic that just blows me away.

Song to the Siren
This Mortal Coil
1983 • 4AD

>> This Mortal Coil was 4AD Records' revolving, early-indie supergroup, which indulged in multi-artist sessions, often with various permutations of the label's acts. 'Song to the Siren' finds Elizabeth Fraser and Robin Guthrie, two-thirds of the Cocteau Twins, offering a lush and melancholy cover of a Tim Buckley original, thanks to Fraser's haunting vocals and Guthrie's distant synths. It gives the gothic lyrics a life beyond mere poetry, adding a depth of off-kilter emotion that according to David Lynch, inspired Julee Cruise.

The Cutter
Echo and the Bunnymen
1983 • Korova

 **LIZ KERSHAW'S CHOICE** >> The Bunnymen sound – muscular, intelligent post-punk pop with clear references to 1960s psychedelic rock – was fully formed by their third album, *Porcupine*. One of its stand-out tracks, 'The Cutter', launches into a kicking groove, the bass and drums backed up with a nagging guitar riff. Before any of that, though, it opens with a synth approximation of Indian strings, playing what sounds like a woozy lift from Cat Stevens' 'Matthew and Son'. Then strings sporadically reappear, elevating a hardworking dance track into something much more intriguing and informed.

She's in Parties
Bauhaus
1983 • Beggars Banquet

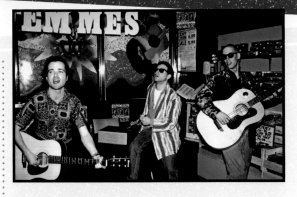

≪ There was always more to goth than simply being whey faced and a bit out of sorts most of the time. Here one of the genre's figureheads, Northampton's Bauhaus, turn out a vast baroque sound with all manner of spires and turrets and gargoyles in the form of fuzz-drenched, echoing guitars, all built on a robust, determined dub-reggae bass line. It rattles the stained-glass windows, borrowing from the more pompous end of prog to produce superb, enjoyable decadence. It's positively Byronic in its careful elaborateness, and has the confidence to throw in a spooky dub section with a *Dance of the Vampires* feel to it, showing enough character not to let Peter Murphy's vocals dominate proceedings.

A New England
Billy Bragg
1983 • Go! Discs

Blister in the Sun
Violent Femmes
1983 • Slash

≪ The great thing about America's early indie scene was that it encouraged acts as apparently ramshackle as Violent Femmes just as warmly as it welcomed the slicker Blondie or the more powerful Ramones. The Femmes had a minimal, acoustic(ish) DIY sound that was really garage rock personified, of which 'Blister in the Sun's jaunty, vaguely hoedown-ish feel is comfortably inexpert and irresistibly disarming. Gordon Gano's similarly untutored vocals run through another commentary on the baffling stresses and strains of adolescent life. Which was something the group's first album, *Violent Femmes*, reflected with enormous empathy as Gano wrote most of its songs while still a teenager.

STEVE LAMACQ'S CHOICE ≫ At this early stage in his career, Billy Bragg was a lesson to us all: making your point exactly how you wanted to make it was paramount, even if it involved more work and less glamour. Bragg was the punk fanzine or the pirate radio of the record business, and it allowed him to convey the sort of socially parochial politics that matter so much to people. In 'A New England', backed only with his rockabilly-ish electric guitar, Bragg's plaintive vocals are seemingly about a broken romance, but also hint at disenchantment in general. This sort of disillusionment doesn't make particularly grand or saleable gestures, but it still made sense to so many of us.

Blue Monday
New Order
1983 • Factory

 The crucial watershed between what Joy Division were and what New Order became, the dancefloor endurance test 'Blue Monday' played a huge part in convincing the mainstream rock world that the electro end of hip-hop had real lasting value. As a result it went a long way to establishing dance music as a bona fide genre. There was genuine cleverness in how they did this: while the synthesizers, sequencers and a 4/4 beat whip up a groove Planet Patrol would have put their name to, it's partially cloaked with regular New Order sounds and a poker-faced, very English vocal from Bernard Sumner. Ridding themselves of conventional verse/chorus constraints, the song's beat builds irresistibly over seven-and-a-half minutes, but shrewdly, and presumably for the uninitiated, New Order sugar the pill with familiar-sounding, attention-grabbing punctuation; a guitar fill, a keyboard riff, and a doubled-up drum pattern. It worked – this remains the best-selling twelve-inch single of all time.

Progress
Flux of Pink Indians
1983 • Spiderleg

GIDEON COE'S CHOICE » Among the last true punks in town, Flux of Pink Indians never adhered to compromising what they did, and when the art world or the music mainstream of the early 1980s was courting so many former street warriors, they became even more anti-establishment. 'Progress' is about a minute-and-a-half of two-chord broadside, a throat-shredding tirade against the evils encroaching on the lives of citizens in the modern world. As with all of Flux's work, it's brief, to the point and an appropriate, unashamedly oikish rallying cry that was needed in 1983.

Double Dutch
Malcolm McLaren
1983 • Charisma

From McLaren's *Duck Rock* album, an epic of cultural tourism, borrowing ideas, rhythms and melodies from Africa, North and South America and the Caribbean, 'Double Dutch' is a double header that grafts the New York street skipping game of the title – a big part of early hip-hop culture – on to the kwela-ish mbaqanga music of South Africa's Zulus. Whatever side you come down on in the exploitation vs exposure debate you have to admit this works as a lively piece of transnational pop, westernizing an African style just enough for popular consumption, with an engaging video of New York double dutch crews in action. Petrus Maneli (the South African writer of the appropriated melody) won an out-of-court settlement from McLaren and producer Trevor Horn.

Easter Parade
The Blue Nile
1984 • Linn

GIDEON COE'S CHOICE The Blue Nile's debut LP, *A Walk Across the Rooftops*, came about when superior hi-fi manufacturer Linn asked the group to record a song to use to demonstrate their products' sonic capabilities, and the result was a whole album. It was, however, much more than an extended test record for the deep-pocketed audiophile, and encompassed an eclectic range of sounds and musical presentations, from orchestral to synth-pop to jazz-funk to modern celtic, all united by Paul Buchanan's mournful vocals. 'Easter Parade' is a very low key, largely acoustic offering – with only a couple of pianos and a distantly swooshy synth washing in and out – but subtly textured enough to create an intriguing and super-relaxing experience.

Just Fascination
Cabaret Voltaire
1983 • Some Bizarre

This song, and the album it appears on – *The Crackdown* – showed the average rock fan how industrial post-punk didn't have to be something that needed to be endured; it could be enjoyed without sacrificing its core values. 'Just Fascination' has the same portentous tempo and big echoey arrangements of all the best industrial electronic music, it allows synth textures and interestingly distracting breakbeats into a track which could've been a wasteland. It's a shrewd acknowledgement of parallel computerized music developments – electro – and lifts the whole piece, anticipating the more mainstream rock-friendly dance music of their next album, *Micro Phonies*.

Upside Down
The Jesus and Mary Chain
1984 • Creation

>> On hearing this for the first time, as part of a music landscape populated largely by hip-hop derivatives, synthesizer bands and art pop, the Jesus and Mary Chain sounded like a throwback to livelier times and the berserk guitar rock of the Ramones and suchlike. But while it deliberately nodded back towards those bygone days and the simplicity of bass, drums and guitar, 'Upside Down' possessed an extra bite. It wrapped the guitar riffs in screaming digital fuzz, overdubbed some extra squealing in the background and pushed the mix to the edge of reason. Against this rambunctious racket, Jim Reid contributed a surprisingly calm, sober vocal, and the whole thing blew a breath of fresh air through the glossy pop scene of the time.

Smalltown Boy
Bronski Beat
1984 • London

<< Jimmy Somerville's powerful falsetto vocal was the instant talking point when Bronski Beat's debut single emerged out of nowhere. Also present, however, was an intelligent and cleverly constructed dance tune, which was fully aware of club sounds from both sides of the Atlantic and both sides of the racial divide – techno, hip-hop, electro, that tipping point between disco and house. That alone would have made it a hit, but what set 'Smalltown Boy' apart was its unflinching narrative about homophobia, bullying and how the resulting feelings of isolation can destroy a young life. Indeed, such fearless, articulate work would make Bronski Beat lead the dance-music pack for a couple of years.

Keep On Keepin' On!
The Redskins
1984 • Decca

>> Not the gentle Curtis Mayfield song of the same name, but a high-octane heartfelt diatribe about revolution and how not to be tricked or bought out of it. The Redskins were a militant Trotskyite band, dedicated to worker power and unseating the government of the time, playing every benefit for striking miners, and any anti-racism/anti-fascism festival going. Their uncompromisingly radical politics tended to overshadow the fact they were exciting vibrant musicians. Indeed, in November 1984 (during the year-long miners' strike), they attempted to have a striking miner make a speech in the middle of Channel 4's live TV pop show *The Tube*, and as a result nobody can remember if their perfomance was any good or not. But they were very good, as this punk-fuelled Northern soul stormer, complete with horn section, testifies.

So. Central Rain (I'm Sorry)
R.E.M.
1984 • IRS

>> By the time they'd got to their second album, *Reckoning*, R.E.M. had worked out that they wanted a life beyond college radio and cult acceptance, and settled on what they were best at – modern-day country rock with a perceptible new wave edge. So while they smoothed off a large amount of their debut album *Murmur*'s spikey spontaneity, it gave them a framework to become far more subtly absorbing. Ironically, shedding so much self-conscious 'indieness' allowed them to set the template for what would be known as indie rock. 'So. Central Rain' is a rich and gorgeous example of R.E.M.'s scope for refined mood manipulation. Ostentatiously sunny with a 12-string guitar and jangly piano, it's (most likely) a break up song – and the minor chords give it a mournful undercurrent, while the musical arrangement builds to a bawling climax of melancholy. Never has unhappiness been so catchy.

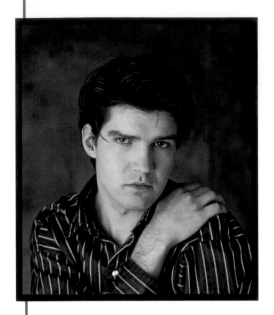

Forest Fire
Lloyd Cole and the Commotions
1984 • Polydor

« The standout track from Lloyd Cole and the Commotions' first album, *Rattlesnakes*, one of the few on which both singer and band sound like they're trying to be themselves rather than imitating Bob Dylan or Lou Reed or somebody. Which means we are treated to a musically literate, slow-building four minutes of ebbing, flowing soul, but soul confident enough in itself not to try to sound American – they even had the cheek to play the song out with a twangy, thirty-second guitar solo. Though a smaller hit than its preceding single, 'Perfect Skin', 'Forest Fire' reinforced Cole and his group as one of the most sophisticated, musically literate bands of the time.

The Boy With the Thorn in His Side
The Smiths
1985 • Rough Trade

LIZ KERSHAW'S CHOICE » An upbeat, almost janglingly cheerful number that finds the vocalist in celebratory mood, but as this is the Smiths and said vocalist is Morrissey, there's a sarcastic sting in the tail. In this particular narrative he or the group are the titular 'boy', while the 'thorn' is the music business in general and the lyric relates how nobody believed the band and their music could ever amount to anything in the 1980s pop-and-rock climate. During a period when relations between band and record label were starting to sour, they felt they could talk this way about the industry because they'd proved themselves on a big scale. That the Smiths were able to get away with making such an inward-looking song is a testament to the music and their bond with their audience.

Who Comes to Boogie
Little Benny and The Masters
1985 • Elektra

One of the Washington go-go originals, the late Anthony Harley (a.k.a. Little Benny) got into this brand of parochially unique, hyper-rhythmic funk as a teenager watching the genre's founder, Chuck Brown. It was a style that began as percussion-only breaks – congas, cowbells, timbales, snare drums – employed in between numbers at live shows, in the same way a DJ would, to encourage club crowds to keep dancing. 'Who comes to boogie?' is a simple enough question, and the answer would be pretty much anybody who hears this tune and not because it's hardcore go-go. Most interestingly, Benny scatters go-go breaks across a crisp, largely irresistible funk track, which had the effect of welcoming in the uninitiated.

Walls Come Tumbling Down
The Style Council
1985 • Polydor

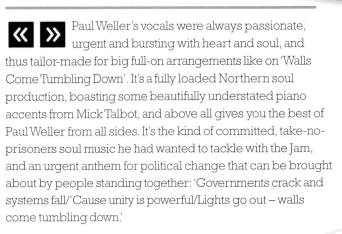 Paul Weller's vocals were always passionate, urgent and bursting with heart and soul, and thus tailor-made for big full-on arrangements like on 'Walls Come Tumbling Down'. It's a fully loaded Northern soul production, boasting some beautifully understated piano accents from Mick Talbot, and above all gives you the best of Paul Weller from all sides. It's the kind of committed, take-no-prisoners soul music he had wanted to tackle with the Jam, and an urgent anthem for political change that can be brought about by people standing together: 'Governments crack and systems fall/'Cause unity is powerful/Lights go out – walls come tumbling down.'

She Sells Sanctuary
The Cult
1985 • Beggars Banquet

The Headmaster Ritual
The Smiths
1985 • Rough Trade

  When the superb non-album single 'How Soon Is Now?' charted in early 1985, it seemed as if the Smiths' next album was certain to capitalize on all of the strengths of their first one. Not really. If anything, *Meat Is Murder* was a bit of a mess, attempting to move in too many directions – but a few tracks stood out. One was 'The Headmaster Ritual', and it is one of the very highest spots in the group's entire canon. Ignore the moaning about his school days, and you have one of Morrissey's finest vocal performances, both engaged and engaging as he soars and even yodels. The true elegance of this song, though, emerges via Johnny Marr's expansive guitar work which isn't doing anything particularly tricksy, but shows off his musical craft nonetheless, and makes the track hugely accessible to all.

The group's most iconic song, from the album, *Love*, that saw the Cult finally shifting away from their semi-underground, quasi-goth origins, to embark on a journey on the road to stadium rock. And they did it very well too: having learned their musicianship in smaller surroundings, they had the nous not to add or take away too much, just magnify every musical gesture and accent so it would make sense from 50 metres away. On 'Sanctuary', everything was tightened up, the tracks were separated, the drums became snappier, the guitars added fuzz to careen through the riffing, and the singing removed any subtlety of emotion in favour of power – but to great effect.

(You Gotta) Fight for Your Right (To Party)
The Beastie Boys
1986 • Def Jam

When Def Jam's Russell Simmons and Rick Rubin started blending rap and heavy metal as a kind of multi-culti exercise in extreme obnoxiousness, one of the natural conclusions was the rapid rise to stardom of the Beastie Boys. But away from the media spin on the trio's on-the-road anarchic exploits, they rode the hybrid and produced some excellent music, 'Fight for Your Right' being a great example. It was never really a rap record, but closer to hard rock fused with sharp hip-hop sensibilities, which absolved the Beasties of the necessity to sing. The backgrounds of Simmons and Rubin, doyens respectively of hip-hop and heavy metal, worked perfectly. Neither form was diluted: a methodology that changed the way both styles were approached in the wider world.

E=MC²
Big Audio Dynamite
1985 • CBS

After leaving The Clash in 1983, guitarist Mick Jones founded a far more contemporary-sounding outfit, which combined his gift for a clipped melody with an affinity for technology, and created some of the mid-1980s' most attention-grabbing rock. They weren't afraid to absorb their musical surroundings then look further afield for other styles to include – for this reason B.A.D. were closer to New York's new wave than most of their peers in the UK. 'E=MC²', for instance, took sampling to extremes, including many snatches of dialogue from the Nicolas Roeg film, *Performance*. As a result it's a smart, sparsely populated dance track with electro leanings, and with some unique sounds giving it a wonderfully mad off-kilter spin.

Brilliant Mind
Furniture
1986 • Stiff

There's a good reason why 'Brilliant Mind' (unluckily Furniture's only hit) crops up on so many 1980s compilation albums: in so many ways, it typifies the decade, being essentially synth-pop, but also totally unafraid to let its disco and jazz-funk influences show. With its driving bass line, funky keyboard flourishes and a menacing sax break, the song summed up soul-boy pop and balanced a good-time beat with an angsty and sardonic lyric delivered by singer Jim Irvin. Much of this was down to some inspired, disciplined songwriting, which enabled the band to convey such a cleverly layered piece so fluently.

My Adidas
Run-DMC
1986 • Profile

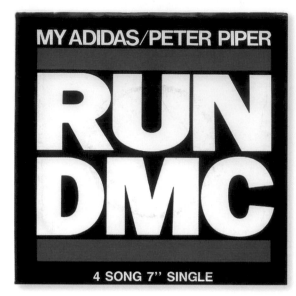

>> Hot on the heels of their collaboration with Aerosmith on the genre-busting, worldwide hit 'Walk This Way', Run-DMC's follow-up was pure New York B-Boy rap. 'My Adidas' wasn't simply a matter of escaping their novelty status, nor confounding any critics who could accuse them of riding Aerosmith's coat-tails. It was about establishing unadulterated rap as bona fide pop music. The record achieved this, but its greatest significance was to herald the modern age of rap, in terms of aesthetics, music and commercial potential. Almost minimalist in production – little more than very live, very forceful turntablism – 'My Adidas' showed Run-DMC's ghetto-slick street style leave behind the P-Funk influenced fringed- and raccoon-tailed-leather nonsense that had been holding rap back. Meanwhile, the sports and leisurewear company Adidas would pay the trio over a million dollars for an ongoing association.

Sign o' the Times
Prince
1987 • Paisley Park/Warner Bros.

<< >> If people had to pick the best Prince album – not necessarily their favourite, but his technical and artistic best – *Sign o' the Times* would probably come out on top, with its title track most likely voted its finest song. The double album as a whole finds Prince impressing with his soul credentials, and 'Sign o' the Times' itself strips things back to such basics – a beatbox, sparing bass synth and occasional guitar – that his vocal has nowhere to hide. Not that it would need to; it's urgent, pleading and, above all, soulful as he runs through a sharply documented litany of 1980s social and political ills. Never has an impending apocalypse sounded so attractive.

Charity, Chastity, Prudence and Hope
Hüsker Dü
1987 • Warner Bros.

  With their final studio album, *Warehouse: Songs and Stories*, Hüsker Dü had evolved into a fully fledged post-punk hard-rock band, with relatively high production values. 'Charity, Chastity' sounds far slicker than the Hüsker Dü of old – layering the guitars, laying on the fuzz tone and seemingly doubling up the drums – but drew a degree of critical ire for it. In retrospect, though, close listening to earlier releases suggests the band was always pointed in this direction, just like so much other US punk of the 1980s: it was poised to fill a gap at the grungier end of the hard-rock genre, vacated by so many groups migrating towards big hair and MTV.

Pump Up the Volume
M/A/R/R/S
1987 • 4AD

>> Built on little more than a monster drum machine and abbreviated bass-riff rhythm, 'Pump Up the Volume' was embellished with scratch-mix effects and countless music and speech samples (even its title is sourced from an Eric B. & Rakim track). A number-one hit in the UK, it kicked open the door left ajar by Coldcut's 'Say Kids, What Time Is It?' almost a year previously. And even if M/A/R/R/S – a collaboration between rock duo A R Kane and electronic trio Colourbox – would never follow it up, 'Pump Up the Volume' kick-started a British-made hip-hop boom; DJ-led acts like Bomb the Bass, S'Express and Coldcut devised witty and inventive tracks crammed with samples, but which usually dropped the often embarrassing reliance on British voices rapping.

Paid in Full
Eric B. & Rakim
1987 • 4th & Broadway

<< Probably hip-hop's most under-appreciated act, Eric B. & Rakim's approach to the genre was jazzier, and showed how a combination of discipline and spontaneity could create the best music. Here, Eric B.'s solid beats are essentially unfussy beatboxing and scratching, bolstered by the seductive bass line from Dennis Edwards' 'Don't Look Any Further', and a perfect anchor for Rakim's rap. One of the most lyrical writers, Rakim delivers unexpected rhymes that dodge in and out of the beat, while never losing the swing. This was from their first album (also called *Paid in Full*) and for two more they continually raised the bar.

Hit the North
The Fall
1987 • Beggars Banquet

» The Fall's line up was – and still is – such an unsettled situation, you never really knew what you were getting, other than the ever-present Mark E Smith and a bristly musical attitude. With 'Hit the North', though, you get much of the best they had to offer, and one of the most accessible singles in their capacious back catalogue. Smith always had a way with the repetitive, knowing exactly what points to embellish; but this track further benefits from cowriter Simon Rogers' production as well as his bass playing, bringing a crisp, almost pop-friendly discipline to what could have been an unwieldy rhythmic stack. Sitting on top of each other, the slightly wonky horn phrasing, a synth, a bass line, guitar riffs and a slapping snare all create something suitably dense, but which sounds dangerously like a groove – there's more than a touch of Kraftwerk here. As for the lyric, it might well be an example of Smith's trademark flinty Northern humour, while the accompanying video is hilariously, dourly deadpan.

We Care a Lot
Faith No More
1987 • Slash

« Once you dodged the poodly hair cuts of the more MTV-friendly end of the US heavy metal spectrum, you could stumble across all sorts of hard rock communities that developed more interesting hybrids from a range of influences. Some might just experiment with new styles for a few songs, but others would make a career out of it. Faith No More seemed to have listened to a lot of funk and very early rap and allowed it to filter through into their output, not dissimilar to the Run-DMC/Aerosmith collaboration, 'Walk This Way'. 'We Care a Lot', Faith No More's earliest hit, had an edge as well, being a funny and damning attack on the 'caring' image that had sprung up in the wake of Live Aid.

Caribou
The Pixies
1987 • 4AD

›› A shimmering example of what can be done with a true punk attitude, a Pentecostal Christian upbringing, a wry sense of humour and a grab bag of musical ideas that take in surf, psychedelia, rock 'n' roll and the garagey end of folk music. Recorded on the cheap – one of 15 or so tracks cut for $1,000 – 'Caribou' is an eerie, screechy, big production number, driven by huge-sounding drums and a churning guitar, which despite some sweet-voiced vocals never quite puts the listener at ease. Indeed, the drawn-out screams of 'Re-p-e-e-e-n-n-t' in its coda are not entirely unexpected. Remarkably, although The Pixies would massively influence the US alternative rock scene of the 1990s, in their time they were always much more appreciated by European audiences.

Travelling at the Speed of Thought
Ultramagnetic MCs
1987 • Next Plateau

‹‹ In the post-Def Jam rush of rap creativity, Ultramagnetic MCs were probably the most progressive and most eager to elevate the art into an alternative rock situation. With clever sampling choices, strikingly original lyrics and a unique delivery by Kool Keith, the MCs were instrumental in shrinking the gap between street culture and New York new wave. 'Travelling at the Speed of Thought' is an early example: still largely intuitive, full of in-jokes, self-deprecating humour and off the cuff ideas, combined with a cut up of 'Louie Louie' and an almost primeval beatbox. In all respects it was raw ghetto wit and open-minded cleverness, leaving no doubt of what was to come.

Birthday
The Sugarcubes
1987 • One Little Indian

>> Possibly the best debut by any band at any time (and bilingual too – the Icelandic original was the flip of the English A-side), the Sugarcubes' 'Birthday' was a lyrical and musical feast: whimsical, experimental, frisky, darkly mischievous and streets ahead of the competition. It brings to mind shades of Angelo Badalamenti scores and echoes of The B-52's, while Björk's unique, vaguely scary lead vocals made the end result as bonkers as it was beautiful, and as sexy as it was sardonic. It was single of the week almost everywhere, and its impact hinted at a great deal of potential in the group, and especially in its singer.

There She Goes
The La's
1988 • Go! Discs

« » Most people would be hard-pushed to name another song by the La's, but when the one they do know is this good, it scarcely matters. A lovely, jangly, sunny love song, and structurally very simple (it's really a recurring chorus), the song owes a debt to the Byrds and Velvet Underground, and is totally contagious without ever getting irritating. Everything you'd want from an indie anthem, in short. At the time of its release, the song caused an extra curricular sensation when, despite the band's increasingly weary-sounding denials, journalists pestered them about it being an ode to heroin, merely proving that some people have far too much time on their hands.

Love Buzz
Nirvana
1988 • Sub Pop

Like Patti Smith's cover of 'Gloria' or Marvin Gaye's cover of 'I Heard It Through the Grapevine', Nirvana's debut single takes a song that's essentially innocuous, even a bit whiny – in this case, a 1969 album track from Dutch rockers Shocking Blue – and retools it as something far darker, built around an almost scarily internalized focus.

'Love Buzz' was hardly an obvious debut single for Nirvana, but that in itself illustrates why the album it pre-empted, *Bleach*, is so revered. This is Kurt Cobain prior to wider expectations or external pressures – Nirvana are trying to please nobody but themselves. Such freedom means that, instead of simply listening to their contemporaries, they delve back into their musical memories. Influences from Led Zeppelin to the Stooges to Black Sabbath to Metallica percolate through, providing a vehicle for the sort of melodic tendencies rarely heard in proto-grunge or modern metal.

Most intriguing, though, was how these obviously musically sophisticated ideas were grounded by a basic approach. The drumming is all over the place and it's not really that hard to see why they replaced Chad Channing with Dave Grohl. Elsewhere, the band may have learned three chords, but they're only using two of them; to stay in front of the banshee guitars the inexperienced vocals regularly descend into a Lennon/Morrison-esque howl; and high production values aren't a priority when recording costs for the song's parent album would total a mere $606.17.

The Theme from Starsky & Hutch
The James Taylor Quartet
1988 • Urban

  Jazz-funkers the James Taylor Quartet always had a sharp ear for a good tune, hence their initial obsession with film and TV themes from the 1960s and 1970s like *Blow Up* and *Mission: Impossible*. In this instance, it was what they did with that source material that counted: the original tune – Tom Scott's 'Gotcha', one of three signature tunes from the 1970s cop series starring Paul Michael Glaser and David Soul – was, by the standards of the day, ridiculously thin (unsurprising as it developed out of a piece of the show's incidental music). The James Taylor Quartet beefed it up. This revamp puts it in touch with its inner monster: fully orchestrated, with churning guitar, careening piano and a gutsy Hammond organ pushing it all forwards.

Suedehead
Morrissey
1988 • HMV

 On the face of it, Morrissey's first solo offerings weren't radical departures from his work in the Smiths with Johnny Marr – a shrewd move, given his tightly focused fanbase – but there was still enough of a shift to let you know development was occurring. The music for his solo debut 'Suedehead' was written by Durutti Column's guitarist Vini Reilly, who supplemented it with keyboards and a cleverly balanced arrangement. While still sounding comfortingly Smiths-like, it expanded a sound that had started to become stale, and in turn inspired one of Morrissey's lighter, most enjoyable performances. The best song the Smiths never did?

Don't Believe the Hype
Public Enemy
1988 • Def Jam

The definitive Public Enemy track offered a short-lived glimpse of how important rap could be as a marriage of high art and strong statement. From the group's second album, *It Takes a Nation of Millions to Hold Us Back*, the group are at a point where, musically, they're still discovering what they can do. You can hear them surprising themselves and each other, all the while mastering a frightening, edge-of-the-Apocalypse sound of Spartan discipline and chaotic freeform.

The Chuck D/Flavor Flav axis echoes this approach: questioning as much as preaching; urging as well as protesting; bringing you the big picture while picking out the tiny details;

distracted and off-the-cuff yet totally focused – it was impossible to ignore. But then why would you want to? Out of the late-1980s global sociopolitical maelstrom, this record suggested that Public Enemy were the guys to lead us all to safety and sanity.

Where Is My Mind?
The Pixies
1988 • 4AD

  From The Pixies' first full-length album *Surfer Rosa*, this song is perhaps less left-field than it could have been, but even in retrospect, not a disappointment at all. With the help of producer Steve Albini, 'Where Is My Mind?' finds the quartet testing the limits, and wondering which of their more experimental ideas actually made musical sense. And most of them did. A straightforward and teasingly melodic track, in true Pixies fashion, it rises and falls in dynamics, and in doing so, at the turn of a chord, shifts from being hard-edged and quite menacing to soft, if not quite cuddly. This, in the context of a song that's apparently about fish, makes it all the more unnerving.

Destroy the Heart
House of Love
1988 • Creation

House of Love had, in Guy Chadwick, one of the best songwriters of English indie rock at that time. Light, catchy melodies appeared to come to him effortlessly, but he'd undercut them with strength of purpose in the rhythm's riffing to give the tunes a strength of purpose lacking in so many peer groups. The mildly psychedelic rocker 'Destroy the Heart' brought out a sense of adventure in the band's guitars, giving their sound the sort of intricate muscularity that should've seen them succeed on a much bigger stage. However, after their wonderful first album they left Alan McGee's Creation Records for a major label, and away from McGee's guiding hand seemed to creatively collapse in on themselves.

Pacific 707
808 State
1989 • ZTT

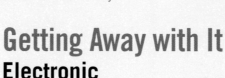

» There was a joyous apex around the end of the 1980s when electronic dance music creativity and technology met on equal terms, allowing hip-hop, electro and house ideas to fuse at a time when techno musicians still wanted their stuff to sound *like* music. Note: that's *like* music, not *exactly the same* as. 808 State (named after a drum machine) were the UK masters at this and the anthemic 'Pacific State' finds them at their peak. Quite rightly, 'Pacific State' (named 'Pacific 707' for its single version) became one of UK techno's most influential tracks. The layering of the rhythm track assembles a groove that is largely bass but with all sorts of quasi-melodic counterparts it could carry the tune on its own. On top of this there's an endearing soprano sax line, but because it's been electronically processed, it sounds unexpectedly offbeat, especially when it delicately duels with a keyboard. Other synth embellishments and rhythmic loops are present in sub-beats, but the whole sounds like a catchy instrumental rather than a collection of beats.

Getting Away with It
Electronic
1989 • Factory

« New Order's Bernard Sumner and the Smiths' Johnny Marr should've had quite enough to knock up a hit single on their own, but recruiting the Pet Shop Boys' Neil Tennant as a guest vocalist was a masterstroke, as was including a full orchestra, arranged by Art of Noise's Anne Dudley. Such was its combination of resonance, airiness and the catchiest of choruses that it was a near-perfect pop single not only for its time, but for any time. It has everything: a solid beat, sweeping strings, a memorable melody, an unusual guitar solo from Marr, engaging lyrics and a wistful lead vocal from Sumner. However the genius comes in the accessible arrangement – easy on the ear on first hearing, once you're immersed in it, you gradually come to realize quite how rich and rewarding it is.

Me Myself and I
De La Soul
1989 • Tommy Boy

>> You'll never go far wrong if you base something on the main riff from Funkadelic's '(Not Just) Knee Deep', but when you mix it with De La Soul's wit, whimsy and general charm, you'll wind up with a hip-hop classic. 'Me Myself and I' put De La Soul at the forefront of an attempt to counter rap's increasingly aggressive image with empathy, humour and heart, which led to their being branded 'hip-hop hippies'. But there was always more to them than that and this track, like the rest of the *3 Feet High and Rising* album, displays a keen intelligence amid the mischievous wordplay. Their laid-back open-minded hip-hop came close to becoming a bona fide genre in its own right, but the group were ultimately foiled partly because of copyright issues caused by their overuse of samples.

Fools Gold
The Stone Roses
1989 • Silvertone

THE STONE ROSES

FOOLS GOLD 9.53

Constructed on a drum loop borrowed from Bobby Byrd's 'Hot Pants (I'm Coming, I'm Coming, I'm Coming)', produced by James Brown, and with a bass line inspired by Isaac Hayes' 'Theme From Shaft', 'Fools Gold' was destined to be a champion of a tune. The Stone Roses were smart enough to make the most of such a solid foundation: they had been prepared to bravely ditch their recent debut album's attractive and appropriate pairing of 1960s psychedelia ideas and modern acid-house methods – very much a 'See Emily Play' for the dawn of the 1990s – in favour of a relatively straightforward take on early-1970s funk. Or perhaps it wasn't that brave after all. 'Fools Gold' was originally a B-side – the first copies pressed actually had 'What the World is Waiting For' as the A-side – it was veteran producer John Leckie who convinced the band to switch them over.

The band totally turned around the way they worked for 'Fools Gold', too: rather than recording as live as possible, the track was built up over a period of time. The basic groove was established first, then band members added ideas and flourishes as they thought of them. Next it was mixed to make sure there was enough space to maintain the funky vibe of the original rhythm – John Squire's wah-wah guitar licks were put on last, so as to embellish rather than dominate, an approach reflecting how George Clinton recorded P-Funk, and one which particularly suited the Roses. An expansive combination of spontaneity and fussiness, with plenty of scope for trying things out, the masterstroke of 'Fools Gold', was it running for nearly ten minutes. This allowed all their ideas to develop, and the groove to completely envelop anybody paying attention. A top-10 hit in the UK, it was for many the group's pinnacle; such a shame that legal wranglings with their record company delayed the making and release of their second album.

Portrait of a Masterpiece
The D.O.C.
1989 • Ruthless

  'Portrait of a Masterpiece' was a perfect hip-hop storm. Produced by Dr. Dre it had an inherent musicality: it was lyrically old-school brag, but it was also sharply inventive – the D.O.C. wrote many of the lyrics for N.W.A's *Straight Outta Compton* album; and his unique rapid-delivery style was always accessible. The album *No One Can Do It Better* topped the rap charts in the US, and took rap back to when it was still fun. It could've opened up a whole new avenue – interestingly, you can clearly hear early UK garage in there – but only months after it came out, disaster struck. The D.O.C. had his larynx crushed in a car accident and it would be five years before he could record again.

The Beat(en) Generation
The The
1989 • Epic

For the first time in years Matt Johnson assembled a proper band for the *Mind Bomb* album, resulting in a cohesiveness that had been lacking on its predecessors. As a consequence – and thanks in no small part to Johnny Marr's guitar – the whole album was moodier, less focused on dance music, and all the better for it. 'The Beat(en) Generation' was almost a jaunty pop tune on which Johnny Marr's harmonica had a starring role, but its smoothly dark lyric painted a dystopian tale of a manipulated and terrorized society.

Kennedy
The Wedding Present
1989 • RCA

When The Wedding Present – an indie rock group from Leeds who became favourites of John Peel and his listenership – came to make their *Bizarro* album in 1989, they had a major label deal, plus enough experience and sufficient recording budget to beef up the sometimes flimsy sound characterized by its predecessor, *George Best*. What they didn't mess with was the up-tempo three-chord attack and the stories centred on love, lust, and the inherent problems thereof; all told from an everyday point of view, which was as comical as it was poignant. 'Kennedy' in particular (which was a breakthrough hit in the UK) benefited massively from a more muscular production, as the music now provided a much stronger framework, meaning frontman David Gedge could inject more feeling into lyrics about local scandal, and bring the line 'too much apple pie' into the mix, while still sounding vaguely sinister.

Hallelujah
Happy Mondays
1989 • Factory

 If any band pointed the way towards the sea change that has taken place in the British music business during the last 20 years, it was Happy Mondays: years before the Internet, they pretty much removed the need for record companies as cultural and stylistic gatekeepers, by reflecting their audience with an unfiltered honesty. There was an anarchy to how they made music, drawing on bits and bobs of whatever they fancied – acid house, funk, disco, punk, psychedelia, rock and so on – that was little different from how most people consumed music, rather than arriving at it as the end product of a series of marketing meetings. As long as it was all done with skill and gusto and had the band's trademark edge of bedlam about it, it would get over.

'Hallelujah', in four different manifestations, is the Essence of Mondays in this respect. The club mix is a groove-ridin', uncomplicated six-minute beast of house-esque funk; the MacColl single mix (featuring the late Kirsty MacColl on backing vocals) is an urgent, chiming, guitar-driven rocker. A subsequent live take (captured on the 1990 video release *Call the Cops*) deftly pulls together elements from both studio versions. The cut on the *Hallelujah It's the Happy Mondays* release (a much later live recording) does the same – but it's not what you'd call deft; more like barely controlled chaos with an irresistible backbeat. All this plus lyrics like 'Bez has got no belly 'cos he's made of fuckin' jelly.'

I Am the Resurrection
The Stone Roses
1989 • Silvertone

CHRIS HAWKINS' CHOICE « More than perhaps any other Stone Roses' song, 'I Am the Resurrection' best explains why they made such an impact at the time they did: straightforward, mid-1960s influenced, swirly guitar pop that doesn't strain to ape house or dance music, and is not swamped with drum loops. It stood out from the Roses' Madchester peers because it just washes over you with hardly any expectations, allowing you to enjoy it without having to muster up anything as energetic or coordinated as dancing. Although quite rousing in tempo and chord progression, it's got a marvellously lazy feel to it – baggy even – and if the four minutes of guitar histrionics that close the full-length version can't quite summon you to your feet, you can still do air-guitar accompaniments slumped in an armchair.

Express Yourself
N.W.A
1989 • Priority

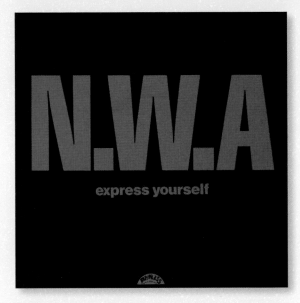

>> The parent album to 'Express Yourself' introduced the next wave of rap: quite literally *Straight Outta Compton*. Laced with profanity and tales of random hood violence in Los Angeles, it was as ideologically distant from the peace-sign-wearing New York Native Tongues Collective as it was geographically. 'Express Yourself', though, is the album's clever, non-cussing anomaly, dealing with freedom of speech and censorship within the music business – both self- and industry-imposed. Its intelligent, reasoned, witty and sharply phrased discourse got lost beneath the more glamorous and notorious likes of 'Fuck Tha Police' and 'Gangsta Gangstas', but the sheer funkiness of this track, including a killer cut-up of Charles Wright's 'Express Yourself' (see page 46), is a fascinating glimpse of what N.W.A might have been.

This Gift
Mudhoney
1989 • Sub Pop

<< >> Early singles on Seattle's Sub Pop label, when the local sound was starting to translate onto record, found the scene at its most interesting and diverse. At this point, Mudhoney were none too bothered about being subtle, preferring to capture the screaming swagger of what they did live, then packing in even more guitar distortion, and anchoring it all with thunderous drumming. Because 'This Gift' is unaffected and even a bit naive, it connects on a far more visceral level. It was grunge as hard rock first and foremost, rather than grunge living up to a set of preconceived ideas about itself.

THE 1990s

Dance music made itself heard beyond the confines of clubs in the 1990s, and made stars of its pioneers. Grunge grew up with a song about teen spirit, and eclectic influences made artists increasingly hard to categorize: was PJ Harvey an indie goddess, alt-rocker, folk heroine, electronica artist or punk? No one really cared when the resulting sound was this good.

Bonita Applebum
A Tribe Called Quest
1990 • Jive

>> For about 20 minutes or so, as the 1980s slipped into the 1990s, certain areas of hip-hop went all summery and laid-back – Digital Underground, Queen Latifah, Jazzy Jeff and the Fresh Prince and so on – and it was so much fun it was a real shame when it didn't continue in this direction on its own terms. 'Bonita Applebum' shows how Tribe excelled at the woozy arrangements and jazzy samples – this illustrates both points with a sitar taking centre stage at times – and although usually looking to make a sociopolitical point, they had a lovely way with a love rap. This is playful, funny, wistful high-school hip-hop that could have so easily cut it as mainstream pop.

The Wagon
Dinosaur Jr.
1990 • Sire

<< The contradiction at the centre of Dinosaur Jr. always made them one of the most interesting bands from the far end of indie rock, where the 'rock' carried more weight than the 'indie'. 'The Wagon' illustrates it vividly: while the music was its usually brisk self and carried its own weight in fuzzed-up, grunged-up distortions, J Mascis' singing is far less urgent, and even tinged with longing, on a song that seems to be about looking for love. It puts an unashamed contemporary folkie hippieness into the mix – some of the grunged-up guitars are acoustic and a few of the speedy hooks are almost jangling – giving the group a measure of intrigue and welcome nuttiness.

Loaded
Primal Scream
1990 • Creation

 LIZ KERSHAW'S CHOICE A year or so before this, if you'd said acid house DJ Andy Weatherall would have transformed earnest indie rockers Primal Scream into something compelling, most people would have laughed at you. It's to the band's massive credit that they first asked Weatherall for a remix, and then allowed him to take such a radical approach. A complete overhaul of a song called 'I'm Losing More Than I'll Ever Have' from their previous album, 'Loaded' is an instinctive, illogical fusion of guitars, dream-sequence house beats and idiosyncratic samples (most notably a Peter Fonda speech from the film *The Wild*

Angels). Almost overnight, it changed the way indie music looked at indie: suddenly the dance music rave-culture world was welcomed in. As for Primal Scream, a few years later they would be recording with George Clinton.

Kool Thing
Sonic Youth
1990 • Geffen

>> The brilliant thing about Sonic Youth was a musicality bordering on the virtuosic, and a taste for post-punk heavy metal that happily absorbed the grungier end of indie rock. On 'Kool Thing' they make use of all the punk moves and noises – discordant sounds, ricocheting drums, loads of fuzz, relentless guitars and suchlike, but within all that apparent chaos was a shrewdly constructed conventional song. It meant the music drew you in, in a way that proper pop songs had done for years, but then hurled you around inside with an excitement that might have felt threatening were it not for Kim Gordon's comforting voice. This is what made Sonic Youth so artistically subversive; Gordon was as striking and sexy as any lead singer should be, but all too often (as on 'Kool Thing') seemed almost ready to collapse into laughter.

Chime
Orbital
1990 • FFRR Records

>> After two summers of love and a wearyingly predictable tabloid fury introduced rave culture to a wider British public in the late 1980s, the music itself still had a ways to go before it became socially acceptable – in other words, the mainstream industry had yet to decide if they could sell it back to us or not. Into this gap arrived Orbital, the Hartnoll brothers, with a debut so straightforward and life-affirming it was impossible not to pay attention.

'Chime' doesn't actually do much, but nevertheless it does it with complete confidence and absolute understanding of what happens on and off a dancefloor. Every instrument involved becomes a rhythmic device, meaning a series of riffs, hooks and beats form their own internal melodies and, while never letting up on the groove, the song offers a substantial yet almost subliminal tunefulness. This afforded it a real usefulness away from the clubs, with or without drugs. And, apparently, 'Chime' cost only £2.50 to make.

Head Like a Hole
Nine Inch Nails
1990 • TVT

>> Trent Reznor developed the NIN notion while working as a recording studio caretaker, mucking about with the equipment when nobody was using it, thus affording himself massive and single-minded creative freedom. He carried through this autocratic approach to his group, meaning NIN was never more than 'Reznor and some other blokes', but he pushed heavy metal in all sorts of interesting directions. On the *Pretty Hate Machine* album (which spawned 'Head Like a Hole'), he shared production with UK dub adventurer Adrian Sherwood and hip-hop futurist Keith LeBlanc. 'Head Like a Hole' itself is a rousing alternative rock escapade that has all the marauding fuzzed guitar expected of modern metal, but spaces and beats and loopy synth hooks firmly and precisely place it in that late-1980s moment.

This is How It Feels
Inspiral Carpets
1990 • Mute

CHRIS HAWKINS' CHOICE << Always the *other* Madchester band, the Carpets were never quite as hip as the Mondays or the Roses no matter how hard they tried; in their early days they were less well-known for music than for the obscenity prosecutions of those sporting their stoned-cow-logo T-shirts emblazoned with 'Cool as Fuck' slogans. But when they stopped trying to be overly baggy and focused their sound into this mildly psychedelic/ mostly melancholy vibe, they set themselves apart from the Manc pack and found an enduring niche. 'This is How It Feels' is a downcast commentary on the despair brought on by literal and figurative redundancy, made all the more poignant by an aching organ and carefully phased guitar. Twenty-five years on, the song survives as a football ground taunt, along the lines of: 'This is how it feels to be Tottenham/This is how is it feels to be small.'

Been Caught Stealing
Jane's Addiction
1990 • Warner Bros.

GIDEON COE'S CHOICE >> This track has dogs barking on it. In the background, during the intro, for no apparent reason. And because it's Perry Farrell's Jane's Addiction, nobody was really surprised: Farrell founded the Lollapalooza Festival in 1991 which was dedicated to bringing together like-minded souls from different genres, to ensure all of the audience experienced something potentially unfamiliar. Before that, though, he had applied the same ethos to his alternative rock band, and they were as likely to do straight-up thrash metal as a perky, funky number such as this. Riff-tastic, hook heavy and deeply catchy, 'Been Caught Stealing' is an uplifting ditty about the joys of shoplifting.

Infinity
Guru Josh
1990 • BMG

GIDEON COE'S CHOICE << >> The post-acid house scene at the dawn of the 1990s possessed a sense of wonder, as artists discovered what they could do with technology that was now affordable. That sense of wonder was implicitly understood by audiences, and the genre's simply constructed tunes let people think there was no real gap between performers and punters. Anybody could make music in the early rave scene – the movement's Guru Josh was studying to be a dentist when bitten by the showbiz bug. On 'Infinity', he seems to be surprising himself as he sprinkles apparently random synth twiddles, jazz-funk piano phrases and eastern-ish electronic signatures onto a straightforward dance rhythm. The overall effect is so disarmingly cheerful it's still being revived 25 years later.

Mama Said Knock You Out
LL Cool J
1990 • Def Jam

>> Astonishingly, by the turn of the 1990s, LL Cool J was already an elder statesman of hip-hop: he'd been around since the mid-1980s, was still having hits, and had put out four albums – yet was still only 22. After his previous ballad-heavy set, his career experience told him he needed a tough, B-boy rap album, full of the enthusiasm, dumb posturing and bragging that made old-school hip-hop so entertaining. It's a mark of LL Cool J's skill and genre intelligence that he could balance all of this so precisely, and 'Mama Said' tied together all his experience, in the process giving him a massive across-the-board success. He had the musical nous to use the sharpest producer of the day, Marley Marl, and mix modern and old-school samples: James Brown, Sly Stone, Digital Underground and – via 'Rock the Bells' – even himself.

What You Do to Me
Teenage Fanclub
1991 • Creation

>> There's an awful lot of bands – and the word 'awful' has been carefully chosen – from the 1980s and early 1990s that could learn a thing or two from this song: it's got three chords, four lines of lyrics and it's two minutes long. Absolutely no messing about here. 'What You Do to Me' is a simple but effective hymn to the singer's girlfriend: 'What you do to me/I know I can't believe/There's something about you/Got me down on my knees' Repeat to fade. Its bouncy tempo is robust enough to drive it along, and Teenage Fanclub are sufficiently slick to leave us wanting more.

What You Want
My Bloody Valentine
1991 • Creation

GIDEON COE'S CHOICE After years and years of fairly insipid but usually touchingly melodic guitar pop – what they used to call 'shoe-gazing' before it became a genre – Irish indie rockers My Bloody Valentine signed with Creation Records and eventually got the kind of lavish budget they needed to make *Loveless*, the album they'd been striving to achieve. From it, 'What You Want' never sacrifices the delicate, inherent tunefulness of the quartet's songwriting, but they also add fuzz, distortions and layered vocals to produce something far more arrestingly muscular. *Loveless* went on to be a massive success, but Creation dropped them, because the budget for the record ended up costing far more than had been initially agreed, and left the label teetering on the edge of bankruptcy for a time.

my bloody valentine

Perpetual Dawn
The Orb
1991 • Big Life

《 **》** The Orb were probably the founding fathers of ambient house as it grew out of the mellow, ecstasy-comedown soundtracks they would programme when deejaying in rave chill-out rooms. Rather ironically, those spaces became self-defeating, populated by enthusiasts for less-animated pharmaceutical use, but The Orb didn't stop there: 'Perpetual Dawn' is the Jamaican stop-off on an ambitiously produced and blissed-out world cruise of a double album *(Adventures Beyond the Ultraworld)*. 'Dawn' is nine minutes of laid-back, slightly loony, all-electronic dub ideas and methods, which despite the brisk tempo, don't really have to work that hard to relax the listener.

Alive
Pearl Jam
1991 • Epic

》 The acceptable face of grunge? US radio seemed to think so when Pearl Jam took the embryonic sound of Seattle and applied it to a far more traditional blues-based rock framework. Drenched in fuzz tones and effects, 'Alive' is certainly contemporary, if structurally closer to Deep Purple or Led Zeppelin – even the solos wouldn't be out of place in that bygone era. A heads-down rocker that was dirty enough for the flannel shirted masses, but sufficiently familiar to the more mature radio executive not to frighten him (and it inevitably would be a 'him'). Their choice of broadly socially aware subject matter helped in this respect too – 'Alive' is about family betrayal and incest – as it advanced the notion of maturity and responsibility as opposed to behaving like brats.

Go
Moby
1991 • Instinct

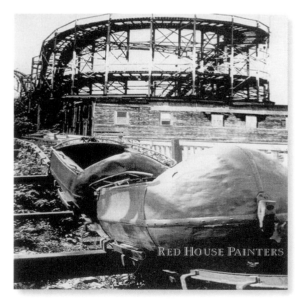

Although acid house and rave culture had the liberating musical effect of allowing pretty much anybody to do pretty much anything over a kicking dance beat, there were acts that stood head and shoulders above the pack, like Moby. As 'Go' proved, he could put down a pumping beat, punctuated with vocal snatches and piano riffs, then ambient the whole thing up – or should that be down? – with floaty *Twin Peaks* samples. Others could have done this, but what set Moby apart on 'Go' (and everything else from his first self-titled album) was that musically he did it so casually and persuasively, without having to bang you over the head with how clever it was.

Mistress
The Red House Painters
1991 • 4AD

Somebody once described the Red House Painters' deeply introspective indie rock as 'sadcore', a statement made even funnier because it's spot on. Here's a band so disaffected with their world in general that they put out two consecutive albums (their second and third) they couldn't even be bothered to name. Both self-titled – not even 'I' and 'II' – they have been dubbed *Rollercoaster* and *Bridge* because that's what's pictured in the gloomy, sepia-tinted sleeve design. From *Rollercoaster*, 'Mistress' is a delicately-shaded wistful guitar rocker, but the kicker is, like the sleeve, all of those tones are different shades of brown.

Smells Like Teen Spirit
Nirvana
1991 • DCG

>> By autumn 1991, the mainstream rock audience were hungry for grunge as part of their music experience, and were keen to decide for themselves which groups should and shouldn't be considered valid. TV and radio, a step or two behind the public as usual, relegated this track to late-night, *alternative* alternative rock shows or college broadcasters – and even the record company didn't push it too hard because they didn't think the market was there. However, from the very first whiff, 'Smells Like Teen Spirit' made a massive impact (entering the UK top 10 in its first week) and its album, *Nevermind*, blew up in an explosion of punk energy, doubled-up, fuzzed -up power-chording, surly lyrics and unglamorous hard-wearing clothing.

Unfinished Sympathy
Massive Attack
1991 • Wild Bunch

JEFF SMITH'S CHOICE << That Bristol's Massive Attack built on Soul II Soul's conscious hybrid of dub reggae methodology, soul music melodies, a string section and a 'collective' mentality wasn't too surprising – Jazzie B's North London outfit regularly worked with the Wild Bunch sound system Massive Attack grew out of. Less expected was what they did with those ideas. By scaling back on any dancefloor obligations, they could mellow the sound to a woozy, chilled state of affairs. When embroidered with overstated, unfinished vocals and snatches or samples of detached instrumentation, it took on an agreeably surreal aspect. It was with good reason the style they developed and perfected became known as trip-hop.

Counting Backwards
Throwing Muses
1991 • 4AD

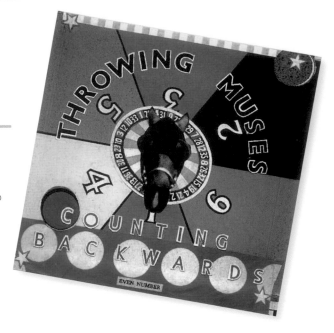

>> Both Kristin Hersh and Tanya Donelly were still with new wave rockers the Throwing Muses when they made *The Real Ramona* album, which found them about as close to daytime radio as they were ever going to be. Thus 'Counting Backwards' may not be nearly as emotionally unfettered as the band's previous outings, but it is just about bonkers enough. On the surface it's a lumbering pop song, all twangy guitars, bratty vocals and a slurred rhythm section, but the subtly odd signature shifts and nonsensical lyrics underneath give it a satisfying depth of weird. It was a clever balance that made their songwriting skills far more accessible, but they never quite repeated it after Donelly left to establish herself as the most exhilarating female songwriter of 1990s alternative rock.

X, Y & Zee
Pop Will Eat Itself
1991 • RCA

<< >> It's rare for a band to pull off the whole genre-mashing thing with the aplomb of Pop Will Eat Itself, but then few other acts approached contemporary music with such reverence and an equally healthy disrespect for what it so often ended up as. Their exuberant naivety made their dumb jokes and prosaic politics enormously entertaining, while their 'Why not?' attitude to mixing musical styles was never less than appealing. 'X,Y & Zee' has a crisp, rumbling house track, with barrel-house piano breaks, bits of fuzzy guitar and a daft rap about nothing that makes too much sense. You get the idea they only want to amuse themselves and if we get the joke, great.

As We Come (To Be)
The Young Disciples
1991 • Talkin' Loud

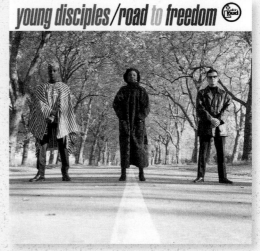

   In the wake of Soul II Soul, London's soul and jazz-funk scenes eagerly embraced the notions of applying reggae and hip-hop techniques to what they did, and used digital technology to supplement (rather than replace) old-school ways. The whole concept tended to baffle major record companies, meaning that smaller labels like Gilles Peterson's Talkin' Loud allowed enterprising, forward-looking groups such as the Young Disciples to get on with whatever they, as gigging musicians, felt people genuinely wanted. 'As We Come' weaves a mix of drum loops, samples and real instruments into a particularly mellow vibe, sensitively cushioning Carleen Anderson's soulful singing. A very modern take on traditional jazz ideology.

You Love Us
Manic Street Preachers
1992 • Columbia

>> By 1992 and the second incarnation of 'You Love Us', the Manics had largely given up the ongoing goth-tinged soap opera and were sensibly concentrating on the musical side of things as heads-down hard rockers with a sound ready-made for the stadiums. Re-recorded for the *Generation Terrorists* album, 'You Love Us' is a virtual Guns N' Roses tribute – modern(ish) heavy metal, with the rhythm pared down to the basics, with what's left compressed and brought into the mix, providing a crunching platform for some wild guitar work. James Dean Bradfield provides a powerful vocal performance that does a great deal to shift attention away from the title's refrain and shine a light on the oblique social commentary that makes up large portions of the verses. It gives what was assumed by some to be an exercise in vanity a far more interesting dimension, something which could also be said for the group's new ethos.

Leave Them All Behind
Ride
1992 • Creation

⟪ ⟫ A carousel ride of guitar-powered pop that could've been little more, and just gone round and round until it ran out of steam, but Ride were too canny to let that happen. 'Leave Them All Behind' may be over eight minutes long, and may be sparing with vocals, but they punctuate the fuzz guitar and big slappy drums with enough nods to Townshend on guitar and organ – indeed, the opening could be the start of the *CSI* theme – and strategically add in solos. Ride could be unfairly labeled as 'shoe-gazers' sometimes, and a track like 'Leave Them All Behind' shows them to have more sense of purpose than that.

Falling on a Bruise
Carter USM
1992 • Rough Trade

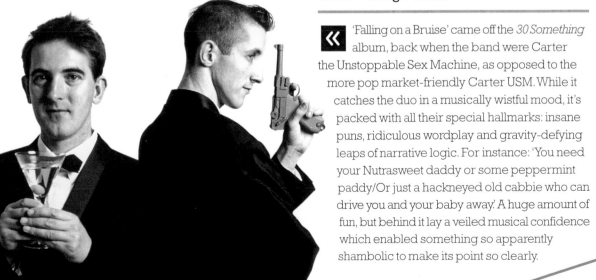

⟪ 'Falling on a Bruise' came off the *30 Something* album, back when the band were Carter the Unstoppable Sex Machine, as opposed to the more pop market-friendly Carter USM. While it catches the duo in a musically wistful mood, it's packed with all their special hallmarks: insane puns, ridiculous wordplay and gravity-defying leaps of narrative logic. For instance: 'You need your Nutrasweet daddy or some peppermint paddy/Or just a hackneyed old cabbie who can drive you and your baby away'. A huge amount of fun, but behind it lay a veiled musical confidence which enabled something so apparently shambolic to make its point so clearly.

Killing in the Name
Rage Against the Machine
1992 • Epic

>> They inherited the original Beastie Boys' mantle to some extent, but Rage Against the Machine opted for social comment over *Animal House*-type hijinks. From the components of rap precepts and heavy metal procedures grew a soundbed of clipped, tense, overwhelmingly rhythmic power chords, which hurled a sustained bawling attack at so much of what was wrong with America of the time. An entertainingly foul mouthed epic, it had an unexpected second life in December 2009 when a British DJ launched an online campaign for people to download 'Killing' and prevent that year's *X Factor* winner from having the UK's Christmas number one. The campaign was successful, Simon Cowell was apoplectic and homeless charity Shelter got the profits.

Ragda
Khaled
1992 • Polygram

DON LETTS' CHOICE << Khaled is something of an Algerian superstar and popular hero, drawing on his country's traditional folk style of making raï records. When forced to flee Algeria, he used the raï style as a vehicle for protest songs about conditions within his homeland and the rise of political extremism. Once deported, he soon absorbed western musical influences to expand the raï's reach, and to use his music to highlight the plight of Algerians abroad – and subjugated working people everywhere. He had blended raï melodies with hip-hop and soul to great effect, and 'Ragda' does the same with dub reggae, setting up a deeply groovy bass and drum riddim, as a foundation for Algerian instrumentation. Never less than rocking, Khaled's vocals (sung in his native tongue) sound completely at home; when the song drops out and the dub effects move forwards in the mix, it seems the most natural thing in the world, and enhances both the song's power and beauty.

Television, the Drug of the Nation
Disposable Heroes of Hiphoprisy
1992 • 4th & Broadway

» The Disposable Heroes of Hiphoprisy found their sound by compressing their samples so much that they became sludgy and burr-edged, with the unrefined texture appearing to drag them backwards in the mix. Then they'd open up the track enough to leave gaps for live percussion and instrumentation and still have ample empty space. The Disposables' Michael Franti absorbed the political influences of artists such as Gil Scott-Heron and the maverick rap sensibilities of Public Enemy to create something befitting the 1990s generation. Combining a kind of industrial rock approach to hip-hop and lyrics replete with righteous indignation, this record is his finest moment.

Changes
Sugar
1992 • Creation

« » Sugar represented a songwriting redemption for Bob Mould, as the younger band seemed to pull him out of his post-Hüsker Dü doldrums and even managed to cheer him up a bit. A fine showcase for the new invigorated Mould, 'Changes' is a chiming melodic number, with its ringing chords and lead lines cascading down onto a solid punk-styled buzz-saw bedrock. It's a nifty combination that both spurs on and relaxes Mould's guitar playing and singing into something freer and far more welcoming. So it shouldn't really come as too much of a shock to learn that its parent album, *Copper Blue*, sold almost 50 times more than Mould's previous effort, the hearteningly titled *Black Sheets of Rain*.

The Drowners
Suede
1992 • Nude

Suede's debut single is looked back at by many as the birth of Britpop: though it wasn't quite that simple, it certainly marked the birth of Suede as a tangible entity, with the band's recorded output arriving to meet the prefabricated legend. 'The Drowners' fell perfectly into step with the hysteria that had already swamped so much of the music press. At a time when the charts were dominated by anonymous dance acts, scruffy heavy metal bands and Bryan Adams, Suede and their frontman Brett Anderson offered an irresistible combination of the glamour of a proper rock star and the kind of sexually confused, generally misunderstood teen-boy angst that had been in short supply of late; in this landscape of macho rock and carefully inoffensive pop ditties, even the sleeve for their debut album featured a deliberately ambiguous cover shot of a gender non-specific couple

kissing. One rock journalist, Danny Kelly (then editor of *Q Magazine*) was moved to describe Suede as, 'skinny white boys speaking to other skinny white boys about their inadequacies'.

Of course, regardless of how much the rock press needed a band like Suede, the paying public tends to be more discerning. But the group had them gripped from this very first single, thanks to shrewd musical choices and often under-appreciated playing. Anderson's theatrically tortured and carnally-hesitant-yet-still-debauched persona manifests itself in a vocal delivery unashamedly recalling Bowie at his most camp, but it is the muscular glam-rock recollections that give the band substance. In particular guitarist Bernard Butler, supported by a rhythm section that effortlessly creates a suitably louche mid-tempo signature, smoothly shifts between crisp glam-era riffs and chiming melodic lead lines. The strength of the rest of the set-up meant that Anderson could concentrate on becoming a romantic poet for the late 20th century.

Popscene
Blur
1992 • Food

Like Suede's 'The Drowners', 'Popscene' was a single hailed as a crucial moment in the birth of Britpop. A compete anomaly in the Blur catalogue, it sits as a watershed between 1991's *Leisure,* an album whose Madchesterisms felt too little too late, and their reinvention on 1993's *Modern Life Is Rubbish*, a far more mannered approach to making obviously English music. 'Popscene' is a spiky, energetic offering, seemingly closer in spirit to New York's new wave of a decade earlier than anything particularly British, and certainly nothing at all like the music Blur became well known for. Stranger still, it sounds considerably more instinctive than so much of their other work: in spite of its uncharacteristic rush, they make something intrinsically complicated sound almost effortlessly throwaway. Like most of the best art-school post-punk, it's a mash-up of 1970s and 1980s influences, which are balanced on a quickly revolving fuzzbox that runs all the way through undercutting the whole thing with casual griminess.

On top of all this, and against an unfussy drum pattern, Graham Coxon's furious guitar work – breakneck riffs and splintered lead lines – is reminiscent of the livelier bluesier end of prog. It's a furious pace, lashed into an even greater frenzy by horn punctuations that sound like a compressed, foreshortened take on what you'd expect to find on a more expansive Teardrop Explodes track. Most surprising, perhaps, are the lyrics, given what Blur would become within the next couple of years – apparently dashed off at the session, they launch a blistering attack on the then self-servingly elite London indie rock scene and the music business that was scrabbling to get a grip on it.

Remedy
The Black Crowes
1992 • Def American

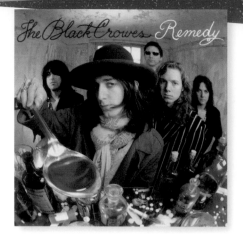

HUEY MORGAN'S CHOICE ›› American musicians of a certain age will tell you that it was the post-Beatles British invasion – Cream, Humble Pie, Free and so on – that revived youthful interest in the blues. From that starting point, some budding young artists delved further back to the original music of the Mississippi Delta. By contrast, the Black Crowes opted for the Thames Estuary. The Crowes' music was closer to British blues rock, and by their second album *The Southern Harmony and Musical Companion*, they'd mastered it sufficiently to allow their own southern-fried flourishes into the mix and to sound like they're having fun. Backed by a powerful, big drum sound, the two guitars talk to each other, either picking or with an open-stringed jangle, but always with a pronounced southern drawl, while the organ props everything up. Even in the early 1990s it was all a bit anachronistic, but it's so all-round joyous that it scarcely matters.

Cannonball
The Breeders
1993 • 4AD

‹‹ ⌄ Any side project put together by Tanya Donelly (Throwing Muses) and Kim Deal (Pixies) is going to be big on ideas and not too keen on rules. When you stir a second Deal sister into the mix – Kelley, on guitar, who had no clue how to play the instrument – you're unlikely to end up with a conventional pop song. Which is where the magic begins on 'Cannonball'. Packed with spontaneous musical wit and invention, at its heart it's a series of apparently unrelated hooks and riffs, plus some enticing phrasing that would frustrate you with their transience, if another equally enticing phrase didn't come along right after. It's a huge tribute to the Breeders' skills that they can stitch this all together into a cohesive, anthemic single.

50ft Queenie
PJ Harvey
1993 • Island

>> Two-and-a-half minutes of storming Steve Albini-produced power-trio rock, nearer to MC5 than Big Black, and while you'd never expect it to be the easiest listening experience, as relative to the rest of the abrasive *Rid of Me* album this came as light relief. Even without the toe-tapping, almost countrified boogie beat, it's as funny as hell with Harvey opting for sarcasm and mockery over straight-up anger. The idea of a 50-ft B-movie-style female guitar hero, rampaging through the heavy-metal world, tearing up speaker stacks and laying waste to egos is hilarious, gaining massive currency with the ambiguous increasing measurement on the last line of the last few verses: 'You come on and measure me/I'm 20 inches long…/…I'm 30 inches long' and so on, right up to 50. It was having the confidence to produce moments like this that raised PJ Harvey's game above the legions of wannabes that trailed in her slipstream.

Laid
James
1993 • Mercury

« Sometimes, especially when you hear a song as gawky and unassuming as this, it's easy to forget how big James had been only a couple of years previously – supporting Neil Young in the US and selling out the UK's 30,000-person-capacity Alton Towers theme-park. Their success also manifested itself in surprising ways: onstage brawling, drug problems, cult membership, and so on. The *Laid* album, however, found James in calmer waters as new members had joined to flesh out their arrangements, and Brian Eno was producing. These two factors made a substantial difference – the fuller sound was a mellower departure, some way from the group's often brash noise of the past – and rescued 'Laid' from being excruciatingly adolescent, by awarding it a grown-up ambience.

Feed the Tree
Belly
1993 • 4AD/Sire

» Shimmering melodies, glorious catchy hooks and sparkling harmonies… this was the pop songwriting goal Tanya Donelly had previously been aiming for on the Throwing Muses album, *The Real Ramona*, but had narrowly missed. Her new group Belly afforded her the freedom to go for this very traditional approach, while modern studio technology gave the production a depth and a tangy crispness. Fundamentally, though, underneath all that sunshine, the previously hardcore-punk Gorman brothers (Tom on guitar and Chris on drums) stopped things getting too fluffy and helped keep 'Feed the Tree' moving along smartly.

Passin' Me By
The Pharcyde
1993 • Delicious Vinyl

 It was lovely to have seen a group such as the Pharcyde develop the kind of playground, fun-loving end of hip-hop into something with a slightly more adult sense of humour. Along with the post-P-Funk Digital Underground, they served as a reminder that, whenever possible, grown-ups also enjoy sitting about ridiculing each other and the world for no particular reason. Some hysterically mundane lyrics – in this case, about unrequited love – are delivered with a self-possession that allowed for all manner of verbal gymnastics. Their music was no slave to convention either, this is a sultry, slinky melange of Quincy Jones, Jimi Hendrix and Weather Report. Never has messing about sounded quite so sophisticated.

Waterfall
Atlantic Ocean
1993 • Eastern Bloc

 Dutch duo Atlantic Ocean understood that trance is a balance somewhere between the necessarily soporific and the frenetic, if only to stop dancers from actually snuggling down for a little sleep. 'Waterfall' is a classic of the genre – beats with dense internal layers of sound that, while keeping things ticking over, are intriguing enough to create interest beyond the dancefloor. On top of this they drift elements in and out of the mix – particularly an ascending piano scale – and occasionally strip it all back to a bare-bones rhythm track. It's a kind of 'dub technique meets Eurodisco at the roots of house', a combination that seemed to happen with regularity in continental Northern Europe.

Rez
Underworld
1993 • Junior Boys Own

» If a tune is nearly ten minutes long and constructed wholly for the dancefloor, take it out of that intended situation and it risks becoming an endurance test rather than pleasurable listening. No such problems with 'Rez', a rare instrumental: indeed, it's because Underworld aimed themselves so squarely at their primary market – chemically-enhanced rave crowds – that the track had a better chance to make itself at home in your living room. The group always stood out in the crowded and bewilderingly splintered world of post-acid house music because they cultivated an in-depth understanding of that environment: they would take their fans on a restrained musical rollercoaster of cleverly smoothed-out emotional and rhythmical highs and lows.

In 'Rez', it's that same approach which, if allowed to, will deftly manipulate the armchair listener into the work's internal sense of drama and carry them along with a sense of anticipation. It's all down to Underworld's three essential qualities: pacing; a delicate touch on the desk; and no small amount of all-out bravery. Its opening illustrates this perfectly – one simple loop that maintains interest by subtly raising the volume, inducing a sense of expectation that drops away at a point where it's held you for so long you feel you have to know what comes next, therefore you stick with it for the next peak. And they keep this up for two-and-a-half minutes before anything approaching a drop comes in. Few would dare to even attempt that,

let alone have the nous to pull it off, but that same loop then runs for the entire duration of the track, with the mood-shifting brought on by other electronic sounds appearing to vary the tone and tempo, precisely at the points where a change is needed. An 'Autobahn' for the 1990s.

Human Behaviour

Björk

1993 • One Little Indian

>> As part of her previous group, the Sugarcubes, Björk and her ethereal tones had always been one more aspect of what at times had seemed an affected oddness. Okay, so it was a vaguely interesting aspect, but that environment was not doing a great deal for her. On 'Human Behaviour', as a solo artist and collaborating with Nellee Hooper (previously producer of Soul II Soul and Massive Attack), the setting is a funky, trippy exercise built upon a rubberized bass line, a cheese-cutter guitar sample and the occasional sweeping flourish of strings. Together, these components form a laid-back, intelligent interpretation of Björk's love of jazz and dance music. The real trick, though, is the strength of the groove that lurks just beneath the gently rippling surfaces, which throw down such a firm anchor that it allows Björk to be Björk, without worrying too much about everything floating away.

French Disko
Stereolab
1993 • Duophonic

  Even by Stereolab's eccentric standards, 'French Disko' is a bit of an oddity. Whereas most bands might manage one stylistic contradiction per single, in this there's three or four: they start with a platform that echoes vintage Kraftwerk rather than anything then-current, then throw in buzz-saw punkish guitars, then some 'space age' prog twiddles, and lastly add some world-weary vocals straight out of the 1980s. They have the sheer nerve to make it work, too, but most bizarre of all is how the track hurtles along, gaining momentum like a runaway train for over four intensifying minutes. Finally, just when you're sure it's building to a really terrifying conclusion, it surprises you yet again. Genius. Mad, but genius nonetheless.

Disarm
Smashing Pumpkins
1993 • Virgin

>> When an indie-type guitar band isn't constricted by the image of an indie-type guitar band, it can lead to all sorts of fun in the studio. Of course, if you're the Smashing Pumpkins, 'fun' may be a relative term, but the experimentation involved in their music at least suggests a degree of enjoyment. The album this comes from (*Siamese Dream*) involves a full string section, a mellotron, psychedelic leanings, some dabbling in goth and lashings of prog rock. 'Disarm' is typically unrestrained, with timpani drum breaks, orchestral aspirations, and what sounds like tubular bells. It reaches a fabulous climax, where such is the drama of the music that the vocals are all but drowned out.

Red Right Hand
Nick Cave and the Bad Seeds
1994 • Mute

   Nick Cave and the Bad Seeds' albums are masterclasses in interlocking narrative. Many a novelist could learn from Cave's ability to tell the bigger story while sweeping you along with individual episodes. To take a track out of one of these dark epics and expect it to stand on its own would be like asking the same of a single chapter of *The Big Sleep*. 'Red Right Hand', though, extracted from *Let Love In*, gives it a darn good go. As close to metaphorical Cave as you're going to get, the cheerfully bubbling backing uses very little to construct drama so startling it should be wearing a frock coat and have LOVE and HATE tattooed on its knuckles. Then the singer himself layers on the menace for a terrifying crescendo, while warning us, 'He'll appear out of nowhere/ But he ain't what he seems.' No, he's really not. Along with all that, this track's big achievement was that it made it alright for us to admit to liking lounge music.

Grace
Jeff Buckley
1994 • Columbia

« In 1997, when Jeff Buckley drowned while taking a fully clothed swim in the Mississippi, he had only released one complete studio album. *Grace* showed the breadth of his singing and guitar playing, and its title track is its standout number. Richly melodic, its restrained and subtle string backing means that nothing gets in the way of Buckley's vocals. What ought to be a melancholy song – is it about a double suicide? – soars at times to theatrical proportions, and he delivers an emotional epic that borders on the overwhelming. As a pointer towards the kind of expressions Buckley was capable of in his writing and performing, it makes his death at such a young age (30) an even greater loss.

Sabotage
The Beastie Boys
1994 • Capitol

» The *Ill Communication* album found the Beastie Boys at their most interesting – they'd matured, grown up from the obnoxious frat-boy rap of *Licensed to Ill*, but hadn't quite become the sensitive, creative types of recent years. They appeared to be reassessing their hardcore punk roots, from a perspective that absorbed so much of what they'd learned from their adventures in hip-hop. The Beastie noise during this period reflected the attitudes of the Lollapalooza generation, for whom it seemed compulsory to acknowledge as much of the musical stratosphere as possible. 'Sabotage' is a furious marriage of thrashing guitars, scratch mixing and throat-shredding vocals, winding up as a very outward-looking take on heavy metal.

Do You Remember the First Time?
Pulp
1994 • Island

⏬ Away from the Blur/Oasis face-off of the mid-1990s there was Pulp, Sheffield's own shrewder take on Britpop. Intelligent, eccentric and somehow more British, they mostly avoided becoming interminable tabloid fodder and could enjoy a much lower profile. Having slowly developed their style under the radar over many years, by 1994 they had honed their style into sophisticated guitar pop that possibly sounded retro simply because it put playing first. Of course it helped that founder and frontman Jarvis Cocker was one of the most incisive and witty British lyricists of the period. Set to a frantic, mildly psychedelic jangle, 'Do You Remember the First Time?' is an acidic missive to a mistress – or is that soon-to-be-ex-mistress? – that only Pulp would have wanted to put to music.

Buddy Holly
Weezer
1994 • DGC

⏫ The bridge between grunge and guitar-based, shoe-gazing alternative rock was never going to be a particularly easy structure to put up, but Weezer pulled off the challenge quite brilliantly. The basis of their sound was as flannel-shirted as anything coming out of Seattle – 'Buddy Holly' does not want for fuzzed-up guitars – but that attitude gets deflated with the addition of gentle and pensive flourishes and solos, and, notably in this case, the whole mix has an almost disconcerting buoyancy to it. Musically the union succeeds, but what made Weezer special was an unabashed cheerfulness – happy love songs instead of groaning about their world made them much more attractive to a mainstream market.

Caught by the Fuzz
Supergrass
1994 • Parlophone

>> Supergrass and their tight, supercharged guitar pop were like a force-nine blast of fresh air: here was a bunch of kids – two members were still in their teens when they made their first recordings – who sounded like they could barely believe this was their job and were going to have enough fun for everybody. 'Caught by the Fuzz' is a rollicking, power pop-driven account of being busted for possession of weed at age 15, where the biggest cause for concern is what mum is going to say. However, there's such a gleeful spirit to the whole thing – in spite of sitting in the 'back of the van' with 'head in my hands', they still manage to sound like they're getting away with it.

Connection
Elastica
1994 • Deceptive

<< Indie pin-ups Elastica inspired a new generation of guitar bands. Their brazen, androgynous front woman, Justine Frischmann – queen of Britpop to partner Damon Albarn's king – trailblazed the way for other female indie lead singers, such as Sleeper's Louise Wener and Republica's Saffron, challenging preconceived ideas of just what a 1990s guitar band could be. The band wrote accessible songs with a modern punky-rocky feel that could have – and a few years later did have – wider airplay.

'Connection' is unabashedly derivative – it sounds like Wire fronted by a Debbie Harry wannabee – but it's presented with such overwhelming self-belief the band get away with it.

The World is Yours
Nas
1994 • Columbia

The son of a jazz musician, Nas always had a strong bent for a good tune, but even during the mid-1990s when rap and hip-hop were reaching their melodic apex, his debut album *Illmatic* raised that particular bar. 'The World is Yours' uses a brooding piano riff, made darker with off-key scratching but buoyed up with taut drumbeats. Low key and completely hypnotic, it gives Nas just the right impetus to surf the rhythms. His lyrics are equally skilful, cataloguing the problems of his hometown New York – or as he puts it, 'the Rotten Apple'. Is 'The World is Yours' chorus blaming those around him for such a state of affairs, or urging them forwards to take control of their own destiny?

Strangers
Portishead
1994 • Go! Beat

GILLES PETERSON'S CHOICE

A thoroughly deserving winner of the Mercury Music Prize, Portishead's 1994 album *Dummy* moved trip-hop's dancehall ideas further into the mainstream, with a take on rock music that absorbed its contemporary environment rather than simply shifting the tempo. 'Strangers' is such a subtle combination of samples (opening with a lift from Weather Report) and original instrumentation that the two are often indistinguishable – what you're convinced is a snatch from a Curtis Mayfield number is, in fact, a specially composed guitar line. Together, these two components have a finesse that transports the track away from any form of rave culture, along with a compelling, floating vocal from Beth Gibbons. With the ethereal quality of the spaced-out backing, the song approaches Julee Cruise territory, but instead of remaining ambient, commands attention.

Just Lookin'
The Charlatans
1995 • Beggars Banquet

» On their self-titled fourth album, the Charlatans seemed to have finally reached their potential after several years, as they fully embraced their modernized take on blues-based soul. It's as if being from just outside Manchester allowed them a little room for manoeuvre within a genre that was becoming increasingly stylized – extra bagginess, perhaps? They adopted a more soulful sound thanks largely to Rob Collins' spiralling, Memphis-style Hammond organ work. 'Just Lookin'' exploits that feel, but also gives it a country tinge to sharpen any southern soul focus.

Inner City Life
Goldie
1995 • FFRR

GILLES PETERSON'S CHOICE « ∧ When jungle, a largely underground, almost exclusively sound-system style, knocked off a few of its rough edges and became the more commercially amenable drum 'n' bass, Goldie was at the forefront. With tracks like this – come to that, the entire *Timeless* album – he took it a bit further, adding quasi-orchestral arrangements, jazz instrumentation and a soaring soprano singer to the basic beats-centric formula. It was a masterstroke, because introducing these textures brought a soft depth to an often hard and brittle environment, meaning the drum 'n' bass elements could remain uncompromising, and the melodies could still find a place in a more conventional rock environment.

Da Funk
Daft Punk
1995 • Soma

>> Described by the French duo themselves as being their nod to G-Funk – they maintained the tune came about after serial spinning of Warren G's 'Regulate' – 'Da Funk' is more a take on New York in the early-1980s than the West Coast of the 1990s. Not that this does the end result any harm at all; indeed the disco-ish time signature and a big bass line has a real 'Rappers Delight'/'Good Times' flavour to it, making it very easy to like because it's just so easy to follow. It's what Thomas Bangalter and Guy-Manuel de Homem-Christo excelled at: taking contemporary styles like electro, house, techno and acid house – often within the same track – and simplifying them for popular consumption around a prominent bass line and a slapping drumbeat. The clever part was that while so much of what they did had an interestingly old-school feel to it, it was only ever retro and never repro, meaning it sat comfortably within modern dance music.

'Da Funk' is a case in point. Big drums bang out a four on the floor, while a bouncy bass guitar lopes throughout – Daft Punk would record themselves playing instruments then sample the results – leaving the obvious electronics to punctuate with counter-riffs and percussive scratching effect beats. It's a testament to the pair's love of straightforward funk and early hip-hop in its character as much as its arrangement, as there's a brash energy and an ad-hoc feel to it that conjures up an exultant block-party vibe. It was a huge hit all over Europe and introduced Daft Punk to the US, but, most importantly, 'Da Funk' influenced Continental dance music to such a degree that it prompted a welcome shift away from Eurodisco traditions.

Acquiesce
Oasis
1995 • Creation

Original
Leftfield
1995 • Hard Hands

Originally B-side to 'Some Might Say', 'Acquiesce' became so popular as part of Oasis' stage set that a live version was issued in the US as a radio-only promotional single, and it's this rendition that brings out the best in the song. More than just a rousing, beery power-pop sing-along it has a depth and strength of musical and emotional communication that goes a long way to explaining the group's appeal. It's also one of the few recordings on which both Liam and Noel take lead vocals – the former sings the verses, the latter the choruses – and leaves you wondering why the older Gallagher didn't do more singing.

Leftfield's Paul Daley and Neil Barnes elevated themselves above so many in 1990s electronic music through a combination of enthusiasm and innovation. 'Original' kicks off with a ridiculous looping bass line and towering organ chords, but how it builds is truly inspired – it owes everything to dub reggae even if it never sounds like it's been anywhere near Jamaica. Skittering jungle accents, techno and breakbeat snatches, weird disjointed keyboard ideas pop up then disappear, while the echo machine gives it all great depth. All that, plus the near-disembodied vocal of Curve's Toni Halliday. This could sound dark, but with Leftfield, you get the feeling they were laughing out loud.

Olympian
Gene
1995 • Polydor

The title track of Gene's first album, made just after the leap from tiny independent label Costermonger to a major record company, represents in so many ways the quartet at their best. OK, so the shadow of The Smiths looms large, but there's a sense of discovery and independence about what they're doing, with an adventurous feel to the song's arrangement. For a large part the piano and guitar have an interesting dialogue, while other ideas – gutsy guitar solo, strings, vocal crescendo – are stirred in and made to work with a clever, sympathetic production.

He's on the Phone
Saint Etienne
1995 • Heavenly

On first hearing, the Eurodisco beat of 'He's on the Phone' seemed less interesting than Saint Etienne's previous work, but knowing the track's history makes it more intriguing. It's a remix of the more obscure 'Accident', itself a revamp of 'Weekend à Rome' by the French singer-songwriter Étienne Daho (who himself appears here), yet each mix retains elements of the previous while still making it its own. Lurking in the background are all sorts of catchy hooks and countermelodies, which all help to lure the track in a woozier and altogether less frantic direction, offering precisely the right harmonious support needed to bring out the best in Sarah Cracknell's lead vocals.

Leave Home
The Chemical Brothers
1995 • Junior Boys Own/Virgin

Formerly called the Dust Brothers, Manchester University graduates Tom Rowlands and Ed Simons were obliged to change their name when the more established American dance music duo the Dust Brothers objected – hence the Chemicals' debut album title, *Exit Planet Dust*. Going at it as hard rock rather than via traditional dance music – above the rhythm track, 'Leave Home' almost entirely consists of synthesized, pitched guitar sounds – they helped modernize the hip-hop/heavy metal fusion popular a few years previously. If it now sounds of its time, it was doubtless forward-looking enough to inspire the likes of Fatboy Slim and Mylo, and established Rowlands and Simons as dance music mainstays for many years.

Black Steel
Tricky
1995 • Island

This bold cover of Public Enemy's 'Black Steel in the Hour of Chaos' succeeds so brilliantly because at no point does it even attempt to be Public Enemy. Instead it values the original's rebellious spirit, but channels it in a different direction. It's become a rock song, and not a rap-meets-rock song but an up-to-date, heads-down heavy metal monster, and paired up with a looped sample of an Indian drum. Easily chaotic enough to get the job done, Martina Topley-Bird's incongruously plaintive guest vocals only add to the madness.

The Changingman
Paul Weller
1995 • Go! Discs

The third stage of Paul Weller's career (the solo artist years) didn't fully distinguish itself until his third solo release, *Stanley Road*. Prior to this, his first two solo albums were so similar to the Style Council in feel and approach, but thereafter he felt satisfied with his mixture of psychedelia and quasi-vintage soul – and so had the confidence to allow the musicians and himself to go off-piste and improvise a little. 'The Changingman' is a wonderfully loose, guitar-laden and swirlingly funky piece that chugs through on its own momentum as Weller and his backing musicians bounce off each other. The rhythmic foundation is so solid and Weller's songwriting was so effortlessly impressive that his band didn't need to worry and could relax into the moment.

This is a Call
Foo Fighters
1995 • Capitol

Former Nirvana drummer Dave Grohl played and sang almost everything on the Foo Fighters' eponymous first album. Recorded in under a week, and made up of a backlog of songs either from notebooks or fresh from his own head, 'This is a Call' is typical of the record: Grohl pulls off a tricky balancing act between alternative rock and mainstream aspirations with quite a flourish. Nirvana's move from the underground to daytime radio had given his solo project a head start, but nonetheless this shows off his gift for a melody that, while submerged beneath a speedy grunge-esque fuzz, wasn't held under long enough to drown.

Inbetweener
Sleeper
1995 • Indolent

After several years of the Live Aid generation of pop stars wearing their austerity on their sleeves, Britpop seemed happy to promote Excess All Areas as a philosophy. All the same, when it came to Britpop's musical output, its practitioners could be just as po-faced as, say, Annie Lennox or Morrissey. Sleeper, on the other hand, had a self-awareness and never took themselves too seriously. Breakthrough single 'Inbetweener' proves this: it's a barrelling, swampy guitar song that elevated itself above the pack with a crisply sunny disposition and inspired soloing. Best of all, though, came when the music press decided the group was simply the very glamorous Louise Wener and some backing musicians, and applied the term 'Sleeperbloke' to anybody who played behind an obviously charismatic frontperson. The band introduced a range of merchandising including T-shirts with slogans reading 'Sleeperbloke' for the men and 'Just another girl-fronted band' for female consumers. Sales of each were brisk.

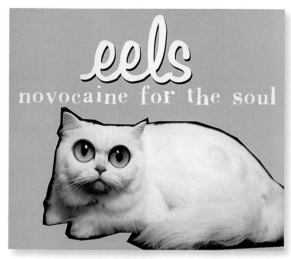

Novocaine for the Soul
EELS
1996 • DreamWorks

<< When you get a band who work as hard to be quirky as EELS do – there are even three choices of typesetting for their name – you fear for the absolute worst. Thankfully EELS had their priorities sorted from the start. Before they turned the quirkometer up to 11, they had already got to grips with the exact requirements for an enduring pop song. The core of 'Novocaine' is hook-heavy and catchy, with enough compelling riffs and flashes drifting in and out to keep you on your toes, and it's in these beguiling extras where they shade the song into something much darker and spookily peculiar. It's rare you get this level of effort put into spontaneous eccentricity.

Fade into You
Mazzy Star
1996 • Capitol

>> For a group that effectively rose via LA's mid-1980s Paisley Underground – a low-level psychedelic folk revival – Mazzy Star took an unexpected turn when they frequently supplemented their jangly, Byrdsian and generally upbeat rock with something much darker. 'Fade into You' was one such number, and, yes, it's prettily countrified (the pedal steel guitar makes sure of that), but it's also probably the bleakest break up song you'll ever experience: 'I look to you and I see nothing/I look to you to see the truth.' Primarily, though, every element in the song seems to be weeping – not just gentle sobs, but those introverted floods of tears that happen almost silently, and with immeasurable emotion. It was far and away Mazzy Star's best-selling record.

No Diggity
Blackstreet featuring Dr. Dre and Queen Pen
1996 • Interscope

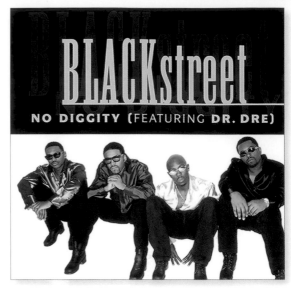

>> From the late 1980s, producer Teddy Riley had been at the forefront of New Jack Swing, which married the beats and production techniques of hip-hop to harmony soul singing. Riley founded Blackstreet in 1991 and, with 'No Diggity', stretched the possibilities of the hybrid to the limit. The harmonizing is real on-the-corner stuff, chopped up sharply but beautifully delivered and carrying the melody, while the backing is a series of spaced-out beats and seemingly random piano samples. Ultimately, though, once you've absorbed the rapping break from Dr. Dre and Queen Pen, you have to wonder how this hard-edged instinctive music evolved into what, in this century, gets called R&B.

Patio Song
Gorky's Zygotic Mynci
1996 • Fontana

>> 'Patio Song' is a love song set on a patio, and a genius piece of psychedelic folk. Once you come to terms with an approach that's that suburb-accepting, it's much easier to appreciate the essence of Gorky's. From an album which consistently juggles near-Bonzo Dog levels of whimsy and banality, it tells the tale of a blissful Welsh seaside summer, and at no point do they neglect the craft of songwriting. Using all manner of instruments, from conventional guitar, bass and drums, to strings, medieval woodwind instruments and a hurdy-gurdy, Gorky's weave a sweet-natured, organic, magic-mushroomy tune around a tender narrative. It all conjures up the kind of summer days that probably weren't nearly as nice as you remember.

Devils Haircut
Beck
1996 • DGC

>> Anybody that can sample MC5, Them and Bernard Purdie, put them in the same track – 'Devils Haircut' – *and* make the inspired result sound like something from out of *Scooby-Doo* has to have something going for them. On his *Odelay* album Beck showed how potent a force musical talent can be when it collides with imagination and the bottle to actually use it. Also crammed into these three minutes is a creeping bass line, a stop-start tempo, clattering drum breaks, and a general vibe of weirdness, all of which flit in and out like bats in a haunted house. The music itself is such a glorious fairground ride of bucking loopiness, it almost doesn't need the self-consciously wacky lyrics like 'Love machines on the sympathy crutches/Discount orgies on the drop-out buses'…

She Cries Your Name
Beth Orton
1996 • Heavenly

<< The late-1980s and first half of the 1990s was a brilliant period for music in general, because it enabled somebody like Beth Orton, with a folk background but also immersed in hip-hop, rock and dance culture, to make an album like *Trailer Park* which could comfortably unite all her influences. 'She Cries Your Name' is pure folk-rock recalling Fairport Convention, but has an injection of ambient electronics mingling with the strings. Elsewhere, there's a kind of acoustic breakbeat segment, and at one stage, even some drum 'n' bass skittering going on in the background. For Orton to make the record in the first place was triumph enough; even better was that Heavenly Records saw fit to release it, and radio was open-minded enough to play it.

Something for the Weekend
The Divine Comedy
1996 • Setanta

Does anybody know why more groups don't make records inspired by ribald British comedy films? It certainly worked beautifully for Neil Hannon's Divine Comedy, who had previously struggled for widespread appreciation, but whose profile rose when they provided the music for the Graham Linehan and Arthur Mathews' TV sitcom *Father Ted*. Then came 'Something for the Weekend', a hilarious double-entendre-laden pop epic, complete with Terry Thomas-style chuckling, as part of an album that as its title *Casanova* suggested, was pretty much dedicated to sex. Suddenly, via the patronage of Chris Evans (then hosting Radio 1's breakfast show), they were famous. Deservedly so, thanks to a beautiful orchestral backing evoking the 1960s, and a modern, softly galloping Eurobeat.

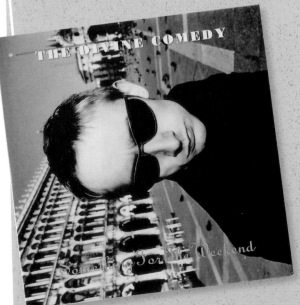

Wide Open Space
Mansun
1996 • Parlophone

The story goes that drummer Andie Rathbone initially refused to join Mansun because he lacked enthusiasm for Britpop, but the demos for their debut album, *Attack of the Grey Lantern*, changed his mind. Taking 'Wide Open Space' as an example, it's easy to see why he quit his car-showroom day job more or less immediately. It's an astonishingly confident tune, revolving around its central guitar riff, growing in strength as it does. It builds to a towering arrangement incorporating a choral chorus and some shimmering synth lines and fuzzy chords that tumble over each other as they get pulled into an alternative orbit. It's effortless in its complexity since none of the elements get in the way of each other, and this allows the tune to cruise to a climax that undercuts any notion of pomposity.

Firestarter
The Prodigy
1996 • XL

≪ As big-beat pioneers, the beats didn't come much bigger than those of the Prodigy. With 'Firestarter', you suspect it was only ever meant to be banged out at a rave, and that actually recording it was a mere afterthought. It's an absolutely furious piece of music, simply constructed around a looped drum sample hinging on a bass drum, and ushering in hooks which work as sirens – the ones that sound like passing cars even have somebody shouting at them. It's so explosive it can hardly be contained within the grooves, and so belligerent it sounds loud even when the volume is turned right down. As a result it's one of the most compelling dance records you're ever likely to be subjected to.

Midnight in a Perfect World
DJ Shadow
1996 • Mo' Wax

≫ This is what DJ Shadow does best: atmospheric hip-hop comprised entirely of samples, and compiled in fascinating depth, where the listener is lured into a private spectral place. He does livelier stuff very well too, which is why 'Midnight' is so effective – seductively smokey and moody, it still always manages to stay subconsciously upbeat so you want to keep engaging with it, rather than stop listening, without realizing. This is down to the usually jazzy samples he uses – here they include Pekka Pohjola and David Axelrod – and how he manipulates the material into making sure the whole mix has a continuously underlying buoyancy, all compiled with the utmost care.

Paranoid Android
Radiohead
1997 • Parlophone

   While not the longest single ever released, in terms of scope and ambition, 'Paranoid Android' is certainly the biggest and bravest of the last twenty years – an epic of near symphonic proportions. The idea that a band could fuse together three very different songs into a single work is nothing new, nor is splitting rock songs into movements – witness early Isaac Hayes or so much prog rock – but it's rare these things are done so engagingly, perceptibly and concisely.

Much has been made of the influences of 'Bohemian Rhapsody', 'Happiness Is a Warm Gun' and, albeit less so, 'Shine on You Crazy Diamond', but really these are just reference points, as 'Paranoid Android' sits comfortably next to them rather than simply *because* of them. It's a unique product of an approach that says 'let's see what we can get away with', which could so easily have come across as merely obnoxious, but doesn't here because of the care with which it's been put together. However the canvas shifts – from delicate acoustic refrains, to baroque synth twiddles, to guitar histrionics – whatever the tempo and however complex the melodies, the underlying vibe doesn't change, thanks to the recurring themes and a fairly constant bass line. It's obviously the same band telling the same story, just split into four sections; revealing a bit more of itself with each listen. Of course the musicianship and arrangements are of the quality needed to pull it off, but really the only way Radiohead were going to end up with something this impressive was to have the fearlessness give it a go.

Nancy Boy
Placebo
1997 • Universal

« With grunge pretty much dead and buried, and most heavy metal taking either the rap 'n' rock route or dumbing as far down as possible, the door was wide open for a rock band like Placebo. Fronted by Brian Molko, a bisexual whose voice is as androgynous as his look, and Stefan Olsdal a gay Swede almost two metres tall, a song like 'Nancy Boy' was packed with intelligence and irony. It's unclear if it's about a man or a woman, and is proudly punk influenced, but its buzz-saw rage niftily has its own melodies and has many of the hallmarks of traditional rock 'n' roll.

Shady Lane
Pavement
1997 • Domino

» An apparently bright and breezy guitar pop song, 'Shady Lane' ambles along pleasantly enough with nothing strikingly original or memorable to mark it out, but on closer inspection, you realize Stephen Malkmus' cheerfully batty lyrics and chiming guitar are a cover up. The melodies are so cunningly constructed that there's a deep beauty to their easy-going nature and the delicate hooks start reeling you into something that has far more going for it than sunshine and lazing about. Its ending – after the helicopter has flown through the mix – won't be what anybody was expecting.

Lazy Line Painter Jane
Belle and Sebastian
1997 • Jeepster

Beefing up their sound was possibly the best idea Belle and Sebastian ever had: prior to the *Lazy Line Painter Jane* EP, their songwriting (while always great) had left the impression that it wasn't being pushed hard enough to show what they could properly do. The EP's title song is given an extra impetus by the presence of a rich Hammond organ, allowing the guitars to open up and it all comes together with a truly groovy 1960s feel. Furthermore, when Thrum's Monica Queen accompanies Stuart Murdoch on vocals, the coaxing dialogue between them brings out a gloriously pop-friendly sound. Throughout, it never loses the quirkiness which was integral to Belle and Sebastian's indie ethic.

Come Together
Spiritualized
1997 • Dedicated

It's probably not a good idea to sit down to listen to 'Come Together' in isolation, as it risks sounding like pure bombast serving no particular purpose other than massaging the band's self-importance. Returned to its original context – the *Ladies and Gentlemen We Are Floating in Space* album – and such musical verbosity makes perfect sense. The album's opening track and title song serves as this song's overture, gradually preparing the listener for the experience of hearing a full brass section, strings and a gospel choir stacked on top of wailing guitars and a circular bass line. This is a vast rock 'n' roll circus, and Spiritualized deserve considerable credit for not letting the end result become an unfocused sprawl.

Brown Paper Bag
Roni Size/Reprazent
1997 • Talkin' Loud

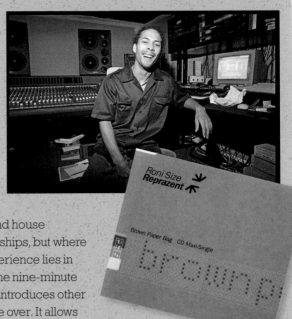

Extracted from the Mercury Prize-winning *New Forms* album, 'Brown Paper Bag' serves as evidence that Roni Size transplanted jungle from underground clubland to the nation's living rooms without, essentially, changing a great deal of it. The style always nodded towards hip-hop and house and 'Brown Paper Bag' subtly highlights these relationships, but where it surges ahead as a listening rather than dancing experience lies in its use of jazz. Not as a sound per se, but as an idea – the nine-minute original version of the track establishes its beats then introduces other elements as solos, stepping aside when their spots are over. It allows the whole to stay as true jungle, while its various components reach for wider appeal.

Celebrity Skin
Hole
1998 • Geffen

According to Hole's front woman Courtney Love, Smashing Pumpkins' Billy Corgan was vital to the recording of the *Celebrity Skin* album, helping the group to create and nurture its songs. Indeed, Corgan is credited as cowriter on the title track (alongside Hole's regular writing duo of Love and guitarist Eric Erlandson), and the sheer Californification of it tumbles out of sparkling hooks and sun-drenched riffs. However, before anybody imagines they're listening to the Bangles by mistake, they're smacked smartly back to reality by a careful measure of pre-Corgan Hole's hot fuzz, plus an underlying punky propulsion of the rhythm.

Kelly Watch the Stars
Air
1998 • Virgin

⌄ Air are so casually but effectively French the government should ask them to remix 'La Marseillaise'. 'Kelly Watch the Stars' embodies all the elegance, good taste and effortless sexiness of a stroll along the Champs Élysées, with nothing at all louche about it. The duo beef up a simple, slinky revolving synth riff with an oozing bass line and bring in a succession of shimmering instrumental cameos, conjuring up the romance, the beauty and the unpredictability of stargazing in the summer as both the prelude and the postscript to a memorable night. Not exactly ambient, but certainly not foreground music either, it's what you'd want if you could have your own theme song playing as the soundtrack to your daily life.

Whippin' Piccadilly
Gomez
1998 • Hut

⌃ Why we listen to popular music in the first place: a well-written melody: something to surprise us; and a sense of fun throughout. What kicks off as a basic rock 'n' roll riff is ingeniously augmented with a series of bouncy hooks. It's a lively state of affairs and all very familiar, but as time goes on, increasingly arresting and unusual sounds begin to invade the track. These include clanking percussion, what might be a sitar and some bizarre electronic squiggles and whoops. All in all, they enhance the tune rather than distract from it, and mean that, while genuinely experimental, 'Whippin' Piccadilly' (about a night out in Manchester) avoids taking itself too seriously.

Goddess on a Hiway
Mercury Rev
1998 • V2 Records

>> There's more than a touch of Buffalo Springfield's first album about 'Goddess on a Hiway'. It succeeds in being disarming without being toadying, and bleak without being pessimistic. It's a gentle brew of jangling guitars and a discreet organ, forming a suitably preoccupied-sounding soundtrack for an absorbing song as cerebral as almost anything Neil Young ever wrote. On the face of it, it's about a break-up or a departure, but one verse in the middle shifts the focus to ecological matters and our destruction of the planet, and you can see why the song was so widely embraced at the twitchy ending of the millennium.

Concrete Schoolyard
Jurassic 5
1998 • Pan

<< As late-1990s rap was getting more and more about proving how tough you were – lyrically gangsterish and musically hard-edged – it was refreshing to find an alternative: hip-hoppers like Jurassic 5 who still wanted to recall its days of innocence. 'Concrete Schoolyard' does exactly that with the help of rhymes such as 'Let's take you back to the concrete streets/Original beats with real live MCs/Playground tactics/No rabbit in a hat tricks.' It's all delivered in such a fun, hanging-out-on-the-porch, line-swapping kinda way to an ultra laid-back but straightforward beat. An obvious enjoyment that gravitates through the grooves to the listener and will delight all but the hardest of hearts.

Ice Hockey Hair
Super Furry Animals
1998 • Creation

A.M. 180
Grandaddy
1998 • Will

 The long-standing problem with plenty of slacker rock – it lives up to its name. It doesn't put in the effort and as a result tends not to hold your interest: the creators can't be bothered, so why should you? Grandaddy, however, are different. The music verges on jaunty, attending to details like a nagging little electronic keyboard riff, a persuasive churning hook and the occasional doubled-up drumbeat, which sounds like it's been added to nudge the listener. The lyrics are similarly intriguing, telling of characters who revel in the notion of inertia, but aren't completely disengaged with the world at large as they haven't lost their sense of wonder.

   Super Furry Animals' vocalist Gruff Rhys once described this song as a 'Badfinger power ballad' and he's not wrong – it really does recall 'No Matter What You Are' with worrying clarity. And although 'Ice Hockey Hair' makes all the right noises – overwrought vocals; towering chord progressions; loads of fuzz; verbose drum fills; and a nebulous swirliness about it – it's far more knowing than that. It recalls the heady early-1970s but does so in a subtly modern way, so as not to stumble into parody or even tribute. By the way, it's great that a group should write and record a song dedicated to the mullet – 'ice-hockey hair' is slang for that iconic 1980s cut – but did it have to be so negative? Surely such a barnet is maligned enough?

JEFF SMITH'S SELECTION

(See Jeff's song choices on pages 85, 179 and 260.)

Twenty years ago I was choosing the tunes for the then new Radio 1 *Evening Session* and to be able to play music like that now all day long is something I have to say I never thought would happen.

Our station now is constantly going forwards but it's important to know where the music came from. I'd like to offer a few additional thoughts from the decades based on some of my favourite tunes and how they might fit into *BBC Radio 6 Music's Alternative Jukebox*.

In the book we highlight the Byrds 'Eight Miles High' as an influential example of psychedelic rock, but I personally particularly like their song 'Chestnut Mare'. To my ears it signalled the move from the 1960s Beatles and Dylan influence to this band helping create a new sound for the 1970s. I think it is one of the first country rock records, a sound that would also be picked up by the likes of Gram Parsons and the Flying Burrito Brothers and, more commercially, by Poco and the Eagles.

Moving genres, Idris Muhammad's late 1970s, 'Could Heaven Ever Be Like This', is a song I recall buying but I never thought would be as influential as it has become in being a key part of how jazz-funk and then chill-out evolved. I think it ultimately gave birth to artists such as Massive Attack and Portishead.

I go back with Primal Scream to their first album *Sonic Flower Groove* but it is their second album that

> 'WE DON'T KNOW WHAT THAT NEXT EXPERIMENTAL BIG THING IS AND WHO IT MIGHT BE FROM BUT YOU CAN BE SURE YOU'LL HEAR IT ON BBC RADIO 6 MUSIC.'

gave us 'I'm Losing More Than I'll Ever Have'. This song is the root to their massive hit 'Loaded' due to a seminal Andrew Weatherall mix. Again this move led to a new take on the concept of remixes and a launch pad not only for the Primals but also for On-U Sound System, Underworld and Junior Boy's Own.

Dipping into the early 1990s and I've always been taken by what Richard Russell did with his XL imprint and the success of The Prodigy was early testament to it. But another track from his label – 'UHF' by UHF – I think really defined techno and dance in the 1990s and to my mind continues to do so.

Coming to 6 Music has really helped me become aware of some brilliant and sonically challenging artists but I think we were all amazed when we heard Bon Iver for the first time. 'Skinny Love' is in this book and I'd just add his importance to the above list of influences as he opened the door to the more experimental side of pop that would in fact crossover as pop music today. You can hear his influence on artists such as Lana Del Rey, Lorde and James Blake.

Music keeps being redefined but often in the shape of what has come before. From time to time something truly different or a radical take on it appears. It's great to know that we probably don't know what that next experimental big thing is and who it might be from but you can be sure you'll hear it first on BBC Radio 6 Music.

Independence Day
Elliott Smith
1998 • DreamWorks

It was testament to Elliott Smith's strength of character and arrangement skills that once he landed his major label deal – which then led to the *XO* album – he involved big string and brass sections, but didn't desert what had secured him the contract in the first place: delicate songs, affectionately performed. Boosted by Smith's falsetto vocal, 'Independence Day' has all the ebbing and flowing acoustic guitar you could possibly wish for, and the orchestrations and harmonies sympathetically act as support rather than threatening to take over. Smith's own life would end tragically early. After years of drug addiction and frequent paranoid episodes, in 2003 he was stabbed to death in his own apartment in a bizarre incident that was originally thought to be suicide. The memory of his life and work is impeccably preserved by wistful, tender, slightly odd songs like this.

Take California
Propellerheads
1998 • Wall of Sound

Propellerheads lay at the more elementary end of big-beat techno, but in many ways that made them more enjoyable than their more cerebral peers – too much attempting to justify the sound as music with superfluous melodies and twiddles could have obscured the primary purpose. As big beat, 'Take California' will satisfy the literalists, as this is exactly what it is – a huge thump of a drum loop and a creeping, underlying bass line. They're joined by sporadic electronic enhancements and speech samples, but throughout, the big beat pounds away, relentlessly and completely compellingly.

Everything is Everything
Lauryn Hill
1998 • Columbia

The kind of song neosoul was invented for, both entirely of the moment and yet steeped in a bygone age. 'Everything is Everything' achieves that by not being self-conscious either about the 1970s funk it harks back to, or the post-hip-hop era it was created in. It uses the technology and sounds of the present day to fit the music of the past by looping and scratching *within* an old-school groove, as a substitute for the usual rhythm section. Lauryn Hill herself stitches the two together by switching from singing to rapping with impressive ease. Meanwhile, playing piano on the session was one John Legend, in one of his first professional jobs, still a teenager and still answering to the name of John Stephens.

Windowlicker
Aphex Twin
1999 • Warp

MARY ANNE HOBBS' CHOICE >> There was a cleverness about so much of Aphex Twin's catalogue that while he could be having an *Emperor's New Clothes* laugh at the expense of so much of the music business – make the most impenetrable electronic twaddle and dare people to say they didn't like it – his music is so carefully crafted that it can work without following conventions. Of course, this requires a degree of effort on the part of the listener, but it pays back in the end. The jagged 'Windowlicker' is jumpy and illogical, and once a conventional melody emerges it's overpowered by seemingly random sounds and time shifts. Yet if you take it as ambience and dip in and dip out as it drifts by, it becomes perfectly agreeable and really rather fascinating.

Rendez-Vu
Basement Jaxx
1999 • XL

« ⌄ Chicago house music, which developed out of disco in the mid-1980s, never really made it to the mainstream in its own right. Sure, many enterprising pop producers took bits of it and grafted it onto what they were doing, but the heart of it stayed underground, only emerging after it had evolved into something else. In the late 1990s, though, with 'Rendez-Vu' being a particularly vivid example, London duo Basement Jaxx took pure house as a musical core, then played with both contemporary and retro pop sounds, striking a perfect balance between the sheer energy of Chicago-style 'old house' and the familiarity needed to move it into the broader arena. As a bonus, because old house had never really made it into the wider world, it came across as 'new house' to many people.

Tender
Blur
1999 •
Parlophone

By the recording of 'Tender', Blur had long tired of the Britpop wave, and had matured both as musicians and people, a development which handily coincided with Damon Albarn's break-up with long-time girlfriend Justine Frischmann of Elastica. Albarn's burgeoning interest in a wider range of music was evident on 'Tender', a long way removed from the tomfoolery of 'Parklife' five years before. With backing from the London Community Gospel Choir it's musically thoughtful, and lyrically dark, as it deals with the glories of love and the pain of separation. New producer William Orbit helped to broaden Blur's palette, and on 'Tender' he created a soft, echoey environment that seems to be reassuring Albarn that everything's going to be alright.

Race for the Prize
The Flaming Lips
1999 • Warner Bros.

Among the modern dabblers in psychedelic rock, the Flaming Lips thankfully preserved its wild orchestral side that produced so much swirly, paisley-clad, and often quite loony music – a fearsome spectrum that ranged from Jimmy Webb to the Nice. 'Race for the Prize' is a lush, sweeping pop song buoyed by soaring synthetic strings, epic-sounding keyboards, and some dramatic stop/starts in the bridge of the song. It relocated that 1960s sound to the late-1990s with great emotional weight, and came just after the Lips' madly experimental quadruple album that, for optimum effect, needed to be played on four separate stereo systems at the same time. Even Robert Fripp had never thought of that.

Cold Blooded Old Times
Smog
1999 • Domino

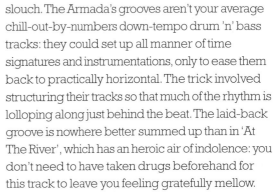

Singer-songwriter Bill Callahan, a.k.a. Smog, leans more to the latter than the former. That isn't to say his none-too-tuneful baritone lacks appeal or soul, but just that his songwriting was simply astonishing. On 'Cold Blooded Old Times' he communicates emotion through lyrics that avoid the clichéd, and comes up with lines that not only require a verbal and tonal dexterity, but also demand the listener's full attention. By not limiting himself to the obvious, his narratives can be far more involved and precise, meaning the stories – this one's about childhood – can operate on a truly absorbing level. Plus, he has the good sense not to let the music get in the way, and the unfussy guitar with a few piano fills is really all that's needed.

At the River
Groove Armada
1999* • Tummy Touch Records

As the acknowledged Sultans of Chill, this North London duo took loafing to new levels with such an innate understanding of sonic repose that even their higher octane tunes have a seductive slouch. The Armada's grooves aren't your average chill-out-by-numbers down-tempo drum 'n' bass tracks: they could set up all manner of time signatures and instrumentations, only to ease them back to practically horizontal. The trick involved structuring their tracks so that much of the rhythm is lolloping along just behind the beat. The laid-back groove is nowhere better summed up than in 'At The River', which has an heroic air of indolence: you don't need to have taken drugs beforehand for this track to leave you feeling gratefully mellow.

* General release – a limited 500-copy edition was available in 1997.

THE 2000s

Possibly needing a comedown from the rave culture of the 1990s, things found a smoother edge in the succeeding decade: dreamy electronica and songs with wistful lyrics that demanded you listen, not jump around to them. A more thoughtful breed of indie rockers emerged, from Franz Ferdinand and Kings of Leon to experimental bands like Sigur Rós, reflecting perhaps a more reflective public mood.

Since I Left You
The Avalanches
2000 • XL

There's really no reason why sampling records have to be so beat oriented, except that, possibly, so many producers are DJs with an ear for dancefloor potential. The Avalanches from Australia show it needn't be that way. 'Since I Left You' takes samples from Rose Royce, the Duprees, Lamont Dozier, and plunders from songs like 'Do the Latin Hustle' and 'By the Time I Get to Phoenix', resulting in a gorgeous, sparkling Philadelphia-sounding dance tune. It doesn't neglect any rhythmic requirements, but simply wraps them up in disco sophistication rather than assume them as the be-all and end-all.

Aisha
Death in Vegas
2000 • Concrete

With over a decade of success for the marriage of heavy metal and hip-hop, it was remarkable it took so long for anybody to combine hard rock and electronica, but luckily, when the time came, it arrived with the astuteness of Death in Vegas' 'Aisha'. The DJ and production duo didn't merely splice some bleeps and beats onto a thrash core, but approached electro from a hard rock direction, using the same balance and intensity of sounds but creating them obviously electronically. With a 'Monster Mash'-style vocal from Iggy Pop telling a serial-killer story in the first person, it's all as much fun as the best Hammer horror films.

Hate to Say I Told You So
The Hives
2000 • Burning Heart

In the somewhat sniffy worlds of British and American alternative rock, Swedish bands rarely break through, but the Hives managed to bypass any cultural embargo. 'Hate to Say I Told You So' shows why, as it keeps itself as simple as possible: a blitz of garage-style power-chording, enlivened with some nifty guitar scratching, fuzz effects and a big bass break. It's effortlessly high-octane and exciting, and although there's a suspicion the lyrics are there for their phonetics rather than their actual meaning, there's nothing to object to. In fact the Hives go a long way to making reparation for European music back in the 1980s.

Up with People
Lambchop
2000 • Merge/City Slang

« Taken from *Nixon*, an album that was supposedly a series of related songs about the disgraced former US President, 'Up with People' is lyrically bewildering (as Lambchop songs tend to be), but that still didn't prevent it breaking the group in the UK. This is country soul at its best, powered by handclaps and a rolling bass line, with horn punctuations adding colour and drama, while a gospel choir echoes the philosophy of singer Kurt Wagner. What's remarkable about the philosophy is that, against the upbeat and optimistic music, the lyrics and phrasing suggest the world is going to hell – at one point, the choir's apparently cheerful chorus splits a line so it's phrased: 'We are screwing/Up our lives today'.

The Ballad of Cable Hogue
Calexico
2000 • City Slang/Quarterstick

« It's hard to imagine you could place surf guitar, a spaghetti Western soundtrack and Parisian torch singing (complete with accordion) in the same three minutes, and have anything remotely listenable. Thanks to a clever production that doesn't let any of the elements collide, Calexico pull it off, stacking things so they overlap to bleed into each other and make the musical connections through similar tone. It's a big-sky Western tale of a lovesick miner, Cable Hogue, swindled out of his gold mine by the woman he thought he loved. Like the music, it's a story as ludicrous as it is absorbing.

Lovely Head
Goldfrapp
2000 • Mute

» There's not nearly enough whistling in pop or rock music today, and as much as the whistled intro to 'Lovely Head' lifts your heart it does little to prepare you for the sumptuousness of the track itself. From the *Felt Mountain* album – the duo's John Barry period and by far their most creative – it's a lavish approximation of a never-made classic *James Bond* theme. Although largely synthesized (unlike much of the album which used a full orchestra), this in no way held it back. Over that creeping, view-over-Monte Carlo tempo, the strings sweep through while Alison Goldfrapp sings like the daughter Shirley Bassey never knew she had. It's extravagantly atmospheric, with a brilliant late-1960s touch of a recurring harpsichord motif – and Goldfrapp herself is responsible for the whistling.

Look Good in Leather
Cody ChesnuTT
2001 • Ready Set Go!

  Legend has it that neosoul adventurer Cody ChesnuTT recorded and mixed all 36 tracks of *The Headphone Masterpiece* album in his bedroom on a four-track recorder, playing all the instruments, then, after failing to interest any record companies, putting it out as a double album on his own label. Within that set is a great album struggling to get out, and although 'Look Good in Leather' is an excellent advert for the DIY recording approach it's not hard to see why the mainstream industry wouldn't touch it with a bargepole. Unashamedly lo-fi, and sharply acoustic, it's a hilariously ironic piece about the ridiculous cow hide-based wardrobes once favoured by rappers and funkateers. Perhaps it was a push to expect the record business to have a sense of humour.

Clint Eastwood
Gorillaz
2001 • Parlophone

The concept of Gorillaz as a cartoon group proved a bit of a barrier for many grown-up music fans, but the best way to approach it was to compare it to early Monkees, with characters created to front a series of songs, which didn't stop said songs standing up by themselves. This was Damon Albarn doing stuff he couldn't do in Blur and doing it really well, as 'Clint Eastwood' demonstrates. It's progressive hip-hop as it ought to be, and more about the tune than the beats – the core is an impossibly low and oozing piano riff, doubled up with a depth charge bass line and with synth melodies slinking through its shadows. The masterstroke was to invite Del Tha Funkee Homosapien to take over the rap, as he brings to it just the right degree of levity.

Witness (1 Hope)
Roots Manuva
2001 • Big Dada

Jungle wasn't the only part of urban Britain's musical landscape where Jamaican dancehall reggae crept in, and Roots Manuva took it to the edges of the mainstream, as tracks like 'Witness (1 Hope)' updated what Soul II Soul had been doing ten years previously. The key to being accepted was assimilating local syntax, but as that couldn't be achieved without altering the music to fit the vocals, then suddenly, toasting about pints of bitter in London street talk makes sense. 'Witness' rocks a relentless, slightly slowed down, dancehall-style bass line, all big enough to support woozy keyboard snatches that drift through, and the perfect support for Roots' nimble rhyming.

F.E.A.R.
Ian Brown
2001 • Polydor

It was a bold move for Ian Brown to opt for minimalist electronica as the basis for most of his *Music of the Spheres* album, but, mostly, it was a rewarding decision, thanks to his unerringly reliable way with a hook: even in the most Japanese of the soundscapes he created had something to draw you in. 'F.E.A.R.', though, really was one for the Stone Roses fans. After 30 seconds or so of bleak synth swirls he drops a big rolling beat that powers the song along as a *prêt-à-porter* anthem, while the most memorable riff comes from the repeated backing vocal of, 'F-E-A-R…F-E-A-R…' Supported by computerized strings and a hint of drum 'n' bass, it's among the best of Brown's work as a solo artist.

Weapon of Choice
Fatboy Slim
2001 • Skint

It's almost impossible to think about 'Weapon of Choice' and not think of Christopher Walken in the video wearing a suit and dancing in a deserted hotel lobby, but focus and you will be rewarded. It's an ingeniously constructed big beat number, reminiscent of an old fashioned funk song, bouncing a straightforward bass and drum rhythm track all the way through. It's punctuated by brass and samples from the likes of Sly Stone, but this is window-dressing compared to Norman Cook's guest vocalist – Bootsy Collins. The lyrics may be random cultural references but the performance is about as funky as you could ask for.

Destiny
Zero 7
2001 • Ultimate Dilemma

« Zero 7's blending of electronics and actual instrumentation is something Britain seems to do particularly well, probably something to do with wanting to embrace the future but being scared to let go of the past – well, would any other nation actually have discussions about 'modernizing' a royal family? 'Destiny', like much of Zero 7's repertoire, is a delightful expression of delicate jazz-funk staying just the right side of being over-elaborate, while still showing off the studio flourishes and the musicianship – the flute, for instance, is a joy. It's a warm, lazy vibe, and gains a persuasive strength thanks to the soulful harmonizing of singers Sophie Barker and Sia Furler.

Sunlight Hits the Snow
I Am Kloot
2001 • Wall of Sound

« In the cluttered world of acoustic, shoe-gazing rock, a trio with a name as pointlessly clumsy as I Am Kloot would have to work hard to make an impact, but they succeeded by taking as simple an approach as possible, and this allowed space for the plaintive Mancunian tones of their frontman John Bramwell. 'Sunlight Hits the Snow' is Kloot's simplicity epitomized – modern-day folk with tinges of cool jazz from the rhythm section, while a multi-layered acoustic guitar can converse without having to shout.

The Modern Age
The Strokes
2001 • XL/Rough Trade

» Timing was everything for this Strokes debut. What had been exciting in the world of US popular music through the late 1980s had curdled and become jaded and clichéd (alternative rock), or overly corporate (grunge), or just largely unpleasant (rap). The Strokes' emergence with what you could call melodic garage – DIY music that opted for tunefulness rather than noise or beats – sparked something of a revival of musicianship and put New York back on the cultural map. 'The Modern Age' is an attractively shambolic acoustic rocker with a disarming lo-fi production that does nothing to inhibit the joyous harmony of the song itself.

Remember Me
British Sea Power
2001 • Rough Trade

« 'Remember Me' is rather aptly titled, simply because it's pure nostalgia. Had it come out 20 years previously it would have slotted so neatly into that buttoned down post-punk caucus of bands like the Jam or Nine Below Zero. In 2001, though, three minutes of crisp, impeccably played, and well-produced power pop came as a welcome distraction from the norm. In truth, it wasn't quite representative of British Sea Power's sound – their album *The Decline of British Sea Power* delved into glam, psychedelia and even included some touches of thrash – but they seldom sounded more convincing than this.

We Come 1
Faithless
2001 • Cheeky Records

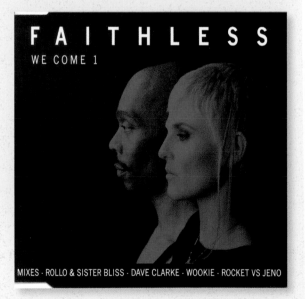

LIZ KERSHAW'S CHOICE » Always a vastly superior dance music act, Faithless offered a depth and a musicality to what they did that never neglected the rhythms, but produced them from such a subtle array of sounds that the group would tease melodies out of material that other acts would use as beats. Such listenable results would give a tune like 'We Come 1' a life beyond the dancefloor, supporting Maxi Jazz's intoned vocals as a fitting piece of poetry with the auxiliary riffs interweaving so well it kept it interesting even if you were only on your sofa. In addition, 'We Come 1' could stand any number of remixes and alterations that could move it into straight-ahead dance territory without ever losing sight of its essence. For evidence, check out the live version or Wookie's UK garage remix.

Pyramid Song
Radiohead
2001 • Parlophone

MARY ANNE HOBBS' CHOICE >> Later-period Radiohead could start to stretch your patience, as they made spinning a couple of tunes into something as taxing as studying for an exam, and since it required so much of the listener, it was tempting to think, 'Why bother?' But on reflection, it all becomes obvious – they put so much into each song so you'd get a proportionate amount out. 'Pyramid Song' came with its own back story involving such disparate themes as Buddhists, Stephen Hawking, Egyptian relics in Sweden and Charles Mingus, while the production featured a French electronic instrument from the 1920s called an ondes Martenot. Still with us? Questioning whether the song would be any different without any of that isn't the point; the weepy track had massive care put into it, giving it a strength of purpose that's hard to resist.

Rockin' the Suburbs
Ben Folds
2001 • Epic

There should be room on everybody's Monday morning playlist for a Ben Folds tune or two. If they're not just plain funny then they're life affirming, and 'Rockin' the Suburbs' is both in equal measures. It all hangs around a big guitar riff – something that might come as a shock to Ben Folds Five fans – but it's all part of the irony involved, as this is a sharp satire about rock groups complaining about their lot that doubles as a send-up of middle-class angst in general. In the first person, Folds talks of how he'll 'Take the cheques and face the facts/That some producer with computers fixes all my shitty tracks', and hilariously whining, 'Y'all don't know what it's like/ Being male, middle class and white.'

Burn Baby Burn
Ash
2001 • Infectious

CHRIS HAWKINS' CHOICE

'Burn Baby Burn' came from the *Free All Angels* LP, which represented a comeback album for Ash after near bankruptcy and all sorts of stress-related issues brought on by too long on the road and the relatively poor performance of their second album. They'd returned to their native Northern Ireland to reconnect with the old Ash, writing and rehearsing this set of songs in the garage belonging to one member's parents, and reverting to the simple guitar pop they did best. 'Burn Baby Burn' is gutsy but remarkably lively given it's about a romance gone stale. They don't neglect the detail, though, and the tune sets itself apart with the subtly shimmering quality of the playing, just enough deft soloing and a thrilling ending.

Plug in Baby
Muse
2001 • Taste

>> As one of the three songs recorded while they were still touring their debut album, 'Plug in Baby' is far more like standard Muse than the bulk of *Origin of Symmetry,* an album that found them messing about with electronics and notions of classical music that had only been hinted at on 1999's *Showbiz.* Not that there's anything wrong with progression, but Muse's intelligent, open-minded take on heavy metal was something most of us were grateful for and 'Plug in Baby' brings all of that back. Riff-tastic and packed with distorted guitars, it also possesses a strongly melodic undercurrent, which gathers all the more percussive elements together with a neat touch.

Squares
The Beta Band
2001 • Regal

<< Another of those gorgeous, slow, dreamy semi-electronic tunes that is far too attention-grabbing to be palmed off as ambient, and owes so much to hip-hop and electro production methods that nobody's going to call it rock. Consequently, no one is sure how to categorize 'Squares', but really, unless your job is to put it in a rack in a big store somewhere – and that's not very likely these days – it doesn't really matter where the track lies. When you're wrapped up in this woozy, heart-beat paced echo-fest, complete with sampled strings and a choir, it's like being in a musical flotation tank and you're not really sure of your own name, let alone what to call this music.

Weak Become Heroes
The Streets
2002 • Locked On/XL

TOM ROBINSON'S CHOICE

'Weak Become Heroes' sounds somewhat downbeat, so it takes time to realize just how much it's actually an optimistic statement from a forward-looking album. Essentially it's a mundane snapshot of 1990s rave culture narrated by a youngster on his way out to a party, and Mike Skinner's frequently cryptic attention to detail is so committed it becomes a fascinating examination of the night, observing characters, customs and colloquialisms. Then the narrative fast-forwards five years, and it becomes a misty-eyed celebration of bygone days, with the message of how we should cherish our histories. All of this is set to a soulful and tuneful piano-based UK garage soundtrack that, quite appropriately, is much more suited to listening than raving.

No One Knows
Queens of the Stone Age
2002 • Interscope

By their third album, *Songs for the Deaf,* Queens of the Stone Age had honed a persona that had started off somewhere between Nirvana and ZZ Top and become much edgier and, at times, explosive. It also found Nirvana and Foo Fighters' Dave Grohl behind the drum kit, meshing dramatically with Josh Homme's guitar to create a dense and thoroughly modern metal, bristling with punk and thrash references. The album as a whole makes the most of contemporary technology which, like a scalpel, cuts the chords up, so that whatever gets stacked on whatever else, it won't be interfering with anything around it, and the need for speed doesn't sacrifice precision or flatten out the sound too much. As a result, 'No One Knows' (its lead-off single) is a relatively relaxed, riff-tastic piece of bar-room sleaze, which might be looking to get laid, or simply looking for a fight, but has such an air of insouciance about it, it clearly doesn't care which.

DON LETTS' SELECTION

(See Don's song choices on pages 23, 82, 127, 184, 246, 265 and 293.)

What links my choices here is down to the duality of my existence, we're talking black and British, so pretty much a culture clash from the get-go. This most crucial combination tooled me up for life. As a child I had the emerging sounds of Jamaica via my parents in one ear and the whole African-American thing in the other courtesy of my elder brothers – if I wasn't going to a sound system I could just as easily have been tuned into Radio Luxembourg. This was against a backdrop of what was going on in the UK at that time – the Beatles, the Stones, the Kinks and the Who (actually the first band I ever saw live, when I was just 14). All of which captured the imagination of a young black kid growing up in Brixton. I guess another contributing factor was the fact that I went to a grammar school and for many years I was the only black kid there; consequently I'm getting turned on by hip white mates who were looking for more left-of-centre sounds: Led Zeppelin, Cream, King Crimson, et cetera.

'NOWADAYS IT'S ABOUT WHAT FINDS ME — WHAT STRIKES A CHORD. THE WORLD'S A BIG AND BEAUTIFUL PLACE AND I REMAIN OPEN TO ALL IT HAS TO OFFER.'

As a youth I guess I might well have been drawn to a good bass line or I might have been searching for the perfect beat but I'm as old as rock 'n' roll (born in 1956) so nowadays it's more about what finds me – what strikes a chord. The world's a big and beautiful place and I remain open to all it has to offer. I still like my bass…but then again I do love a good guitar riff. Electronics remain in the mix…and what's that weird sound from someplace I never knew existed? Yep I'll have some of that too!

My buying habits were of the records that best soundtracked where I was at ('King Tubbys Meets Rockers Uptown') or where I'd like to be (GMF). Dancing was definitely part of the mix 'cos that was serious currency when it came to getting the girls. Having said that, I realized pretty early on that you can't spend your life on the dancefloor – when the music stops, you gotta face reality and, guess what? There's a tune for that too! I can't be summed up by a single genre of music any more than I can be defined by my colour – I remain the Don.

Goodbye
The Coral
2002 • Deltasonic

<< Produced by the Lightning Seeds founder Ian Broudie and from the Coral's self-titled first album, this tune has a satisfyingly nostalgic feel about it, but still sounds sharp and clear enough to stand up in the modern world. Indeed it's the use of contemporary studio technology that gives the Coral such a spacious ringing to the guitars that it conjures up images of beat groups in matching cardigans on *Ready Steady Go!* in the 1960s. It's all cunningly undercut with a softly swirling Hammond organ, but the real joy lies in the soaring harmony singing on the choruses. If it's all a little anachronistic, it's also a huge amount of fun and you just know a couple of members of the Coral must be smirking to themselves as they share a microphone for these backups.

There Goes the Fear
Doves
2002 • Heavenly

>> When it became clear on the morning of its release that 'There Goes the Fear' was heading for the UK top 10 on advance orders, Doves decided that, just for a laugh, they would delete the single that very afternoon – so if you hadn't got a copy you'd have to wait for the album. It wasn't so much a publicity stunt as a statement about the value of music (and pretty much everything else) in this age of 24/7 availability, but they chose a great tune as an example. 'There Goes the Fear' is sunny, it's open and it's unassuming, but it's wonderfully catchy with a shimmering kwela-ish guitar hook. You'd sorely miss it if it wasn't there.

Obstacle 1
Interpol
2002 • Matador

the seed (2.0)
THE ROOTS featuring Cody ChesnuTT

The Seed (2.0)
The Roots
2002 • MCA

Astonishingly, post-punk had become a vein of nostalgia in its own right by the time the 21st century rolled around. New York's Interpol hark back to Joy Division – both in terms of music and demeanour – with a doff of the cap to My Bloody Valentine and the Cure. On 'Obstacle 1', guitars are compressed and layered on top of each other to form an impenetrable mass, with a nagging rhythm persisting in the background, while singer Paul Banks spins a tale of woe about a lie that's gone so bad somebody ends up getting stabbed in the neck. Even an Arthur Baker remix for a reissue a year later couldn't do much to lift the gloom, and although you might not be able to see them, you suspect Interpol are perpetually wearing long, dark overcoats.

When 'The Seed' began life, on Cody ChesnuTT's *The Headphone Masterpiece* album, it gave unequivocal proof that DIY is not always the best option. ChesnuTT's hyper-neo bedroom-demo style soul music is endearing to a point but, sooner than you'd like, starts to sound gimmicky and grating, and is crying out to be finished. Progressive hip-hoppers the Roots were an excellent choice to do so. Retaining ChesnuTT's vocals and guitar playing, they are sympathetic to the song's melodic ideas and back-to-basics vibe, but by adding some bottom end, a few jazzy samples, some echo to round out ChesnuTT's vocal, and some sharp multi-handed raps, the original is finally given a real strength of purpose.

Sunshine Recorder
Boards of Canada
2002 • Warp

Anybody who imagined that rock stars dabbling in the occult or that giving Beelzebub a production credit was a trend that died out with Slayer, must have slept through the media controversy surrounding Boards of Canada's *Geogaddi* album, which was released four years after their debut studio album, *Music Has the Right to Children*. There are mentions of horned gods, experiments in backmasking – and if more evidence of Satanic involvement should be needed, the album's playing time is 66 minutes and 6 seconds. Of course such suggestions might just be clever marketing for a collection of dark, spookily textured ambient electronics from a band that preferred to be seen as shunning publicity, of which 'Sunshine Recorder' is a fragile and unnerving example.

boards of canada
geogaddi

of canada
he right to children

Fix Up, Look Sharp
Dizzee Rascal
2003 • XL

>> Grime and its original self-contained, under-the-radar world allowed development and marketing of the music with no outside influence. As a result youngsters like Dizzee Rascal – he was just 17 when this came out – had the skills and the confidence to know how to behave when the mainstream came calling. There was no carrot the mainstream industry could offer and an artist like Mr Rascal (as dubbed by broadcaster Jeremy Paxman) was smart enough to know how to gussy it up enough without losing its essence. A tune like 'Fix Up, Look Sharp' – a big, big beat complete with a bonkers, frantic but very funny free-association rap – could never have been conceived in an A&R department. Yet it was Dizzee's first of many top-20 hits.

Milkshake
Kelis
2003 • Arista

 After the disappointing sales of her experimental-ish previous album *Wanderland*, Kelis went back to basics for *Tasty*, on which 'Milkshake' was far and away the most standout track. Produced by the Neptunes, it's a bass-synth loop supplemented by skittering high-register percussion with Kelis in full-on tease mode playground-style rapping – it sounds like a skipping song – about her milkshake. Perhaps unsurprisingly the video, which was set in a diner and runs through virtually every visual sexual innuendo imaginable, elevated it to international attention – even the bread rolls play their part – while an underdressed Kelis gyrates and eat cherries in a manner that has one customer covering her young son's eyes.

Date with the Night
Yeah Yeah Yeahs
2003 • Interscope

  As the Yeah Yeah Yeahs music became more accomplished, and the media attention on vocalist Karen O had calmed down somewhat, the talents of the rest of the group – the magnificent noise whipped up by drummer Brian Chase and guitarist and keyboard player Nick Zinner – were allowed to come to the fore and flourish. Here they produce a battering wave of post-punk on the offensive, one that has no bass player but you'd never really notice. The speedy, crunching power chords are underpinned with just enough bass synth, while the all-out battering served up by the drums practically knocks you over.

Such Great Heights
The Postal Service
2003 • Sub Pop

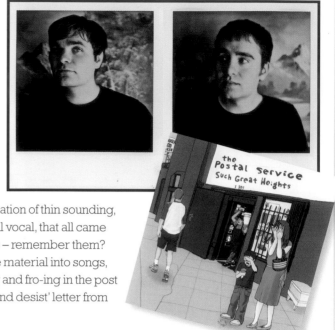

>> This lovely, perky song by electronics wizard Jimmy Tamborello and Death Cab For Cutie singer Ben Gibbard, happily recalls the synth-pop of the 1980s – Tears for Fears, Human League, Pet Shop Boys and so on – which realized it didn't need to be art and could start enjoying itself. It's an engaging combination of thin sounding, rudimentary beats and riffs, with a yearning soulful vocal, that all came about when Tambrello recorded music on to DATs – remember them? – and then mailed them to Gibbard who edited the material into songs, added vocal ideas and sent them back. This to-ing and fro-ing in the post triggered their name and, astonishingly, a 'cease and desist' letter from the real Postal Service for copyright infringement.

House of Jealous Lovers
The Rapture
2003 • Vertigo

<< If heavy metal had continued along its blues-based trajectory there's every chance it might have ended up sounding like the Rapture. While so many of their contemporaries were mucking about with hip-hop and dance techniques, the New Yorkers were fusing 1970s analogue funk with hard rock. Before the first guitar histrionics make an entrance we get almost a minute of percussion – the band lines up with four of their number taking percussion duties – then there's a driving Rick James-ish bass line and a choppy 4/4 drum pattern. Remarkably, this makes 'House of Jealous Lovers' seem both heavier and lighter at the same time, driving the song with such momentum that the squawking vocals don't become an issue.

Seven Nation Army
The White Stripes
2003 • V2

By Jack and Meg White's fourth album, *Elephant*, the White Stripes had finally made the jump from being 'critically acclaimed' to genuinely popular, and they'd done it rather cunningly. Early on they'd arrived at a tasty blues-rock approach, largely familiar to anybody over the age of 40, and persevered with it, gradually increasing their reach by smartly manipulating the media with a tantalizing, evolving mythology. Here they almost went legit as 'Seven Nation Army' became something of an anomaly: it featured what may have been a bass guitar driving the main hook, but because the whole set was recorded using 1950s gear it could have been anything. Another shrewd move, as it made the song far more recognizable to the mainstream, where it reached such a level of user-friendliness that its central riff became a football-ground chant.

Hurt
Johnny Cash
2003 • American Recordings

>> 'Hurt' came from the last album Johnny Cash recorded before his death in 2003. *American IV: The Man Comes Around* was, essentially, a catalogue of regret and compunction about a life as it was lived, told mostly through cover versions. This Nine Inch Nails original was a superb, astute choice, even though its writer Trent Reznor was initially skeptical about the idea. Rick Rubin produced sparingly, leaving plenty of space for Cash's careworn vocals and acoustic guitar, apparently offering self-reparation for previous wrongs. It's a near-naked performance that slowly grows in emotion, while an orchestra swells in the background and lifts Cash up to the possibility of redemption.

All Possibilities
Badly Drawn Boy
2003 • Twisted Nerve

<< After scoring the film *About a Boy,* it was as if Badly Drawn Boy got bitten by the movie bug, as 'All Possibilities' and indeed the rest of the *Have You Fed the Fish?* album, comes across as a soundtrack in search of a film. Not that this is a problem – Badly Drawn Boy's orchestral sensibilities are excellent and here he has the confidence to craft a tune that, from the start, manages to evoke Philly soul with a pinch of salsa, then settles into a groove that is very 1970s caper movie, with the crooks getting away via the Pacific Coast Highway. It's lush, swish, incredibly disco sophisticated. In fact, it's practically everything Badly Drawn Boy's voice isn't, which keeps the song firmly in the indie arena.

Molly's Chambers
Kings of Leon
2003 • RCA

>> It's important to remember how young the Kings of Leon were when they recorded their debut album. Two of them were teenagers, the other two barely into their 20s – and as such they had little truck with musical tradition. They came out of the country and southern rock environment of Nashville, but in true young-person style, were determined to shake things up a bit and infused it with a degree of garage or post-punk rock. 'Molly's Chambers' has the same chugging time signature and twanging southern drawl of good country rock, but it's been punked up a bit by raising the tempo and adding some buzz-saw chords and a relentless drum pattern. What resulted is so effective it's difficult to see why such a melange is so comparatively rare.

Mr Brightside
The Killers
2003 • Lizard King

<< >> A fantastic example of how keeping things simple can work out for the best. 'Mr Brightside' draws more on the disco-influenced new romantic British pop groups of the early 1980s, piling catchy guitar riffs on top of a pulsating bass line to create a shiny but honest pop sound. It doesn't contrive to be arty or clever or even twiddly, and the hooks draw the listener to a point at which they start overlapping, creating melodies that are easy to follow. But the Killers do it with such sparkle and subtle depth you never feel like you've been sold short. That the lyric is a detailed-to-the-point-of-paranoia tale of what may only be imagined infidelity presumably gave it another natural point of entry for so many listeners.

Take Me Out
Franz Ferdinand
2004 • Domino

The best thing about Franz Ferdinand was that they had a genuine musical intelligence but never made a big deal out of it, and weren't constantly foisting this cleverness on you either in interviews or in the studio. They just got on with it and produced apparently simple songs that had the hidden depth to be completely intriguing and have an appeal far beyond student discos. 'Take Me Out' manages to be two tunes in one. It starts off in vintage style, as a windmill-chording thrash rocker, but then segues into a thumping disco-esque groove with such well-oiled precision you hardly notice the join. You could never accuse Franz Ferdinand of being pretentious, and this second single marked their chart breakthrough, both in the UK and in many overseas territories.

Banquet
Bloc Party
2004 • Wichita

During the five years between Bloc Party's formation and their debut album, their sense of confidence grew dramatically so that the *Silent Alarm* set had an inbuilt degree of self-assurance, while also retaining ample freshness and spontaneity from its studio sessions. What they pull off on 'Banquet' is a crisp brand of up-tempo guitar rock that is broadminded enough to assume influences such as dance, funk and punk, but sufficiently disciplined not to allow them anything more than shading. As a result, instead of sounding like a conscious hybrid, Bloc Party's music becomes unique and rather refreshing.

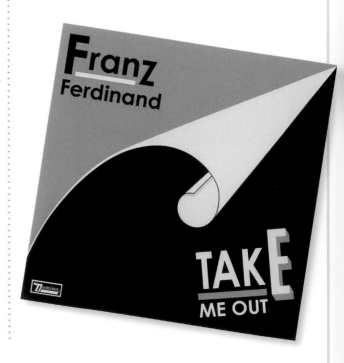

Can't Stand Me Now
The Libertines
2004 • Rough Trade

>> The image of the Libertines as indie rock's favourite soap opera, starring Pete Doherty as a cartoon crackhead, overshadowed the reality that they were a very good band. Although producer Mick Jones, formerly of the Clash, had to hire security to stop Doherty and fellow frontman Carl Barât fighting, he captured a powerful beauty in the guitars and driving rhythms of 'Can't Stand Me Now', which eventually abandon any pretense of delicacy and expand into the soundtrack of open conflict. The narrative is about the pair's relationship falling apart – they sing the same lines at the same time with not even a hint of harmony – and if it wasn't for Jones' relentlessly attention-grabbing production, once again the melodrama would obscure the music.

Club Foot
Kasabian
2004 • Sony

<< What is it about the Midlands and heavy metal? Something to do with the area being Britain's manufacturing heartland and the music lending itself to the rhythms of the construction line? For decades now, the UK's best hard rock has regularly hailed from the middle of England, and Leicester's Kasabian became worthy flag carriers in the mid-2000s. But, thankfully for both the genre itself and its fanbase, the Kasabian approach isn't too inward-looking. Rather than create some sort of living museum of metal, the group has clearly been listening to the Stone Roses and hung out at a progressive rave or two. 'Club Foot' is metal with a very modern dance-music attitude, transporting Madchester about a hundred miles south and introducing it to a more relentless way of rocking. Post-baggy pop.

I Predict a Riot
Kaiser Chiefs
2004 • B-Unique

>> As with so much of the Kaiser Chiefs' output, the lyrics of 'I Predict a Riot' are a vital component. They're so broadly Yorkshire it's almost a cliché, plus there's some of the most deft rhyming this side of the Notorious B.I.G. This is a story of the sort of violent youthful mayhem that happens in most British town centres on a weekend, and on first listen you think it's either a mistake of just plain clumsy. But then you're entranced by the compositional dexterity: couplets like, 'I tried to get in my taxi/The man in a tracksuit attacks me', are just genius. All this backed by power pop guitar and crazy harmonizing.

Oh What a World
Rufus Wainwright
2004 • DreamWorks

« In which the classical-aspiring son of folk singers Kate McGarrigle and Loudon Wainwright III assembles a vast, sumptuous, full-orchestra piece that veers from Jimmy Webb to Ennio Morricone with all the pomp and splendour of both. And that's before we've got to the Ravel's Bolero motif. It's the sort of spectacular piece that deserves to be applauded for its meticulous attention to detail, but like the lyrics – plaintive ramblings about the world as immediately seen by Wainwright – it seems like reverie, existing for its own sake rather than with any greater structural or musical purpose.

Neighbourhood #3 (Power Out)
Arcade Fire
2004 • Merge/Rough Trade

» As part of an album entitled *Funeral*, so named because various band members had experienced familial loss during its making, this was never going to be the cheeriest of songs, but what it becomes is a questioning, eye-opening missive regarding the turn of the millennium. Ostentatiously set in the severe (even by Canadian standards) winter storms of 1998, a week-long power cut becomes a metaphor for mankind's soul or the space where it used to be: 'I went out into the night/I went out to pick a fight/With anyone.' All of this is quite brilliantly set to a molten surging beat that has the sheer nerve to play the central riff on a glockenspiel, as it effortlessly shifts gears between anger and despair.

STEVE LAMACQ'S SELECTION

(See Steve's song choices on pages 30, 89, 143, 220, 249, 257, 284, 288 and 289.)

'Complete Control' is my favourite Clash song: right from the very start it's a statement of intent. It's hard to find a single record that sums up what the punk movement meant to people, and there are lots of records I could have chosen, but the fury of that record and the manifesto it sets out make it the one, for me. It's the one I turn to whenever I need to make a decision about something: I know Strummer will have the answer.

We did a gig for 6 Music as part of the Camden Crawl in 2009, and we put on a couple of gigs with a variety of new bands and a couple of old favourites, so I asked Billy Bragg – not knowing if he'd do it – to play at the Dublin Castle. It holds about 200 people, so it was a tiny venue for Billy, but he agreed to play. It turned out to be my favourite gig of all time. I've got a bootleg of it that I listen to pretty much every week. It's just really inspiring. By the time he did 'New England' at the end of the set he barely need to sing because the crowd was singing along so loudly: it was so rousing.

Generally when it comes to reggae I'm pretty old-school – stuff like Clint Eastwood and General Saint are more my thing – but Damian Marley's 'Welcome to Jamrock' is just one of those songs that I'd play on the radio and it brings things to life: it's just a great song.

I love discovering bands and being there at the start of their career, and the Maccabees was one of those situations. The first time I saw them, they looked like they'd just met for the first time on the way to the gig! There was something fantastically naive about their first record. They have a real romance and sensitivity: there are a lot of clumsy lyricists around at the moment, but the Maccabees manage to get to you, without being too soppy or introverted. 'First Love' is always in my DJ set when I'm playing out.

'I LOVE DISCOVERING BANDS AND BEING THERE AT THE START OF THEIR CAREER...'

Just Like the Rain
Richard Hawley
2005 • Mute

 One-time Longpigs and Pulp member Richard Hawley pulled off a remarkable feat with 'Just Like the Rain' and its parent album *Coles Corner*. It's authentic duck's ass, check shirt and big jeans-wearing countrified 1950s-type American pop, but 'Just Like the Rain' is no museum piece or Conway Twitty tribute act. This bouncy, rockabilly-esque guitar-led number is a song of loss and subsequent regret and pain, the emotions that make up much of Hawley's palette. Such is his marvellous lyrical mix of burdened optimism and contemplative disappointment, that he inspires sympathy rather than pity.

Apply Some Pressure
Maxïmo Park
2005 • Warp

If ever a group has summed up *post*-post-punk, it's Newcastle's Maxïmo Park. That's punk as it was, but two generations removed, having absorbed enough mainstream mannerisms to become almost acceptable. 'Apply Some Pressure' is, probably, some sort of gawky love song, but it's delivered with a youthful enthusiasm and cheerful pogoing thrash that explodes into the room and is so high-end vibrant it can't be ignored. The level of ineptitude that once seemed a punk prerequisite as a part of the anti-musicianship pose, has been filtered out here: by now, it's just another aspect of the indie spectrum, and luckily, it gave Maxïmo Park a following beyond life's mosh pit.

I Bet You Look Good on the Dancefloor
Arctic Monkeys
2005 • Domino

» The Arctic Monkeys' first album (*Whatever People Say I Am, That's What I'm Not*) was the fastest-selling debut by a British act, shifting 360,000 copies during the first week of release. Exactly why was not immediately obvious: it excels at spiky, speedily tuneful power rock, but it's still difficult to see why it was quite so eagerly anticipated. Gradually, though, on repeated listens, the album starts to explain itself – it's a rock opera, if you will, dedicated to almost every aspect of city-centre clubbing and telling the story in minute detail. The single that broke the Monkeys, 'I Bet You Look Good on the Dancefloor', concerns itself with some arcane courtship ritual: the narratives are hilarious, poignant and pointless all at the same time. So many British youngsters could identify with these scenarios, and that may have been the key to why the Monkeys suddenly became such major players in British rock.

Welcome to Jamrock
Damian Marley
2005 • Tuff Gong/Universal

 **STEVE LAMACQ'S CHOICE** **«** Damian Marley is most definitely the smartest of all the Marley offspring. At no point in his career has he tried to be his dad and, as a result, has made contemporary sounding reggae with international appeal to a post-MTV pan-racial generation. His music acknowledged what was going on around it, he performed as a DJ rather than a singer, and the upshot was something as sharp as 'Welcome to Jamrock'. This was built around a repurposed Sly and Robbie riddim – 'World-A-Music' by Ini Kamoze, since you ask – and reborn as a taut, slapping state of affairs that owes almost as much to hip-hop as dancehall reggae. All the while Damian delivers a fire-and-brimstone, righteously Rasta rant that lays waste to ne'er-do-wells from street criminals to corrupt politicians, with an ironic refrain of 'welcome to Jamrock' echoing in the background.

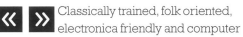

Chicago
Sufjan Stevens
2005 • Rough Trade

 Classically trained, folk oriented, electronica friendly and computer literate, Sufjan Stevens made it his mission to chronicle everyday American life from both a contemporary and historical point of view. 'Chicago' comes from *Illinois*, the second in a series of albums that set out to musically interpret each of the fifty US states, and, through his refined melding of acoustic and rudimentary electronic instruments with an orchestra and some jazzy brass, it connects on a compelling level. 'Chicago' is a road-trip number, about driving across country to start a new life in the windy city. A powerful, big production is full of hope with more than a tinge of regret about past mistakes, and is so relevant to so many real lives it becomes impossible not to be moved by it.

Hoppípolla
Sigur Rós
2005 • EMI

 Experimental musicians Sigur Rós – they use a bowed guitar among their array of instruments – vividly reflect their Icelandic environment. There's a glacial, chilly, light-blue colour to the sound of what they do, but it is never forbidding, while the dramatic splashes of sonic reds and greens bring beauty and excitement. 'Hoppípolla' boasts a sweeping orchestral soundscape, punctuated by drifting figures like clouds in an otherwise clear blue sky, which swell to become hugely uplifting, representing infinite possibilities. It's the Sigur Rós song almost everybody will have heard, as it's been used as music on TV shows from nature to sport to award ceremonies and in movies, adverts, and even at live events such as Sydney's 2013 New Year fireworks.

Midnight Request Line
Skream
2005 • Tempa

GILLES PETERSON'S CHOICE >> As a teenager, Skream worked at Big Apple Records in Croydon, dubstep's spiritual home, and, together with acts like Zed Bias, DMZ and Oris Jay, was at the forefront of its evolution to usurp grime as the underground sound of choice. 'Midnight Request Line' was one of dubstep's early breakthrough records and takes a more melodic approach while staying true to the style's twisting, edgy expressions. Not really what you'd call a dance tune, it's a dark, spooky piece, all about atmospherics and creating an ambience of possible danger and chaos, brought on by unsettling key and time changes, yet all arranged within the neatly ordered boundaries of handclaps and a portentous bass riff. The signatures and ideas sprinkled on it slowly form a fractured tune, but even when you think you've got a grip on it you still can't predict what's coming next.

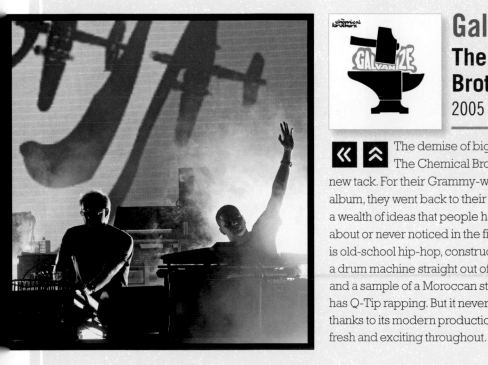

Galvanize
The Chemical Brothers
2005 • Virgin

<< ^ The demise of big beat meant that The Chemical Brothers had to try a new tack. For their Grammy-winning *Push the Button* album, they went back to their roots and explored a wealth of ideas that people had either forgotten about or never noticed in the first place. 'Galvanize' is old-school hip-hop, constructed out of a bass synth, a drum machine straight out of the very early 1980s, and a sample of a Moroccan string orchestra. It even has Q-Tip rapping. But it never sounds out of place, thanks to its modern production techniques, and is fresh and exciting throughout.

First Day of My Life
Bright Eyes
2005 • Saddle Creek

» On the same day in January 2005, Bright Eyes, founded by singer-songwriter Conor Oberst, released two albums: one sensitively acoustic, the other far more robust electronica. The theory for the two projects was that the two aspects of Oberst's creativity could be expressed without either treading on the other's toes. The reality was that the folky and acoustic *I'm Wide Awake, It's Morning* was confident, bright and interesting, while the electronic pop of *Digital Ash in a Digital Urn* sounded like a man out of his depth. 'First Day of My Life' originates from the first set, and sensitive guitar and bass act as an ideal bed for Oberst's aching voice to tell a tale of apparent personal redemption, but which hints at a wider social agenda.

Standing in the Way of Control
Gossip
2005 • Back Yard Recordings

« Less frantic and less tantrum-throwing angry than their previous albums, with *Standing in the Way of Control,* Gossip hit an up-to-date balance of punk attitude, and focused indignation. It did nothing to throw water on what they'd set themselves up as, but made them more accessible. On its title track, here, the arrangements are crisp and spare, giving Beth Ditto greater opportunity to carry the excitement and show off her powerful and emotional voice. Self-penned, the song perfectly suited that voice: it was a comment on a US government proposal to forbid same-sex marriage.

Bro's
Panda Bear
2006 • Fat Cat

» Panda Bear is Noah Lennox of Animal Collective, and this is from his third solo album, *Person Pitch*, which he wrote and recorded after relocating from the US to Lisbon in Portugal. The move had an effect on him, which he described at the time as gloriously elevating. It shows in the music too, and the 12-minute 'Bro's' is a gorgeously sunny, daftly psychedelic number that sounds like something the Young Rascals wished they'd done in the 1960s. It is, in fact, made up from samples of the Tornadoes, Cat Stevens, the Equals and an owl – and that's not a group called 'Owl', it's an actual feathered bird. Taking sampling beyond the traditional dance-oriented world like this opened an entire corridor of doors for post-digital pop.

Lloyd, I'm Ready to Be Heartbroken
Camera Obscura
2006 • Merge

This was written as an answer song to Lloyd Cole and the Commotions' 1984 classic, 'Are You Ready to Be Heartbroken', simply because Glaswegian band Camera Obscura were such big fans of Cole. It's the sort of infectious, dazzlingly happy, fully orchestrated three minutes of pop music we haven't heard enough of since the first half of the 1960s: Herman's Hermits, early Beatles, Freddie and the Dreamers, that sort of thing. Even the narrative of blind young love is so innocent it comes over as endearingly quaint, and appropriately naive: 'Hey, Lloyd, I'm ready to be heartbroken/Cause I can't see further than my own nose at the moment.' Quite literally, they almost never make them like this any more.

Over and Over
Hot Chip
2006 • EMI

The coolest thing about Hot Chip is that they are fully aware that electronic music is a computerized playground, open to anybody for the price of an Apple Mac. Therefore, as success in the rock world has never been more of a lottery, you might as well have a laugh while you're doing it. Mercifully unburdened by any need for street credibility (or whatever the kids call it these days) and not being weighed down with an art rock label, Hot Chip are intrinsically aware of what's required to command attention, while simultaneously pretty much doing what they like. 'Over and Over' is a groove so cleverly spaced out it manages to be insistent without you really realizing it's there, then fills in the gaps with tempo-shifting bleeping, squelchy and twiddly bits, carving out snatches of insane melodies. It's clear Hot Chip set out to please nobody other than themselves, and in doing so provided music so laid-back it's virtually horizontal; a lack of tension that, to the listener, is just as attractive.

Roscoe
Midlake
2006 • Bella Union

It was perhaps for the best that Midlake dumped the gently jazzy psychedelic pop of their first couple of albums and opted instead for a subtle, countrified soft rock approach on *The Trials of Van Occupanther*. Not because there's any more integrity about recreating the 1970s instead of the 1960s, simply that this style better suited their lilting voiced singer, Tim Smith, and allowed the whole group to show off their multi-instrumental talents to more immediately impressive ends. The backing on 'Roscoe' really is a soundbed: acoustic guitars, basses and pianos blend with their electric counterparts, building up layer upon layer of softness with a low-key urgency until it envelops you. It's a perfect environment for a wistful song that seems to be about how modern life has corrupted a long-standing rural village. Most impressive of all, though, is that 'Roscoe' shows us that a place where Radiohead meets the Eagles can be a pleasant and quietly exciting environment.

The Ride
Joan as Police Woman
2006 • Reveal

SHAUN KEAVENY'S CHOICE >> Joan Wasser's stage name is a tip of the hat to the 1970s Angie Dickinson TV series *Police Woman*, and the sassiness, sexiness and humour that came with it. The album this comes from, *Real Life*, has all those qualities, but 'The Ride' is one of its more considered and pensive pieces, bringing out Wasser's wealth of experience in music and life; she was well into her thirties when this was recorded. Gracefully arranged and enhanced by organic-sounding instrumentation, Wasser sings in sultry tones about embarking on a love affair – if not with cynicism then with a certain careworn sense of self-preservation. The song has a lazily self-confident feel that raises Joan as Police Woman above so many of her singer-songwriter peers.

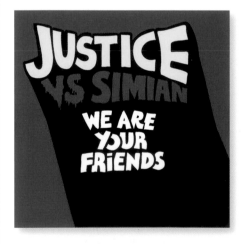

We Are Your Friends
Justice vs Simian
2006 • 10 Records

« When 'We Are Your Friends' first circulated, it was as if some sort of early 1980s-themed fancy-dress-party karaoke track had somehow found its way into proper record shops. It's an inspired mash up of all the flimsy aspects of the synth-pop of that era, and what's so shameless about what it's doing that it has a definite klutzy charm. The verses are made up of simple electronic riffs and drum tracks, countered by impassioned if repetitive vocals, while the intro and a seemingly random break are the sort of tinny, rudimentary electro that kids in matching tracksuits used to dance to. In fact that's the thing about this tune: it's just so dumb and party-friendly it's difficult not to want to dance. Spinning on your head, of course, would be optional.

First Love
The Maccabees
2006 • Polydor

  A gloriously stupid narrative that seems to be taking place in a university bar as it so accurately sums up the awkwardness, the expectation and desires thrust upon young people away from home for the first time. The lyrics run through a disjointed narrative that could so easily be those first clunky conversations and mad leaps of fantasy that go with them, switching wildly from optimistic confidence to twitchy nervousness within the space of a line.

The Maccabees' music, too, soars from sheepish and hesitant to crashing and self-assured, showing the band to be as tight as they are astute, while making sure there's a central melody to stitch these emotional flights of fancy together.

The Greatest
Cat Power
2006 • Matador

'The Greatest' is the title track of an album of countrified southern soul that found the Georgia-born Chan Marshall, a.k.a. Cat Power, returning to below the Mason-Dixon line. She was back recording in Memphis' legendary Ardent studio with a band that included Hi and Stax veterans. *The Greatest* is an album that shows just how closely related black and white music were in the south, and how even traditionally big arrangements can be scaled down to suit a smaller voice with no loss of soul. 'The Greatest' itself is a tender, ultimately pessimistic tale of missed opportunity that might be about a boxer or might be about life in general, and Marshall's sexily weathered tone conveys it perfectly as an intimate late-night conversation.

This Is What You Are
Mario Biondi
2006 • Schema

CRAIG CHARLES' CHOICE « For about half an hour back in the 1980s, this sort of easy-action, jazzy soul with a big arrangement found favour in London clubs, but, as good as some of it was, none of it was at this level. Italian Mario Biondi has a rich, warm voice, and doesn't even break a sweat as he eases through this swinging Latin-seasoned big band number with a verve Lou Rawls would be proud of. The orchestra have been arranged with utter precision too: brisk percussion and interchanging rhythms keep things percolating, allowing the brass and strings to take a more laid-back approach, and giving an easy-going air to what is satisfyingly brisk. It gives Biondi's voice the perfect platform. Fabulous.

Steady, As She Goes
The Raconteurs
2006 • Third Man/V2

» The Raconteurs are a 'supergroup' or side project for the White Stripes' Jack White and fellow songwriter Brendan Benson. It found them teaming up with Patrick Keeler and Jack Lawrence of the Greenhornes, the latter also being in White's other side project the Dead Weather. It was the right time for White to make a shift, too, as the Stripes had been getting a tad stale for a while and this freed him from many of that outfit's self-imposed constraints. Cannily, though, he opted not to alienate his fanbase completely and this first Raconteurs offering wasn't a huge departure. It's still a love letter to classic rock, but this time the contemporary recording equipment and the band's pop sensibilities give a crisp urgency to White's compositional skills.

Crazy
Gnarls Barkley
2006 • Warner Bros.

<< When you send your demo to a record company you only get one shot, so you might as well make it epic, and you couldn't get much bigger than Gnarls Barkley's introductory offering, 'Crazy'. It's underpinned by a dramatic sample from a spaghetti Western soundtrack – the Reverberi brothers' 'Last Man Standing', from the climactic showdown in *Django, Prepare a Coffin*. Producer Danger Mouse looped a snatch of it, allowing room for reverb, and played some of the riff along with it to increase the tension. On top, CeeLo Green's urgent, plaintive singing made it an instant post-hip-hop soul classic. Indeed the A&R man who received the demo claimed to have only played it once before offering Gnarls Barkley a recording contract.

Duplexes of the Dead
The Fiery Furnaces
2007 • Thrill Jockey

>> The Brooklyn brother-and-sister duo Matthew and Eleanor Friedberger typically confound as much as they charm and obstruct as much as they entertain. The album this comes from, *Widow City*, came with a press release explaining how the sounds they had produced were in step with the lyrical narrative. For example, a bassoon signified waiting, monkey noises represented a rooster at dawn and, on this track, an acoustic guitar served to illustrate sunlight, 'through the dirty curtains a duplex of the dead would no doubt have'. But when listening to the tune's whirly, Beatles-ish, jazzy, and psychedelic-in-patches vibe that supports words that could be about anything, the idea isn't to start picking anything apart. Just take it head on, immerse yourself in the intricate strangeness and on repeat listening, different aspects will organically reveal themselves.

Skinny Love
Bon Iver

2007 • self-release (general release 2008 • 4AD/Jagjaguwar)

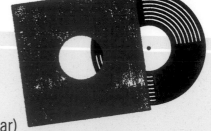

Probably the greatest thing about the best modern folk music is, almost paradoxically, how technology has allowed traditional folk values to shine through in precisely the way the players intended. In this case it allowed Bon Iver's nucleus Justin Vernon to isolate himself in a remote Wisconsin cabin and more or less finish *For Emma, Forever Ago*, a collection of songs of longing, loneliness and heartbreak, without having to get out of character. 'Skinny Love' opens with a barely there concoction of acoustic guitars, over which Vernon forsakes his usual falsetto for something lower and slightly cracked but framed with his own harmonizing. It builds slowly and slightly, with a drumbeat and not much else to an almost shouty conclusion (by Vernon's standards) about a love betrayed, all the while retaining the delicate and essential purity of the singer's ideas.

All My Friends
LCD Soundsystem
2007 • DFA Records

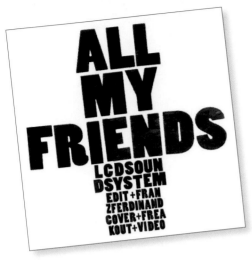

From LCD Soundsystem's second album, *Sound of Silver*, which once again allotted space to James Murphy's unashamed Eno, Bowie and Velvets admiration, but this time it's done with a bit more panache than before. 'All My Friends' is a rattling subway-train ride of a two-fingered synth riff, subtly gaining momentum with rifling drumbeats and countermelodies, heading towards a powerful finale of electronic sound. All the while, Murphy intones a lyric in that half-talking half-singing style favoured by his previously listed heroes. At over seven minutes, it's a fun, interesting ride, showing how he was starting to come to terms with his songs as pop music, as opposed to art rock.

Mig, Mig
Fanfare Ciocărlia
2007 • Asphalt Tango

CERYS MATTHEWS' CHOICE »

Although their music emphasized their Romanian roots, the brass band Fanfare Ciocărlia took a pan-Balkan approach and plundered other neighbouring lands for influences and accents. On 'Mig, Mig', they hired musicians and singers from Serbia, Bosnia, Macedonia and so on, meaning the *Queens and Kings* album was able to incorporate so many new ideas into the sound they had already established. 'Mig, Mig' features Bulgarian singer Jony Iliev and is a lively, percussion-heavy gypsy dance, with the brass coming in for crisp, detached riffs with such gusto it could almost be mariachi.

Men's Needs
The Cribs
2007 • Wichita

In a late-2000s sea of entirely indistinguishable floppy-haired British indie guitar bands, a group like the Cribs were determined not to submerge themselves in it, and were a welcome noise. Especially as, on this evidence, they were barking mad – and most notably so on 'Men's Needs'. It aims to make a lyrical point about men's approach to life as being enslaved to mammon, while women take an altogether more sensitive view, yet it's bellowed out like a drunk at closing time. Likewise the music is equally raucous, with guitars barrelling through the mix as obnoxious as you like, and daring listeners to ignore them, rather than pleading for attention.

Paper Planes
M.I.A.
2007 • XL

While grime and jungle were allowing rappers in London to be themselves rather than an imitation of their US counterparts, M.I.A. developed her own unique strain of hip-hop created around her English–Sri Lankan heritage. It was beautiful because not only did it tap into the original spirit of hip-hop inasmuch as it was a personal expression, and free from corporate interference, but it was it so far removed from anything else it couldn't be ignored. 'Paper Planes' has an inimitable sound palette, as she makes use of Tamil and other southern Asian instruments and samples, resulting in a much perkier feel. In turn this shapes the way M.I.A. can deliver the lyrics – reminiscent of 'Double Dutch' rapping – into a light sing-song – that's clearly having as much fun as we are.

She Can Do What She Wants
Field Music
2007 • Memphis Industries

 MARC RILEY'S CHOICE

Sunderland's Field Music had already shown themselves to be masters of the preposterously catchy hook with hidden and complex depths, and 'She Can Do What She Wants' continued the tradition. Here it's the bass line and the ingenious vocal harmonies that pull you in, but such is Field Music's development that there's far more going on underneath all that. The strings are supplemented by a vibraphone, but as they retreat back in the mix there is more scope for them to behave with a modest virtuosity, while there is a refinement and sophistication present in the brasher riffing.

1234
Feist
2007 • Interscope

'1234' began as a song by Australian singer Sally Seltmann (who recorded under the name New Buffalo), who soon dropped the song from her repertoire because she thought it sounded too much like a Leslie Feist composition. However, a year or so later, when Seltmann toured Canada as the opening act for Feist's side project, the rock group Broken Social Scene, she offered Feist the song. Feist has a cowriting credit on the commercially released version of the song, as it's probably unlikely that what Seltmann played for her on tour had much in common with how it ended up. A ditty about lost love starts off so twee it could be from *Sesame Street* (and indeed it was later affectionately rewritten for that show), but builds up from the banjo, strings – and Feist's truly lovely voice – into a boisterous bar-room stomper complete with a wonderful trumpet. By that point it doesn't seem to care if the lost love ever gets found or not.

Golden Skans
Klaxons
2007 • Polydor

>> Cultural descendants of the Stone Roses and Primal Scream, Klaxons took on rave culture and dance music from a guitar-oriented but decidedly post-baggy point of view. Golden Scan was a state-of-the-art light-show projector so integral to the rave scene it would be namechecked on flyers. Rather than take the samples-and-loop route, they simply play and, in doing so, hark back even further to the sort of soul-based pop that was everywhere in the 1970s. Boisterous as 'Golden Skans' might be, Klaxons aren't of that beery, blokey, often boorish disposition that got in the way of so many post-rave bands, opting instead for a prog rock perspective. Although the lyrics stop short of pixies and hobgoblins, there are still enough fantasy worlds, thrones, Tangian deserts and rainbows to fuel a movie franchise.

Sea Legs
The Shins
2007 • Sub Pop

<< <> The Shins' album *Wincing the Night Away* was inspired by long-standing insomnia – perhaps unsurprisingly, it was less lively overall than its predecessor. Not that you'd guess that if the only track you'd heard was 'Sea Legs'. Here, melody is everything and it's one of those wonderful perky pop songs that's acoustic enough to be charming, but requires some studio technology to give it the power to get noticed in the first place. Although the layered orchestration is satisfyingly dense, it's put together with a light touch and remains engagingly floaty.

Weather to Fly
Elbow
2008 • Fiction

DON LETTS' CHOICE >> Elbow took their name from a line in Dennis Potter's *The Singing Detective*, and the title of the album this track is from, *The Seldom Seen Kid*, is a Damon Runyon character, so it'll be no surprise to reveal that 'Weather to Fly' is witty and literate, both lyrically and musically. It's a supremely elegant, wistful song that looks back with comfortable nostalgia and looks forwards with optimism, absorbing the listener with crafty wordplay. The music is equally impressive: a lilting melody urged forwards by a clever vocal arrangement, a big, loose bass drum and a furtive piano line. The highlight is a stately, restrained brass section that appears towards the end and rounds off the narrative in an entirely appropriate fashion.

Mykonos
Fleet Foxes
2008 • Sub Pop/Bella Union

<< ∨ This was a part of a five-track EP, *Sun Giant*, issued at the end of a successful introductory tour as something for new Fleet Foxes fans who otherwise faced an attention-testing wait for their debut album. As cynical a move as this could have been, track four, 'Mykonos', was a highlight, an enthralling aperitif for what was to come. Fleet Foxes took West Coast folk rock and gave it an Olde English twist complete with medieval-sounding percussion and baroque instrumental flourishes which were so smoothly applied that nothing seemed out of place. The key to this merger is the gorgeous harmony singing that could be the Association or CSNY from the 1960s, but could be equally at home in *Game of Thrones*.

Dog Days Are Over
Florence and the Machine
2008 • Island

>> Perhaps the most pleasing aspect of Florence and the Machine was the idea that a big-voiced female singer could: a) live her life without courting constant tabloid attention; and b) understand that emotional songwriting didn't have to involve inflicting self-indulgence on the rest of us. These amiable qualities shouldn't take anything away from how good Florence Welch and her band are. They are astonishingly varied in approach and style, and 'Dog Days' is a larger-than-life soul number, swelling to the sort of epic proportions that mean Welch has everything to do to keep up. She is more than equal to the task.

Time to Pretend
MGMT
2008 • Columbia

<< Making a career out of rubbishing most of what the modern music business represents may not be wholly advisable. But MGMT (which is an abbreviation of their original name, The Management) bite the hand that feeds them with such infectious cheerfulness it would be churlish for anybody to take issue. The marvellously catchy 'Time to Pretend' combines samples and loops with traditional instrumentation, then ushers in an array of swirly whirly psychedelic sideshows, to surround you with a sound that is then deliberately distressed for a friendly, lo-fi feel. Meanwhile, the lyrics are a hilarious spoof on the cocaine and supermodels rock 'n' roll lifestyle that concludes it's all a fantasy anyway.

Heartbreaker
Metronomy
2008 • Because Music

MARC RILEY'S CHOICE >> Metronomy hail from Totnes in Devon, and their *Nights Out* album, was apparently themed around a dreadful and disappointing weekend in a provincial English town. 'Heartbreaker' kicks off proceedings in appropriately melancholy fashion. It begins with a stark synth and bass line, and what sounds like seagulls cawing in the distance, but it doesn't stay gloomy for too long. Swiftly and silkily, the song transforms itself into a sophisticated electro funk number, but in piling on absorbing layers of sounds and instrumentation, the band keeps everything separate enough to pull it all apart and end play with some subtle dub ideas. Here, it seems, is when the weekend truly gets going.

Calling and Not Calling My Ex
Okkervil River
2008 • Jagjaguwar

<< Named after the title of a short story by Tolstoy's granddaughter Tatyana, Okkervil River, from Austin in Texas, occupy the countrified end of indie rock. They have the good sense and wit to do a classic cowboy-style 'she done him wrong' song but give it a twist by rooting the tale as a 21st century exercise in introspection. In 'Calling and Not Calling My Ex', it's more a case of: 'he got fired the same day as she got her big break and flew off to fame and fortune', so the lyrics are a late-night bar-room cocktail of jealousy, longing and regret. The music, too, is a finely balanced up-tempo big band melange of modern sounds and traditional sentiment, giving the yearning a buoyant feel that makes it all the more poignant.

Say Aha
Santigold
2008 • Atlantic

 Happily, former music graduate and one-time major label A&R representative Santi White, a.k.a. Santigold, draws her inspiration from the New York new wave scene of the late 1970s and early 1980s. Happily not because she overtly channels any of those acts, but instead channels the freedom and curiosity of that era, and experiments with different genres both past and present. 'Say Aha' has a punk-ska foundation at its heart, but brings in art-rock synth, a full-blooded surf guitar, and sews it all together with dub reggae techniques. It's bouncy and fun, and transcends the sum of its parts to create the ideal platform for vocals that implicitly urge that you get up and jump around.

Dancing Choose
TV on the Radio
2008 • 4AD

After seven years and three albums of mostly challenging experimental music under their belts, post-digital avant-garde outfit TV on the Radio seemed to have decided enough was enough and they'd rather reach out to a slightly wider audience. Hence *Dear Science*, a set of tracks that can be called songs without fear of legal action, but will remain a cause for concern with the purists. 'Dancing Choose' sums this up: it begins as otherworldly electro, segues into a sunny West Coast rock, moves back into old-school hip-hop and finishes off giving up the funk. Yet it's somehow none of those things, because it's put together with such a wild collection of unexpected sounds.

Cape Cod
Kwassa Kwassa
Vampire Weekend
2008 • XL

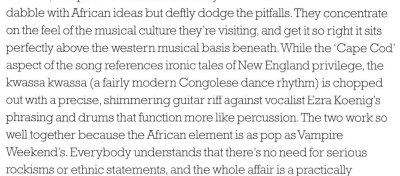

Messing about with music from far-flung lands is never as easy as it seems – it's but a small step from Paul Simon earnestness to 10cc glibness. On 'Cape Cod Kwassa Kwassa', Vampire Weekend memorably dabble with African ideas but deftly dodge the pitfalls. They concentrate on the feel of the musical culture they're visiting, and get it so right it sits perfectly above the western musical basis beneath. While the 'Cape Cod' aspect of the song references ironic tales of New England privilege, the kwassa kwassa (a fairly modern Congolese dance rhythm) is chopped out with a precise, shimmering guitar riff against vocalist Ezra Koenig's phrasing and drums that function more like percussion. The two work so well together because the African element is as pop as Vampire Weekend's. Everybody understands that there's no need for serious rockisms or ethnic statements, and the whole affair is a practically weightless and sunny experience. Incidentally, the video was directed by future film-maker Richard Ayoade, who is also known for the character Maurice in TV show *The IT Crowd*.

Two Weeks
Grizzly Bear
2009 • Warp

>> Grizzly Bear's recording budgets had been increasing considerably, but by their third long-player, *Veckatimest*, the band knew that big didn't necessarily mean better. 'Two Weeks' is a case in point: while it may have big harmonies, driving drums and apparently complex synth arrangements, it's far less dense than their previous work. Sure, the instrumentation is stacked, but there's daylight in between the layers, and it's this space where so much more of the song's internal dynamic is allowed to make an impact. You feel you're listening to the group rather than the production, which had been a bit of an issue in the past; but they don't waste the chance to be heard on 'Two Weeks'.

Airplanes
Local Natives
2009 • Infectious

<< In true indie style, Local Natives financed the recording of their debut album *Gorilla Manor* themselves, and then publicized it just as independently by gigging and blogging. As a result, there's a sense of enterprising freedom about it all: they wrote and produced everything entirely as a group effort and ended up with what *they* wanted, rather than what a major label might see value in. 'Airplanes', for example. The song's sunny harmonies are completely infectious, while the smoothly swelling backing becomes much bigger than you'd expect from an operation of this size. It's amazing what can be achieved when ingenuity takes the place of a big budget, and the approachable, easy-going charm of 'Airplanes' is an added bonus.

My Girls
Animal Collective
2009 • Domino

<< Animal Collective is a side project for a variety of Baltimore-based experimental musicians, of whom only Noah Lennox (from Panda Bear) and David Portner, a.k.a. Avey Tare, are constants. It works quite wonderfully as a meeting place for different influences and favourite styles, expressed on synthesizers and samplers in an unusual manner, but more often than not with a psychedelic bent. Take 'My Girls': looped vocal choruses and twiddling keyboard lines cascade over each other before the rhythm section kicks in to give it an underlying swing that periodically drops below the growing surge of melody. The interplay between these elements is so nimble it ends up with a spinning psychedelic wash and the end product is all the more beguiling for it.

In for the Kill
La Roux
2009 • Polydor

>> A common reaction to hearing *about* La Roux as opposed to actually *hearing* a La Roux track was 'Didn't we have too many 1980s synth-pop duos in the actual 1980s?' But what came as part and parcel of the duo's homage, along with a gravity-defying ginger quiff, was a way with a pop song that was dangerously catchy. Rock fans of a certain age will recognize almost all the musical references on 'In for the Kill', but that doesn't stop them being irresistible, and in the summer of 2009 there was a gap in the market for uncomplicated grown-up electro. Technological developments too meant it had a sonic depth few of the original synth duos managed.

1901
Phoenix
2009 • V2

If you've ever wondered what happened to the bits of Eurodisco that became house music during the 1990s, Phoenix should figure as part of the answer. At the forefront of the French alternative rock scene, they are essentially a guitar band but their excitable dance pop has assimilated Eurodisco's rhythm patterns and translated it to their conventional line-up of instruments. It sounds a little unnerving to start off with, but on a tune like '1901' – that they gave away as a free download to boost their international profile – a bass synth holds it all together, liberating the guitars, and giving their disco licks a touch of punk attitude.

Little Lion Man
Mumford & Sons
2009 • Island

For about 20 minutes at the tail end of the 2000s, the music media invented something called the West London folk scene and scrabbled around looking for some music-based connection, missing the point that the London aspect was the most important feature. The music was London first, folk second, and Mumford & Sons were far and away the best at it, which shows up vividly on 'Little Lion Man'. It's constructed as a rock song, influenced by punk and pop as much as anything Celtic, and performed with total conviction on a blend of contemporary and traditional instruments. And that is the key: this isn't folk music with a bass guitar or a rock song with a bit of banjo, it's a modern and unique London take, and all the sounds present are relevant.

Daniel
Bat for Lashes
2009 • Parlophone

From Bat for Lashes' second album, *Two Suns*, saw a considerable improvement in Natasha Khan's songwriting and, although the arrangements are conflated into a more manageable form, they still dwell in a world of fairies and fantasies and mystical landscapes. 'Daniel' is probably the best example of this leap forwards. The echoey quasi-medieval sounds and melodies carry a lyric about an imaginary lover, and a more straightforward synth line tops it off with 1980s pop-style dance riffs. Although these rhythms remain appropriately delicate, they provide a welcome toughening up without losing the ethereal mood, shifting Khan away from the Stevie Nicks soundalikes and into something far more her own.

THE 2010s

The digital age's impact on alternative music
is undeniable: previously hard-to-source music is
widely available online, and the technology to create
and record music is more accessible than ever before.
It's unsurprising, therefore, that the sonic landscape is
an ever-expanding bed of geographical and historical
influences. Even as music pushes forwards, the past is
rediscovered and offered up anew to the next generation,
providing a connecting thread across the decades as
artists old and new forge the next chapter in the story
of alternative music.

Pumped Up Kicks
Foster the People
2010 • Columbia

« Music with a real swagger about it, as Californians Foster the People neatly bunch together a blend of styles and musical ideas – art rock, early hip-hop, synth-pop, prog rock – into a breezy, easy, swinging, superior pop song. You'll just happily bounce along, singing it in your head until you start to clock the words, which are written from the point of view of a young man contemplating a shooting spree at his school, then coming home to kill his dad. In the wake of the recent US shooting rampages carried out by youngsters in schools, shopping malls and a cinema, writer Mark Foster wanted to explore the issue of teenage depression and mental illness.

Schoolin'
Everything Everything
2010 • Geffen

» ⌄ An apt name for this band, as there hasn't been a great deal left out of this song. 'Schoolin'' isn't so much a mélange of styles as a mash up of musical techniques, concepts and principles, seemingly moon-affected. In essence it's a slice of new age ambient electronica, and a drum 'n' bass approach to percussion, which wouldn't have been too unusual were it not for the bizarre key and time changes. 'Schoolin'' switches to a disco beat, followed by a more ethereal break, before the entrance of some synth power chords and a flash of twiddly guitar, all of which leads to some adventures in bass-heavy jazz-funk. The result could have been an awful mess, but fortunately it's an intriguing example of modern music, topped off with one further incongruous element – a male falsetto vocal from singer Jonathan Higgs.

Am I Just a Man
Steve Mason
2010 • Double Six

» After the Beta Band, King Biscuit Time and Black Affair, Steve Mason was ready to release music under his own name, but only after financial problems and a period of serious depression. Therefore there was always going to be a therapeutic element about *Boys Outside*, his first solo album, and 'Am I Just a Man' is blanketed with a sense of regret at the end of a love affair, which questions his ability to communicate with an ex-lover. The equally eloquent music combines a gently up-tempo folk-funk with a discreetly shaded synth wash, and in doing so, presents a reboot of 1960s West Coast rock.

I'm Getting Ready
Michael Kiwanuka
2010 • Polydor

« Acoustic soul has never been easy to get right. The singer and the song are under a lot of scrutiny, and with no horn section or fat bass line to hide behind, they are exposed and isolated under an uncomfortably bright light. North Londoner Michael Kiwanuka's warm voice contains many subtle tones and textures that communicate impressive emotion without having to overdo things. In this relaxed, easy-action mode, he glides over the unplugged backing with a quiet urgency. The real joy here, though, lies in the song itself, 'I'm Getting Ready'. It's one of those studiedly ambiguous soul classics that could be about a love affair, but could equally have far wider concerns.

Becoming a Jackal
Villagers
2010 • Domino

⇑ ⇒ 'Becoming a Jackal' is beautiful Irish pop music, conveying true soul and passion without recourse to anything remotely diddly diddly. Fronted by Conor O'Brien, Dublin's Villagers play a selection of traditional and contemporary instruments, and apply a balance to them that allows both sides to complement each other and shine through. Here, on 'Becoming a Jackal', a brooding tale that might not be a metaphor, it's an ideal soundbed for O'Brien's light brogue to tell a dark-tinged story with a meticulous attention to lyricism. His writing puts spinning a narrative above all else, and his relish for words and wordplay seems to gives the storyteller as much pleasure as the listener.

I Still Believe
Frank Turner
2010 • Xtra Mile

⇐ ⇒ From an album entitled *England Keep My Bones*, acoustic punk Frank Turner presents a song of such mesmerizing optimism it yanks you out of your chair and gives you a good shaking before sending you out into the world to perform random acts of kindness. Formed around a simple, noisy three-chord structure, 'I Still Believe' somehow feels even punkier because it's acoustic and doesn't need a power supply. An exuberant Turner bawls about still believing in rock 'n' roll and its ability to right almost every kind of wrong: 'Now who'd have thought that after all/Something as simple as rock 'n' roll would save us all?' There's such overwhelming delight and positivity in this infectious tune that you can't see why you stopped thinking that in the first place.

New York Is Killing Me
Gil Scott-Heron
2010 • XL

>> Given a decade of prison terms, crack addiction, alcoholism and an HIV diagnosis before his *I'm New Here* album, Scott-Heron's comeback record (his first in 16 years) could have simply made the statement, 'Look – he's not dead!' It would have been impossible, however, for it to lack power: on 'New York is Killing Me' he might have decided to call it a day in the big city, but there's still no sense of bitterness. The production is spot on, bridging the notions of old and new, rural and urban, innocent and erudite with the main riff being a children's clapping game, supplemented by some dark electronic sounds and pulses. But it's still the philosophy of a beaten man, and so for more reasons beyond the obvious, it's such a shame this was part of Gil Scott-Heron's last recording.

Spanish Sahara
Foals
2010 • Transgressive Records

<< Foals' melodic grip was surer by the time of their second album, *Total Life Forever*, but they still hadn't lost their early talent for recognizing the value of a groove. That is what lies at the heart of this seven-minute epic, allowing it to build impressively slowly – it kicks off with the central riff on a lonely guitar and moves it upwards by packing stuff around it to beef it up rather than obscure it. With a real sense of drama, that same riff grows to a point where the guitars can spar with each other. It's so gripping that you can forgive the lyrics, which are every bit as alarming as you might expect from a band who described their album as sounding like 'the dream of an eagle dying'.

Bloodbuzz Ohio
The National
2010 • 4AD

   Over ten years into a career, the National's narrative – documenting the travails and pressures of the modern man, more out of resignation than any particular angst – was one that could only go so far. On their fifth album, *High Violet*, however, there is a dark, self-destructive quality to the lyrics, as if life has not just caught up with their everyman protagonists, but is in fact starting to pass them by. 'Bloodbuzz Ohio' seems to be about personal and generational financial problems, but of course this being the National, it's all put together in a way that is far from frugal. Matt Berninger's brooding baritone is engulfed in a gently swirling and swelling, semi-orchestral concoction that, if taken on its own, would have been surprisingly upbeat. With the addition of chiming pianos and crisp drumming, there's a depth and a lush urgency that gives the singing a restrained desperation and the overall song a real poignancy.

Crystalised

The xx

2010 • Young Turks

NEMONE'S CHOICE A group who met at school – the same South London school attended by Hot Chip and Pierce Brosnan – here show the sort of confidence brought about by such internal familiarity as they stretch things a little in the often stylized world of British indie rock. Remarkably, their choice to have male and female voices sharing the vocals is what sets them apart – you'd think such interplay would be more common, but it isn't. Not only does their wonky harmonizing have a hugely endearing quality, against this story of a relationship at breaking point, it also brings an air of genuine intimacy. Meanwhile the music reflects all the moody hesitancy and indecision of the lyrics, and consequently creates an absorbing sonic framework.

Tightrope
Janelle Monáe featuring Big Boi
2010 • Bad Boy

The most satisfying thing about Janelle Monáe as a soul singer of the post-MTV age is that, after you've stripped away the alter egos, the tuxedos and the largely entertaining psychobabble she spouts in interviews, she's a superb artist with some excellent songs just below the surface. 'Tightrope' is glittering neosoul with an old-school funk feel: basically, it's a kids' clapping song, of the sort that used to crop up in soul and R&B with regularity, and the bass line, the drums and the horn riffs all copy or fall in with it. Of course it's phased and echoed and looped in a thoroughly modern fashion, but when all is said and done, it's street funk, with Monáe's voice strong enough to stay out front.

Good Intentions Paving Company
Joanna Newsom
2010 • Drag City

MARC RILEY'S CHOICE

It's rare for a list like this to include the likes of Run-DMC, the Ramones and Supergrass alongside a harpist, but if you're thinking that's probably for the best, check out Joanna Newsom. The musician's effervescent, high-pitched voice seems to be merrily mangling iambic pentameters on first hearing, but in truth, she is a marvellous whirlwind of verbal dexterity, twisting and turning to accommodate the wit and wordplay of her lyrics. A title like 'Good Intentions Paving Company' is a useful signpost to how she thinks, and musically she's just as playful. This is dominated by a grand piano (the instrument she learned before the harp) but also ushers in guitars, organ and even a trombone into the mix that's vaguely reminiscent of mountain folk, but which can rock out just as readily. So much fun you may end up a little disappointed there's not actually a harp to be heard after all.

Midnight City
M83
2011 • Mute

<< French electronics band M83 – the name of a far-flung galaxy, not txt spk – decamped to Los Angeles to record an epic double album, *Hurry Up, We're Dreaming*. The results, as witnessed by 'Midnight City', are so 1980s it's as if Lady Diana were still happily married and we're all wearing white socks. Even this track's title sounds like an episode of *Miami Vice*. However, it's far enough removed not to be too reverent, thanks to M83's playful, dry sense of humour. They feed all manner of yelps and bleeps into the arrangement, which undercut the sombre orchestrations, then throw in signature changes to add twists to the straight-ahead synths. While they're clearly not of this century, they're no Harold Faltermeyer tribute act either.

Sophia
Laura Marling
2011 • Virgin

>> It wasn't until her third album, *A Creature I Don't Know*, that Laura Marling properly hit her stride. Hardly surprising, really, given she was still only 21 years old, and was still finding an emotional maturity and artistic self-confidence. 'Sophia' leaves no doubt as to the nature of this new, grown-up Laura Marling: the hook line of, 'Where I've been lately is no concern of yours', leads into a tale of a woman once gravely wronged but who now has the upper hand. There's a boldness about the music, too, starting off with just an acoustic guitar, then adding percussion and cello before slyly seguing into a hoedown that wouldn't be out of place in the Blue Ridge Mountains, while the singer adopts an accent that just stops short of yodelling. This all works better than you might think, as such an unexpected sense of fun stops the ambiguous, intense lyrics from becoming too overbearing.

Youth
Daughter
2011 • Communion

›› None of the three members of Daughter is Scandinavian – English singer, Swiss guitarist, and French drummer – but there's definitely something of a Nordic feel to 'Youth'. The empty landscapes of a lone guitar and minimal, distant drums, which are swept through with strings, give way to swirling wintry storms of keyboards and layered guitars. 'Youth' is a vivid theatrical piece with contrasts so slick and smooth that they obscure the song's lyrics which come across as fifth form poetry – why do so many of today's more sensitive songwriters confuse 'deep' with 'affected'? Regardless, those lyrics are delivered with a delightful lilting falsetto, and become just another interesting tone within the mix rather than anything to distract the listener.

Lonely Boy
The Black Keys
2011 • Nonesuch

›› Forthright, noisy blues-based rock has become a bit of an endangered species of late, what with studio technology becoming more accessible to most musicians. This is a shame, because when it's done with the conviction and gusto of the Black Keys there's little that's more invigorating. With Danger Mouse at the desk, the arrangement is so crisp and precise that it allows the production to fool about a bit – listen out for the bass and drum break about two thirds in – while the choral-style backing vocals are a lovely touch. 'Lonely Boy' is one more example of the Black Keys taking enormous care to give us something sounding totally spontaneous.

The Words That Maketh Murder
P J Harvey
2011 • Island

« A track from the most accomplished and poignant anti-war album of modern times, *Let England Shake*, which was so rounded a condemnation of conflict it examined war from angles many musicians would have overlooked. 'The Words That Maketh Murder' articulately and wittily dissects the failure of diplomacy in the continuing war in Afghanistan. It alludes to the idea this might be deliberate, and cleverly brings in references to World Wars I and II for the same denunciation. Most strikingly of all is the general jauntiness of the music, it's a big rolling rock 'n' roll number, that might be a bit un-Harvey, but has all the more impact for that – it's probably the only peace protest song ever that was granted permission to reference 'Summertime Blues'.

Cash and Carry Me Home
Ghostpoet
2011 • Brownswood

» The UK hip-hop scene markedly improved when a generation of artists stopped looking towards America all the time, and instead carved out music that underlined their sense of Britishness. In some cases – jungle, grime, dubstep – it took on other influences; in others, such as Ghostpoet, it didn't need to. 'Cash and Carry Me Home' has a ghostly bass and drum riddim, laying down an appropriately unsettling all-electronic soundtrack for a tale about the aftermath of a marathon drinking session. Filled with a mixture of regret, confusion and last night's whisky, the rapper is trying to get home, while drunkenly berating his mum and snivelling like a baby because he's lost, befuddled and he's smashed up his phone. A masterly, minutely-observed vignette of an aspect of club culture that's seldom eulogized.

JOE GODDARD

GABRIEL

Gabriel
Joe Goddard
2011 • Greco-Roman

NEMONE'S CHOICE A reworking of a house tune written by producer John Beck and the vocalist featured here, Valentina, 'Gabriel' owes so much to the remix itself, carried out by Hot Chip's synth wizard Joe Goddard, that it would make no sense to put anybody else's name on the title. Goddard has completely deconstructed the song, forensically examined its component parts and then put it back together selecting elements of it more for their potential than what they actually are – it's the same technique used to brilliant effect by Jamaican dubmasters Joe Gibbs and Errol Thompson on their *African Dub* series (see page 60). Goddard works around the basic house beat, moving phrases and riffs backwards and forwards in the mix to shift things from a sparse bass and drum to a towering orchestration, but always with a satisfyingly fat feel to it. Even so, Valentina's vocals, often chopped up, looped or modulated, never let you forget you're still listening to a song.

The Perfect Blues
Jesse Boykins III & MeLo-X
2012 • Ninja Tune

 Contemporary soul music is too often a contradiction in terms, as it's so easy for artists and producers to assume it means simply channelling the past. Jesse Boykins III and MeLo-X, however, move deftly beyond such idle tendencies. With 'The Perfect Blues', singer-songwriter and rapper-producer, respectively, create a light-headedly ambient post-hip-hop groove topped with a feathery vocal that's gorgeously soulful without a valve amp in sight. It's tunes like this – and the rest of the *Zulu Guru* album – that point in precisely the right direction, as modern-day African-American music struggles to find a more cerebral alternative to what came to be called R&B.

Husbands
Savages
2012 • Pop Noire/Matador

MARY ANNE HOBBS' CHOICE ›› In a wider context than this list, it would be easy to appreciate the irony involved in Savages. Here is a band trying to recapture the spirit of punk almost scientifically, labouring to make sure every 'i' is dotted but most of the 't's aren't crossed, even though punk's original purpose was to be spontaneous. Judged on music alone, though, the band is much more than a collection of carefully dishevelled mannerisms. Of course 'Husbands' easily ticks all of punk rock's boxes, but thanks to the ready availability of modern studio technology, in some ways there's a lot more depth and listenability to it than in some of the work of punk's founding fathers. Behind the shouting and the buzz-saw thrash, there's some interesting swirling going on, giving the production a slightly psychedelic feel subtly updating what's on offer.

Hold On
Alabama Shakes
2012 • Rough Trade

›› If you take a fusion of country soul and southern blues as being the basis of the modern-day interpretation of white American rural folk music, Alabama Shakes are among the brand leaders. It's not frozen in aspic, though, and 'Hold On' owes as much to 1970s rock as anything entirely traditional. There's a powerful rhythm section at work, while the guitars have just the right mix of twang and downhome funk to plant it firmly in their home state at Muscle Shoals. It's singer Brittany Howard's voice that takes it all the way back home; although the syntax and cadence is up-to-date, the stretched vowels and the storytelling style are a strong connection back to simpler times. It's a canny reworking of tradition that ought to extend its lineage through at least one more generation.

Lightning Bolt
Jake Bugg
2012 • Mercury

STEVE LAMACQ'S CHOICE Precocious singer-songwriting talent Jake Bugg was just 18 when this tune came out as a track on his self-titled debut album, by which time he'd already appeared on *Later…With Jools Holland* and had his music used in a commercial for beer he wasn't yet old enough to drink. 'Lightning Bolt' is a great example of the confidence and the clarity in his work, a lively rockabilly-like number with a skiffle feel from the acoustic guitar, snare and splash of harmonica. Very crisp, very clean and, although none of it is particularly original as such – the central riff is a little close to 'Bad Moon Rising' for comfort, and Bugg's singing is an homage to mid-1960s Bob Dylan – it's delivered with such joy and enthusiasm you don't really care.

The Bravest Man in the Universe
Bobby Womack
2012 • XL

SHAUN KEAVENY'S CHOICE ≫ Record label XL had already released Gil Scott-Heron's final recordings before it oversaw the rehabilitation of another soul veteran: Bobby Womack's first new material for almost 20 years. This came courtesy of Damon Albarn, who talked Womack into voicing something for Gorillaz, then acted as middleman between the singer and XL to secure a deal, and once in the studio, became the project's co-producer. On *The Bravest Man in the Universe*'s title track, Womack just does what Womack does and the post-dubstep trip-hop fits in around him. All a bit circus horse, but it works wonders, and brings a soul legend into the 21st century with credibility and very little fuss.

Breezeblocks
Alt-J
2012 • Infectious

» The opening lyrics of 'Breezeblocks' are: 'She may contain the urge to run away/But hold her down with soggy clothes and breezeblocks.' Nonsense, perhaps, but even so, nonsense with such commitment it wins you over, and delivered as part of a totally absorbing soundscape; start from a folkie point of view, and then, using dubstep and hip-hop concepts, wash the bass line beats over with a shimmering coating of synthesizers, tinkling bells and strange percussion, then top it off with a perpetually overlapping vocals. This could easily have sounded like so much noise, but Alt-J are smart enough to turn it into so many people's own record collections, all boiled down into a single three-minute package.

Spin That Girl Around
Euros Childs
2012 • National Elf

   Euros Childs, once the frontman and creative force of loveable Welsh nutcases Gorky's Zygotic Mynci, had released seven solo albums in six years after the group's split. Each album had a theme, and this particular one, *Summer Special*, was all about summery, unadulterated pop songs, of which 'Spin That Girl Around' certainly is one. It's built around a mid-tempo, unassuming piano figure, with proper verses and choruses, and a running time of under three minutes. It's not so much for dancing as an accompaniment for lazing around to while it plays in a neighbour's garden, and that's even before Childs' willowy falsetto enters with some whimsical lyrics about being in love.

Little Talks
Of Monsters and Men
2012 • Universal

Exuberant and noisy Icelandic rock from a six-piece folk-based outfit, whose instrumentation included accordion, melodica, acoustic bass, baritone guitars and a glockenspiel. However, in spite of this, and songs that feature all sorts of fey references to Nordic woodlands, Of Monsters and Men approach their songs from an indie-rock perspective. In the case of 'Little Talks', they've come up with a number that really swings. It's a remarkable achievement: the song itself could've simply drifted away, but it not only remains intact – it's been pumped up to a level of genuine excitement.

Emmylou
First Aid Kit
2012 • Wichita

MARK RADCLIFFE'S CHOICE

Given country music's proclivity for broken hearts and damaged souls, it made perfect sense for Swedish folk-sweetheart siblings Johanna and Klara Söderberg to choose the name First Aid Kit. Their Scandi take on this pillar of the US music business is restorative stuff as there's little careworn or cynical about the pair. 'Emmylou' is a charming, playful and innocent expression of love, with wry references to several country icons: 'I'll be your Emmylou and I'll be your June/If you'll be my Gram and my Johnny too.' It's delivered in pealing harmonies, while the acoustic arrangement keeps the pedal steel guitar away from the weepy button.

Elephant
Tame Impala
2012 • Modular

» Tame Impala is pretty much the work of just one man. He is Australian experimentalist Kevin Parker, who describes it as not so much a group as a project. What Parker does harks back to the glory days of psychedelic rock. Although 'Elephant' is recognizably *Piper at the Gates of Dawn*-era Pink Floyd, it's not actual copyism. His allusions lie in attitude rather than in sound, and the song gets away with some startling gear changes as the comfortably fuzzed baroque flourishes arrange themselves into a tune. Riding an early glam groove, it pulls you into a Lewis Carroll rabbit hole, and you're more than happy to take that tumble, even though you've no idea where it might end up.

Genesis
Grimes
2012 • 4AD

« Canadian synth-pop poppet Claire Boucher, a.k.a. Grimes, recorded the whole of her *Visions* album on the GarageBand computer program in her front room, an environment where a lack of outside assistance allowed her to do exactly what she saw fit. As with so much of the album, 'Genesis' boasts a chirpy, disco beat that allows her to show off her music's oddness without banging you over the head with how zany it might all be. The singer gets away with it because she knows exactly what she's doing with conventional pop song structures, and therefore all sorts of strange and smart musical diversions feature organically within the tune rather than being grafted on the outside.

Sixteen Saltines
Jack White
2012 • Third Man/XL

>> For Jack White's first official solo album, *Blunderbuss*, he used flexible crews of highly rated session musicians to bring his ideas to life, often as he was having those ideas in the studio. An inspired move, as it indulges his hyperactive imagination, but also keeps things much tighter than they might have been in a standard band situation. The hook-heavy, riff-tastic, and hard rockin' three minutes of 'Sixteen Saltines' hurtles out of the box as an exhilarating blast of blues and gives White's guitar chops all the room they want. It's tightly produced, contemporary in sound, direct in its desires and is so memorable that it allows all the convoluted back stories and media manipulating to be forgotten.

Hold On
SBTRKT
featuring Sampha
2012 • Young Turks

>> Producer and sought-after remixer Aaron Jerome opted for an alias, SBTRKT, and a Junkanoo-ish mask to cover his own releases. He says he wants the music to speak for itself and, in the case of 'Hold On', it argues that 21st-century post-hip-hop music need not focus exclusively on the dancefloor. Jerome's techniques and sonic balances are rooted in dubstep, but the result here is more urbane than urban, with tinkling beats and bells providing a tender, spacious Japanese-garden feel, and a whisper of a synth in the background. The vocal doesn't perform to type either: guest singer Sampha laments a love recently lost – that afternoon – in a hesitant and almost bewildered fashion.

Storm
Django Django
2012 • Because Music

NEMONE'S CHOICE >> Django Django met at Edinburgh College of Art, formed a band and moved to London. Their next move, if their self-titled debut album is anything to go by, was to set about proving that art rock doesn't have to be loaded with meaning or symbolism, or even be particularly challenging. 'Storm' centres around a big primal-sounding drum groove with guitars easing in and out but never interfering with anything, while also present are Beach Boys-style harmonies singing in rounds. It's a coming together of textures that shouldn't work in theory, but in reality they fit together beautifully simply because of that incongruity.

GMF
John Grant
2013 • Bella Union

DON LETTS' CHOICE

>> Many would have thought that John Grant had reached the nadir of self-loathing with his debut album *Queen of Denmark*. In the *Pale Green Ghosts*, however, he dissects such issues as alcoholism, drugs, coming to terms with his sexuality, a soured relationship plus an HIV positive diagnosis. 'GMF' (a.k.a. 'Greatest Motherfucker'), is a gentle acoustic rock song. As its mood swings between whining self-pity and boorish conceit, looking back in anger on that broken affair, the elegance of the music highlights the intensity and nakedness of Grant's rawness. It's a powerful performance that is neither comfortable nor reassuring but, especially in the current musical environment, has a deeply endearing honesty.

Immunity
Jon Hopkins
2013 • Domino

Soubour
Songhoy Blues
2013 • Trangressive Records

CERYS MATTHEWS' CHOICE Some theories say that the blues originated in West Africa and came to America on the slave ships. If that's the case, Songhoy Blues, a Malian guitar trio, have reclaimed the sound: their love of music grew out of youthful obsessions with Jimi Hendrix, BB King and Howlin' Wolf. The band came together to play music to uplift the spirits of their countrymen during the recent civil war – the title of this tune, 'Soubour', means 'patience'. Indeed there is a suitably languorous blues approach here, as the guitars roll around each other, holding rhythm patterns with interlocking riffs, which give the musicians ample opportunity to show off their licks. Where Songhoy Blues put their own stamp on it is in the Malian vocal harmonizing, with a phrasing and musicality that never left its homeland.

GIDEON COE'S CHOICE >> Jon Hopkins has collaborated with Brian Eno, Coldplay and King Creosote but seemingly kept the best of his oozing, ambient techno-meets-traditional compositions for his fourth solo album, *Immunity*, from which this is the title track. A piano line laps slowly against a shoreline littered with deeply distorted percussion – it sounds like a sticking door being repeatedly opened – and gently carries you out into the gentle sea of a quiet synthesizer and ancient-sounding vocals. Occasionally another vessel of softly computerized woodwind drifts onto the horizon, but there's little to stop you being carried off into the distance.

Are You With Me Now?
Cate Le Bon
2013 • Wichita

MARK RADCLIFFE'S CHOICE   On Cate Le Bon's *Mug Museum* album, classy songwriting meets minimal production from Noah Georgeson and makes the most of modern folkie Le Bon's love of language and witty, evocative lyricism. The album was written not long after her grandmother died, an event reflected in the material, and 'Are You With Me Now?' alludes to the singer coming to terms with it and celebrating a life lived. It's a mood set by the laid-back jangling of the mid-tempo music, and reflects her relocation from Wales to sunnier LA without losing her homeland's darker palette.

Says
Nils Frahm
2013 • Erased Tapes

MARY ANNE HOBBS' CHOICE

Even at the halfway mark of 'Says', an eight-minute ambient epic, it's easy to feel all you've heard is two overlapping piano motifs swelling and ebbing and shifting gently across each other in front of a softly swooshing synth backdrop. Yet you don't feel you've been short-changed. Indeed it comes as a surprise so much of the tune has slipped away. This is the exquisiteness of Nils Frahm's classical-meets-new-age-at-the-grassroots-of-jazz compositions: they follow complex but quite rigid internal rules of composition and emotional manipulation, which permit the melodies to sound riskier than they actually are. He reels you in so completely that, as this builds into its climax, you're moving along with it rather than waiting for it to happen.

The Throw
Jagwar Ma
2013 • Marathon

With 'The Throw', Australian psychedelic rave band Jagwar Ma hark back to two bygone eras yet still manage to sound cutting-edge and relevant. They've revived the idea of guitar music as dance music, in the way it used to be back in the Madchester days, as opposed to music you could probably dance to. As a consequence, there are evocations of the sort of dippy optimistic psychedelia of early Pink Floyd or Traffic. Within the backward guitars, looped drums and stacked vocal harmonizing of 'The Throw', towering melodies unfold to cascade over each other, in order to form their own internalized hooks that firmly snare the listener. It's a distinct arrangement, effortlessly transplanting established ideas to the present day.

Retrograde
James Blake
2013 • Polydor

MARY ANNE HOBBS' CHOICE By the time of James Blake's second album, *Overgrown*, he seemed to have a far better idea of what direction he wanted his music to take, which in turn imbued his songwriting with a fresh confidence. 'Retrograde' is a case in point. It's a gorgeous mixture of acoustic and electronic soul that has simplicity at its essence, which harks back to the sort of thing the more inspired musicians were doing in the 1970s. It is, though, anything but retro: deep bass chords undercut the lone piano, before Blake brings in the synth like a dubstep drop, but without ever disturbing the balanced air of calm melancholy.

Where Are We Now?
David Bowie
2013 • Columbia

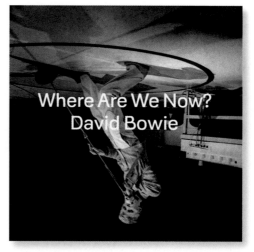

MARK RADCLIFFE'S CHOICE David Bowie's first album in ten years, *The Next Day,* became his first UK number one album in 20 years, and from evidence offered by 'Where Are We Now?' it's easy to see why his return to form was so commercially successful. It's intelligent, thoughtful – to the point of being almost wistful – and the sort of understatedly elegant song that is ideal for a man with almost half a century in the music business. It's not in competition with the rest of the music scene, instead drawing on Bowie's wealth of experience since the mid-1960s and distilling it with a self-assurance that doesn't need to lurk behind a character or a style. The album as a whole took over two years to record, in complete secrecy, and is so much better for its lack of hoo-ha or expectation, as is plain on 'Where Are We Now?' It's the sound of a man setting out to please nobody other than himself. In setting out to please himself, Bowie made a large number of people very happy.

INDEX

ACKNOWLEDGEMENTS

Cassell would like to acknowledge and thank the following for supplying photographs for use in this book.

Key: a above, b below, c centre, l left, r right

Alamy AF Archive 20a; EyeBrowz 56a; Interfoto 60a, 195b; John Bentley 101a, Johnny Greig Portraits 161a, Keith Morris 290ar, M&N 21al; Photos 12 55a; Pictorial Press 9a, 17a, 27b, 29, 46a, 47r, 58a, 66a, 69, 72a, 99a, 103a, 134b, 135a, 154b; SuperStock 144a; The CoverVersion 94b

Corbis Gonzales Photo/Malthe Ivarsson/The Hell Gate 294b; Jeffrey Bender 194b; Joseph Cultice 203al; Lynn Goldsmith 135b; Roger Ressmeyer 119a; Steve Jennings 202al; Ted Shresinsky 10b; Tim Mosenfelder 276a; Bettmann: 63; epa: Joelle Diderich 267a; Reuters 242a

Getty Images Ben Pruchnie 292b, Bruno Vincent 251bl, C Flanigan 287b, Dave Benett 245a, Douglas Mason 292a, Dove Shore 262ar, Frank Hoensch 277b, Frazer Harrison 269b, Fred W McDarrah 25, Graham Denholm 270a, Jakubaszek 282a, Jamie McCarthy 272ar, Janette Beckman 155b, Jo Hale 245b, 258b, 262b, Jon Sievert 6, Jordi Vidal 274, Karl Walter 281, Kevin Cummins 97, 208a, Maurits Sillem 243a, Morena Brengola 258al, Philip Ryalls 261b, Shirlaine Forrest 277a, Simone Joyner 291b, Steve Pyke 154a, 155a, 164b, Tim Mosenfelder 252a, 268ar; Archive Photos: Afro Newspaper/Gado 121b, Maureen Donaldson 126b, Paul Natkin 190 b; Bloomberg via Getty Images 265a; FilmMagic Inc: Jeff Kravitz 188b; Hulton Archive: 24a, 26a & b, 74a, 78a, David Harris 125a, Frank Micelotta 152b, Kevin Cummins 28 a, Martyn Goodacre 156b, 172b, 177a, 187a, 196b, 206b, 207b, 211b, Michael Putland 125b, 146a, 148a, Photoshot 85a, 140a, 145a, 163b, 166b, 176b, 183b, 194a, 225b, 255a, 257ar, 263b, 271a, Scott Gries 227ar, Tim Mosenfelder 191a, 197a, 215a, 218b, Tim Roney 171b; Michael Ochs Archives: 10a, 11b, 13b, 14, 19b, 22b, 23a & bl, 24b, 30br, 31a, 33br, 35b, 38b, 40c, 42ar, 46b, 47l, 48b, 54l, 56b, 59a & bl, 68b, 70a & b, 73b, 82ar, 95b, 110b, 124b, 162b, 170a, Al Pereira 132a, Alison Braun 177b,

Stephen Albanese 224b, David Corio 81b, 122, 127a, 178al, Larry Hulst 35a, Lindsay Brice 172a, Lisa Haun 153a, Paul Ryan 17b, Tom Copi 13a; NBC via Getty Images 77a, 184b, 264b; Photoshot: Martyn Goodacre 227b; Redferns: Andy Sheppard 260, 273, 279 a, 282b, 284a, Annabel Staff 279b, Barney Britton 254 b, 263 a, Brian Cooke 52a, 76a, 92a, Clayton Call 185b, Daniel Boczarski 290b, Dave Tonge 193, 211a, 216b, David Corio 138b, 212b, 213a, 249b, David Redfern 42b, David Reed 62 b, David Warner Ellis 121a, Des Willie 199b, Dimitri Hakke 222, Ebet Roberts 99b, 100a, 107b, 110a, 111, 117b, 124a, 128a, 147b, 205b, 267b, Echoes 43b, 55b, 57a & b, 58b, 136b, Erica Echenberg 150r, Estate Of Keith Morris 27a, 78b, 84bc, 91b, Fin Costello 102b, 106b, 108r, 120ar, 130b, 140b, Frans Schellekens 156a, 160a, GAB Archive 16a, 19a, 32b, 34a, 65a, 100b, Garry Clarke 44b, Gary Wolstenholme 270b, Gems 20b, 38al, 39b, 50b, Gijsbert Hanekroot 79b, Gilles Petard 11a, 16b, 21b, 59br, 65b, 67a, Gus Stewart 91a, Hayley Madden 49ar, 218al, 224a, 248al, Ian Dickson 87, 95a, 101b, 189, Ian Tyas 84a, Jan Persson 50a, Jim Dyson 289, John Rodgers 64al, Jon Super 242b, Kerstin Rodgers 145b, 149b, Lex van Rossen 250ar, 259b, Linda Nylind 238, Marc Broussely 272b, Mark Holloway 264a, Martin O'Neill 115b, Martin Philbey 224c, 291c, Matt Carmichael 248a, Michel Linssen 196a, 200a, Mick Gold 36, 71b, Mick Hutson 165b, 170b, 173b, 175b, 179a, 180b, 181b, 182b, 186b, 198b, 204b, 209a, 214a, 218ar, 220ar, 226b, Neil Lupin 266a, 271b, Nicky J Sims 215b, Ollie Millington 278b, Patrick Ford 200b, 202br, 244a, Paul Bergen 182a, 192a, 209b, 256a, Peter Noble 113b, 131b, 137b, 142b, 146b, Peter Pakvis 228a, Peter Still 127b, 210b, Phil Dent 139b, 148b, RB 8b, 28b, Richard E Aaron 79ar, 96, Rob Verhorst 231a, 268bl, 278a, Robert Knight Archive 40a, Roberta Bayley 77b, 86b, 102a, Simon King 219b, Simon Ritter 167b, Steve

Morley 93b, Steve Thorne 294ar, Stuart Mostyn 174b, Suzie Gibbons 159b, 160b, Tabatha Fireman 243b, 283b, 285b, The Visualeyes Archive 18a, Virginia Turbett 98b, 112l, 118a, 131a, Wendy Redfern 232, 235c, 250bl, 253b, 265b, 276b; Robert Johnson Estate 8a; Sony Music Archive: Mark Barker 184a; Time & Life: Ken Probst 1 85a; UIG via Getty Images 251a; WireImage: Al Pereira 280b, Barry Brechelsen 241a, Chris Walter 90a, EJ Flynn 246a, Gary Gershoff 285a, J Vespa 226a, Kevin Mazur 213bl, 266b, L Cohen 236al, 23al, Paul Natkin 128b, Paul Warner 257al, Ron Wolfson 143a, Skip Bolen 269a, Theo Wargo 233b, 259a

Photoshot Idols 67b, LFI 92b

Rex Features Brian Rasic 137a, 168; Everett Collection 51a, 89a; ITV 158b; Jeremy Sutton Hibbert 220b; Jerome Martin 227al; Pat Pope 216al; Piers Allardyce 201a; Ray Stevenson 104b; Sipa Press 239ar; Steve Richards 109b, 120b; T Tan/BEI 288c

Shutterstock andersphoto 295a; Christian Bertrand 293al

Photo by Roland Hamilton 293ar

Courtesy Savages management 287a

Courtesy The Chamber Group 286

Additional credits

All images are the copyright of their respective owners. Every attempt has been made to acknowledge these correctly. We apologise if any any errors or omissions have been made and will correct any such errors in future editions.

4AD Ltd/Beggars Banquet Beggars Group 180a art Vaughan Oliver, design Dave Coppenhall, 142a art 23 Envelope, 153ar design Vaughan Oliver, 155a design Vaughan Oliver, photo Simon Larbalestier, 188c art Vaughan Oliver, photo Jason Love, 268br art Tunde Adebimpe, Morning Breath Inc, 280a art Mark Fox; **4AD Ltd/Beggars Banquet/Sire** Warner Music Ltd 190bl design V23/Chris Bigg; **American Recordings/Universal Music** 188a; **Ammunition Promotions Ltd** 251ac design Give Up Art; **Ansonia Records Inc** 9b; **Atlantic** Warner Music Ltd 34b, 40b, 44, 72b art Bob Defrin, photo Dennis Chalkin; **Back Yard Music Ltd** 252b photo Carissa Pelleteri; **Beggars Banquet** Beggars Group 143al, 150b design Jaypee, 241 layout Bruce Brand, photo

Pat Pantano, 262ar, 292c photo Dan Wilton; **Beggars Banquet/Sanctuary Records** 127c; **Beggars Banquet/Universal Music Ltd** 236b design Sean McCabe; **Beggars Banquet/Warner Music Ltd** design Patrick Keeler, photo Autumn de Wilde; **Brownswood Music Ltd** 285c; **Calderstone Productions Ltd** 21ar illustration Klaus Voormann; **Chrysalis Records/Union Square** 117a logo Jerry Dammers/Horace Panten/John Sims; **Chrysalis Records/EMI Records Ltd** Universal 126a, 143b; **Columbia** Sony Music Entertainment 73a; **Creation Records Ltd/Sony Music Entertainment** 185c photo Kevin O'Neill, 171a design Chromatone, photo Luke Hayes, 215c art Don Brautigan, **Creation Records Ltd/Ride Music LLP** 182l design Charles Bobbit, photo Jock Sturges; **Daughter Project Ltd** 284c; **Divine Comedy Records Ltd** 208b; **Domino Recording Co Ltd** 211b, 244b, 249a, 277c, 276al design Matthew Cooper, 293b; **Dub Store Records** 41a; **Duophonic Ultra High Frequency Disks Ltd** 194c; **Eden de Luxe Ltd** 225al; **Elektra** Warner Music Ltd 30bl, 42al design Carl Cossick, 83b art Tony Lane, photo Robert Mapplethorpe, 107c; **EMI Records** Universal 10c, 19c, 68a, 74b, 84b, 179b photo Stephanie Chernikowski, 132b, 147c, 167a, 235b, 250c, 225ar art Victor Castelum, **EMI Records/Sony** 77c; **Fat Cat Records** 253a; **Greco-Roman** 296al art Utile Creative; **Heavenly Recordings Ltd** 203ar; **Instinct/Outer Rhythm** 178ar; **InterScope/Polydor** 206a; **Island/Def Jam** 243c design Paul Agar, photos Lizard King Records; **Junior Recordings Ltd/Cooking Vinyl** 192b; **Light in the Attic Records** 38ar; **Lizard King** 268al; **London Records 90 Ltd** 115ar, 147a, 154b graphics Olga Gerrard, 166a art Central Station Design, 200c; **Marathon Artists Ltd** 294c; **Matador Records Ltd/Jeepster Recordings Ltd** 212a; **The Mayfield Family Trust/Warner Music** 49a art Glen Christensen; **Mercury** Universal 66b, 106c, 128ca, 132ar illustration James Rizzi, 151al sleeve CBS Records Australia Ltd, 181a design Ian Swift, 190a, 213ac, 242c; **Mercury Records/Big Cat UK Records** 215ar, **Mercury/Sony** 175a art The Drawing Boards, photo Michael Comte; **Modular Recordings** 291ar art Leif Podhajsky, **Mute**, a BMG company 86a art Timothy Jackson, 105, 114b, 130a photo Rodney Martin, 173c layout Designland, 195a, 246c, 283a; **National Elf** 290al; **Ninja Tune Ltd** 287ar; **Now Twist and Shout Ltd** 94a design Nick de Ville; **One Little Indian Ltd** 144b typography Bernard FAB; 226ac design Sy Acosta, photo Kurt I; **Parlophone** Warner Music 24c, 28, 64r photography Storm Thorgerson, Tony May, Hipgnosis, 98al, 107a photo

Milton Haworth, 109a, 118al, 134a, 138a art James Marsh, 158c art Morrissey, Jo Slee, layout Carin Gough, photo Geri Caulfield, 161b design Peter Saville Associates, 187b design Stylorouge, photo David Grewcock, 198a design Designers Republic, 201b, 210a, 220al art Graham Coxon, 226bc art & design Jamie Hewlett, Zombie, 230a, 231b, 254a design Owen Clarke, Wallzo, illustration Eskimo Square, 261a; PIAS Recordings UK Ltd 215c, Polydor Universal 62a art Don Brautigan, design Charles Bobbit, David Fried Krieger Inc, 91a design Bill Smith, photo Walt Davidson, 104a, 115al design & illustration Bill Smith, 139c, 149c design Simon Halfon, Paul Weller, photo Nick Knight, 156c design Ryan Art, photo Russell Young, 197c, 202bl design Andy Vella, 205a art & design Francesca Restrepo, photo Ann Giordano, 207a art Manuel Ocampo, 213bc photo Jim Goldberg, 233a design Patrick Hutchinson, 239b art Cody Critcheloe, 257, 277c; Polydor/Universal-Island 177a art Rainbow Paterson; Rough Trade Records Ltd 229a, 246br art & design Tracy Maurice, 228b; Saddle Creek Europe 252c art Jason Ulrich; Sanctuary Records BMG 76b; Sena/Sony Music Entertainment/Warner Music 191b; Silva Screen Records Ltd 250a art Divya Srinivasan; Sire Warner Music 81a, 170bc, 235a; Sony Music Entertainment 32a, 48a art & design Ernst Thormahlen, 51b photo Steinbicker/Houghton Inc, 71a, 89c, 120b, 151ar photo Terence Donovan, 151b art Calum Colvin, 152a, 160c, 163a art John Squire, 165a design Designers Republic, 174c design Andrew Biscomb, Peter Barrett, photo Kevin Cummins, 175c, 176c design Designland, photo Angus Cameron, 180c, 182a, 184c, 186a design Andrew Biscomb, Peter Barrett, photo Holger Trülzsch, 199a & c, 202ar art Jonathan Coooke, design Blue Source, photo Derek Santini, 204ar, 229b design Simon Corkin, photo Ellis Parrinder, 230bl, 245bl art Simon Corkin, 277ar, 295b; Stiff Records/Union Square Music 82b; Sub Pop/

Fintage Publishing & Collection BV 157 design Lisa Orth, photo Alice Wheeler, 167br layout Jane Higgins, photo Michael Lavine, 240c art Kozyndan, 264c design & illustration Robert Mercer; Sub Pop/V2 Music 265c; Trojan/Sanctuary Records BMG 33a; Turnstile Partners 294al; Ultimate Dilemma Records Ltd 228al; Universal Music Ltd 30a, 54r; Universal/Island Records Ltd 41br, 42a, 56a design Visualeyes, photo Esther Anderson, 79al photos Motown Record Corporation, 82al, 83a, 90b, 98ar art Island Art, photo Ashworth, 106a, 135c, 153b, 173a design Gary Talpas for Föhn Design, 185a illustration Gray Brothers, 197b art Philip Castle, 203b art Martin Callomon, Richard Baker, Rob Crane, 204al, 236ar, 290c; V2 Music Ltd 255 design Midlake, Tim Carter, photo Tim Smith; V2 Music Ltd/Universal 272al; Virgin Records Universal 118b art Thomas Rathmell, 120a photo by POUR, 140b design Ken at AS, photo Steve Jansen, 145a, 179b, 214b, 251bc, 256b, 128cb, 52 design CCS, photo Karl Stoecker, 85b design Peter Kodic, Russell Mills, 95c, 101c, 110al, 124bl; Virgin Records Ltd/Gut Records Ltd 131c art BEF in association with Bob Last; VP Records 60b; Warner Music Ltd 22 design Ronnie Stoots, 46c, 110b, 112b, 142c, 146c, 148c design Carin Gough, photo Cecil Beaton, 149a, 150al design Carin Gough, Morrissey, 152c, 162a, 164a design Andrew Biscomb, Peter Barrett, 174a design Casey Niccoli, Penny Farrell, photo Victor Bracke, 230br, 262al art Nick Scott, 284b; Warp Records Ltd 219a design Designers Republic, photo Chris Cunningham, 237bl photo Peter Iain Campbell, 237r, 248b art Yes, photo Ian Davies; Welk Music Group/Sanctuary Records 136a design AQ Graphics Inc, photo Hemu Aggarwal; Wichita Recordings Ltd 291al; XL Recordings Beggars Group 219c, 288b design Switzerlandcs.com, photo Jamie-James Medina; Xtra Mile Recordings/PIAS Recordings 276b; Zomba Records Ltd/Sony Music Entertainment 170ac

BBC Radio 6 Music would like to thank our audience and all the artists, labels, pluggers, managers, venues, record stores and festivals who make us the community we are.

Many thanks to those who made this book possible – James Stirling, Jeff Smith, Hannah Knowles, Lloyd Bradley, Leanne Bryan, Justin Lewis, Eoghan O'Brien & Clare Barber, Giulia Hetherington, Claire Jullien, Martha Pazienti-Caidan, Katie Pollard, Emma Trevelyan, Camilla Pia, Lorna Clarke and Bob Shennan.